M000275499

NAPOLEON
AGAINST
RUSSIA

A CONCISE HISTORY OF 1812

A wounded casualty is assisted out of the firing line during the battle of Smolensk by a grenadier and a member of the elite company, 8th Hussars. Faber du Four. Author's collection.

NAPOLEON
AGAINST
RUSSIA

A CONCISE HISTORY OF 1812

DIGBY SMITH

Pen & Sword
MILITARY

First published in Great Britain by
PEN & SWORD MILITARY
an imprint of
Pen & Sword Books Limited
47 Church Street
Barnsley
S. Yorkshire
S70 2AS

Copyright © Digby Smith, 2004

ISBN 1 84415 089 5

The right of Digby Smith to be
identified as Author of this Work has
been asserted by him in accordance with
the Copyright, Designs and Patents Act 1988.

A CIP catalogue record for this book
is available from the British Library.

*All rights reserved. No part of this book may be reproduced or
transmitted in any form or by any means, electronic or mechanical
including photocopying, recording or by any information storage
and retrieval system, without permission from the Publisher in writing.*

Printed and bound in Great Britain by
CPI UK

Pen & Sword Books Ltd incorporates the imprints of
Pen & Sword Aviation, Pen & Sword Maritime, Pen & Sword Military,
Wharncliffe Local History, Pen & Sword Select,
Pen & Sword Military Classics and Leo Cooper.

For a complete list of Pen & Sword titles please contact:
PEN & SWORD BOOKS LIMITED
47 Church Street, Barnsley, South Yorkshire, S70 2AS, England.
E-mail: enquiries@pen-and-sword.co.uk
Website: www.pen-and-sword.co.uk

Contents

Preface

There are literally scores of personal accounts of this great historical disaster that have been published to date, many of them translated into English, mostly from French originals. Some of them were written by highly-placed officers and officials of the *Grande Armée*, who were in close proximity to Napoleon (undoubtedly the single architect of this great tragedy), during the whole adventure. They have left comprehensive accounts of their experiences; sometimes these are extremely controversial, such as that of Count Philippe de Segur. His representation of certain aspects of the Emperor's character so enraged General Gaspard Gorgaud, one of Napoleon's most devoted ADCs, that Gorgaud challenged Segur to a duel over them, in which the latter was wounded.

All the English-language accounts that I have read so far concentrate on the fate of the main body of the *Grande Armée*, under Napoleon's direct command, as he drove them on and on to certain death, either on the road to Moscow, or in the inevitable, humiliating retreat. It is often a surprise to those new to the study of this campaign to realise that almost all the regiments of this central column had lost fifty percent of their march-in strength of 24 June by mid-August, before any serious actions had been fought. Astounding – but true.

In selecting our 'war correspondents' for this work, I have been at pains to:
• Select only the best parts of the most genuinely informative of previously published memoirs.
• Introduce characters new to English-speaking readers.
• Introduce accounts from the flanking formations in Latvia, Polotzk and in Volhynia, all of which have previously been steadfastly ignored.

Research into the Latvian theatre of the war, where Marshal Macdonald's X Corps operated almost independently against the Baltic port of Riga, has revealed an environment so totally at variance with the grim hell of Napoleon's central sector, that one could be forgiven for doubting that the two sequences of events took place in the same year or in the same war.

On the southern front the Austrian auxiliary corps of Prince Karl Schwarzenberg, together with the VII (Saxon) Corps, operated around the area of the Pripet Marshes in Volhynia, now the Ukraine. Their incredibly difficult attempts to fight – even to move – in the largest, most dangerous marshes in Europe must excite our admiration for what they achieved.

Schwarzenberg's somewhat rash, aggressive operations placed his army in awkward predicaments on several occasions; good luck, and clumsy Russian opponents, allowed him to escape just retribution.

Gouvion-Saint-Cyr's army at Polotzk (II and VI Corps) was largely destroyed by the dumb incompetence of Saint-Cyr and the indifference of the Emperor. Together they presided over its demise in the full knowledge of its causes and its effects.

I have not attempted to give detailed accounts of the various battles and clashes that took place; many other books cover them in great detail. This work concentrates on the individuals and their experiences.

As with so many of my recent works, I am deeply indebted to the generous cooperation of many correspondents of the Napoleon Series and Napoleon Series New Forum on the Internet. Gregory Troubetzkoy and Ronald Pawley kindly allowed me to include quotes from their own books to enrich the narrative.

Prologue

Early in 2002, some drab ex-Red Army barracks in Vilnius, capital of Lithuania, were being demolished, when suddenly the driver of the bulldozer stopped his machine. He had seen something. There, tumbled up out of the soil under the blade, were human skeletons – scores of them. Management was quickly called in. Was this another Katyn Wood from the Second World War? Yet another Nazi massacre of Russian prisoners? Gingerly they began to pick about among the bones. What did they find? Here a button with the number '29' within a ring; then another with '61'; then a rhombic metal plate bearing a crowned eagle; a squashed felt and leather shako. The artefacts littered among the bones now began to tell a story. Not of a deliberate massacre, but of a human tragedy of massive scale, which took place 190 years before, in December 1812.

At that time, a starving, terrified horde of sick, injured, disoriented refugees flooded westwards out of Russia, harried by the Cossacks and crushed by the icy winter winds into numbed automata, their only wish – to survive. These few thousands were the unhappy remnants of one megalomaniac's twisted dream of world domination. They were all that was left of his '*Grande Armée*'.

Wilna, as Vilnius was known in December 1812, was a major depot of food, forage, weapons and equipment for Napoleon's army. It was also a major hospital. But the then authorities of the city knew nothing of the almost total destruction of that army in the foregoing months: nothing could have prepared them for the climactic events that were to burst upon them in the next few days.

The tide of human misery washed into the city, hoping to find warmth, rest, food and shelter. The astonished commissary officials refused to open the depots to them, unable to believe that these ragged tramps really were the proud regiments that had marched through the city not six months before, on their way to capture Moscow and bring Czar Alexander to heel.

In the resultant chaos of the next two or three days, thousands died of starvation, frostbite, disease, sickness – and a few from enemy action – in Wilna, before the wreckage of that army shuffled on westwards to Kowno and to Prussia. Thousands of the corpses were hurriedly dumped into the River Niemen, through holes hacked in the ice, and borne away. It is likely that most of the bodies in the building site were buried there either in the autumn months of 1812 (the patients of the hospitals who had died) or in the spring of 1813, when the clean-up operation took care of the corpses exposed by the melting snow.

A museum has now been opened in Vilnius to house the artefacts found in the trench. They bear witness to all the nationalities that went to make up the invading army: Frenchmen, Germans, Swiss, Italians, Portuguese, Croats and Illyrians, Poles and Lithuanians.

What a monument to the incredible human folly of one man.

Digby Smith
Thetford, 2004.

Napoleon I, Emperor of the French. Author's collection.

Chapter 1

The invasion of Russia is decided upon

'The colonial produce placed on the market in Leipzig fair
was conveyed in 700 carts from Russia; which means that today
the whole trade in colonial produce goes through Russia, and that
the 1,200 merchantmen were masked by the Swedish, Portuguese,
Spanish, and American flags, and that were escorted by twenty English
men-of-war, have in part discharged their cargoes in Russia.'
Napoleon, 4 November 1810.

'In affairs of state one must never retreat, never retrace one's
steps, never admit an error – that brings disrepute. When one
makes a mistake, one must stick to it – that makes it right!'
Napoleon to Segur in Moscow, October 1812.

It is generally agreed that Napoleon's invasion of Russia in 1812 was his greatest mistake. To be sure, he made others; the kidnapping and execution of the Duc d'Enghien, his invasion of Spain and his subsequent failure to resolve the mess he left behind there before embarking on the Russian adventure, and – undoubtedly – trying to compete in a trade war with Great Britain.

While the results of the Russian failure were speedily and dramatically evident, the effects of the trade war, carried out equally relentlessly between Britain and France, were much less easily seen but equally – if not more – fatal to his empire. Indeed, it was the continued smuggling of British contraband through Russia into western Europe that was the *real* reason for Napoleon's decision to invade the Russian colossus. It can be argued that he would eventually have been forced out of power by the universal public resentment of his Continental System, which deprived the masses of all the spices, condiments, tea, coffee, cocoa and other colonial products to which they had become accustomed.

With the British government's Order in Council of May 1806, all Continental ports from Brest to the River Elbe were placed under blockade by the Royal Navy. This was known as Fox's Blockade, he being the Foreign Secretary of the day after the death of William Pitt. This sealed off the great Hanseatic ports of Bremen and Hamburg. Napoleon responded with his Berlin Decree of 21 November 1806, which was a much more rigorous policy than France had previously employed. The British retaliated with new Orders in Council in November 1807, banning neutrals from trading with France and its allies. Spencer Perceval, the then prime minister, summed up the aim of these new Orders in Council: 'either the neutral countries will have no trade, or they must be content to accept it through us.'

Alexander I, Czar of all the Russias. Author's collection.

Napoleon then resorted to the first Milan Decree of 23 November 1807. He had declared '*une croisade contre le sucre et le café, contre les percales et les mousselines*' (a crusade against sugar and coffee, against percales – calico – and muslin). Interestingly enough, this was to give a great spur to the development of the European sugar beet industry.

To his brother Louis, king of Holland, Napoleon wrote that his aim was to '*conquérir la mer par la puissance de la terre*' (conquer the sea with the power of the land). Britain was placed under blockade; all trade with Britain was to cease; British goods on the Continent were subject to seizure and no ship – of any nation – could enter any French or allied port if it had previously visited a British port.

This policy was doomed to failure, since any power that aims at world domination – and Napoleon certainly did – must be able to control the world's seas. Britain did so, and was thus the superpower of this age. Soviet Russia's great naval building programme following the Second World War, when she also strained to attain global domination, is further proof of this truth. Nowadays, air power goes hand in hand with sea power to ensure world dominance.

The effects of the trade war on the economy of Holland were disastrous: 1,349 merchantmen entered Amsterdam's port in 1806, but this had dropped to 310 in 1809.

The *Moniteur* of 25 September 1806 gave another reason for the promulgation of Napoleon's Continental System: '*La prohibition des marchandises étrangères de côtes que vient d'ordonner le Gouvernement ne contribuera pas peu à nous faire obtenir le resultat si désirable de fabriquer nous-mêmes la totalité d'articles dont nous avons besoin.*' (The prohibition on the entry of goods of foreign origin, ordered by the government, is designed to favour the sales of all articles made in our own territories).

To replace the trade between mainland Europe and the industrialized production and colonial items, now firmly a British monopoly, Napoleon attempted to create and impose his own 'common market' on all the nations under his control. Naturally, this market was skewed in favour of France, in the same way that Britain biased trade with her colonies in her own favour. The ban on trade with Britain lasted until early 1810, when the Emperor was forced to allow trade with his great rival under licences; Britain rapidly became one of the most significant markets for French goods. But if the French economy had suffered under Britain's blockade, the economies of the other European states were in tatters by this time and the irrepressible smuggling was forcing Napoleon to annex more and more stretches of Europe's coastline in a frantic, but fruitless, effort to stop it. Holland, north Germany, the Hanseatic ports, the Grand Duchy of Oldenburg – the list grew ever longer, France ever larger.

The economy of Russia, too, was suffering under the Continental System, which Alexander had agreed to impose upon his country in 1807. By 1810 the very internal stability of Russia was in danger and the merchants and nobles were in growing unrest. The Czar relented. To have done otherwise would have been too dangerous for him personally.

British merchantmen poured into St Petersburg; colonial produce flooded through Russia and across Europe. Napoleon's spies reported everything. He realised that if he did nothing to stop this impudent flouting of his orders he would become an impotent laughing stock, and he was notoriously short of a sense of humour. He tried diplomatic threats; these were fended off, ignored. He pondered. Since meeting with the Czar at Tilsit three years before, he had been convinced that he could manipulate his Russian cousin like putty. Now this.

What was he to do? Admit that Britain had won? Never! He well knew that such an admission would rapidly be followed by the end of his reign. But there were many who were capable of reading between the lines of the Emperor's much-cherished economic lies, among them the Duke of Wellington. In October 1811 he wrote to Lord Liverpool (then Secretary of State for War):

> I have no doubt but that Napoleon is much distressed for money. Notwithstanding the swindling mode in which his armies are paid, the troops are generally ten and eleven, and some of them twelve months in arrears of pay... It is impossible that this fraudulent tyranny can last. If Great Britain continues stout, we must see the destruction of it.

And again, on 24 December 1811, to Lord William Bentinck, commanding British forces in Sicily:

> I have long considered it probable, that even we should witness a general resistance throughout Europe to the fraudulent and disgusting tyranny of Buonaparte,[1] created by the example of what has been done in Spain and Portugal; and that we should be actors and advisers in these scenes; and I have reflected frequently upon the measures which should be pursued to give a chance of success... I am quite certain that the finances of Great Britain are more than a match for Buonaparte, and that we shall have the means of aiding any country that may be disposed to resist his tyranny.

This was pure prophecy. Denis Davidov (a young Russian officer of spirit and initiative) had heard of the guerrilla warfare that the Spanish people had unleashed on the hated invaders and was keen to try it in Russia. We shall see how successful he was.

For Napoleon, to just let things continue, to try to ignore the creeping destruction of his artificial economic structure, was not an option either. Action was imperative; but Russia? How could he force his will on that giant? Diplomacy had failed; economic counter-measures would be just laughable; French exports to Russia were miniscule. There remained only one possibility – war. But this would have to be conducted on a truly mammoth scale and in a theatre up to 2,000 km away from Napoleon's French base.

He was not worried about fighting the Russian army; he had beaten them in 1805, 1806 and 1807. He overawed all their commanders and his *Grande Armée* was the perfect war machine. The Confederation of the Rhine, Italy, Naples – even Prussia – would provide more or less willing contingents and other assets to support him. His new father-in-law, Kaiser Franz I of Austria, would also be persuaded to lend a sizeable contingent. Napoleon would break into Russia like a tempest, destroy their army and enforce his will in Moscow and St Petersburg. Then? Who knew? Perhaps on to India? Perhaps to eclipse Alexander the Great?

So how did the opponents in this epic struggle measure up to one another in 1812? Russia had a population of some 37.5 million, an army of 516,770 at the end of 1811 and a navy of 67 ships of the line, 36 frigates, over 700 sloops, designed for shallows use, and 21,000 men in the crews. The army was increased by a further 113,275 men in new regiments; a further 185,000 were raised in Reserve Divisions, formed by the combined Reserve and Depot battalions. There were then 63,279 men in garrison regiments and some 100,000 irregular troops. An astounding total of 1,300,000 Russians were eventually mobilised for the defence of their homeland. These were sub-divided as follows:

- 1st Army of the West under Barclay de Tolly – 110,000 men, plus 7,000 Cossacks and 558 guns.
- 2nd Army of the West under Prince Bagration – 45,000 men (including the newly-formed 27th Division) and 217 guns.
- 3rd Army of the West under General Tormassow – 46,000 men and 164 guns.
- The Army of the Danube under Admiral Tschitschagoff – 38,600 men and 204 guns.

Up in Finland and Latvia were a further 26,000 men and 78 guns. In the early part of 1812 the populace was called upon to join the militia or *Opolcheni;* this resulted in a further 330,000 men joining up, although many were armed only with axes and pikes.

France's population was 30 million, considerably less than that of Russia, but her army was the greatest in Europe until Russia mobilised in 1812. Estimates of the march-in strength of Napoleon's multinational army vary; Chambry gives the following totals: 610,000 men, 182,000 horses and 1,372 guns. Doctor David Chandler gives 'more than 600,000 men... 200,000 animals – horses and oxen – of whom 80,000 were the finest cavalry mounts.'

When Napoleon invaded Russia, there were 4,000 men in his headquarters alone. The Imperial Guard numbered 47,000, the twelve infantry corps had 415,000 men, the four cavalry corps 40,000 and the artillery and train numbered 21,500. A further 80,000 men followed on in the 'march regiments'. These totals included all the foreign contingents from Prussia, the Confederation of the Rhine, Italy, Naples, Spain, Portugal, Austria and Illyria. The stunning sum of 607,500 men is reached. In June 1812, however, only just over 500,000 invaded Russia, the rest (IX and XI Corps and the march regiments) were on the lines of communication.

The French navy had been second only to Britain's Royal Navy in 1790. The excesses of the Terror had caused over half the officers to emigrate. Various defeats had steadily reduced it; Trafalgar gutted it. In disgust at its repeated failures, Napoleon had turned his face from what was left. The remaining ships rotted in their blockaded harbours, their crews used for coastguard duties. In 1813 naval gunners formed four regiments of infantry, which fought very well at Leipzig and other battles.

Notes

1 The Duke loved to refer to the Emperor by his discarded birth name instead of the adopted 'Bonaparte'.

Chapter 2

The preparations

'I have decided on a great expedition. I shall need horses and transport on a large scale. The men I shall get easily enough; but the difficulty is to prepare transport facilities. I shall need an immense amount of transport because I shall be starting from the [River] *Niemen* [Russia's border with the Grand Duchy of Warsaw] *and I intend to operate over large distances and in different directions … do not let the question of expense check you.'*
The Emperor to Lacuée Cessac, head of the imperial ordnance department in June 1811.

Napoleon said to a representative from Marshal Marmont from Spain in 1811:

Marmont complains that he is short of many resources – food, money, means etc. Well, here I am, about to plunge with an immense army into the heart of a great country which produces absolutely nothing!

Then he fell silent for some minutes, before asking the nonplussed colonel: 'How will it all end?'

Segur tells us of the contents of some of the Emperor's orders: in one missive he wrote 'For masses like these, if precautions be not taken, the grain of no country can suffice.' In another:

…it will be requisite for all the provision wagons to be loaded with flour, bread, rice, pulse and brandy, besides what is necessary for the hospital service. There will be nothing for them to expect from the country and it will be necessary to have everything within ourselves.

Again, all that he wrote was true.

The entire French empire and her satellites were cranked into action for the invasion; Europe buzzed with activity from one end to the other. As Bernays tells us in his account of the fate of the Frankfurt contingent:

…other convoys carried tools of all sorts and apart from furniture, namely ovens, also building materials, prefabricated sections of wooden houses with windows, collapsible windmills – in addition there were whole battalions of artisans, not only bakers, butchers, tailors, cobblers, but also masons, carpenters, gardeners… also numerous fire engines, as if one had foreseen the burning of Moscow.

Also trekking eastwards from France were 'disproportionally large numbers of beardless novices, the bad horses of the national French cavalry and the wagonloads of young lads clapped into irons for desertion.'

In December 1810 some 80,000 young Frenchmen were called up for military service; one year later Napoleon withdrew all the cavalry and artillery of the Imperial Guard that were in Spain. In January 1812 he further pulled out the two Young Guard divisions and all the units of the Grand Duchy of Warsaw. Thus 27,000 veteran soldiers were withdrawn from Spain, which still left an amazing 232,500 French and allied troops in that country, struggling to hold their own and getting nowhere.

In the spring of 1812 the *Grande Armée* began to form up within the borders of the Grand Duchy of Warsaw. The government there was, of course, called upon by Napoleon to provide massive amounts of food and fodder and the troops were billeted upon the townspeople.

The Regiment Frankfurt, later to form part of the 34th Division, XI Corps, was in Hamburg in April 1812. Bernays gives us this example of the degree of smuggling that then existed:

> Every day the regiment marched out of the city, to drill on the Heiligengeistfelde, which lay outside the customs zone. Before they returned to the city, Danish merchants[1] would fill the barrels of their muskets with coffee beans, cinnamon and the like. When this ruse was finally discovered, the soldiers resorted to hiding the goods in clay busts of the emperor. The Continental System was so detested, that no-one thought to report them.

For the supply of some of the troops marching eastwards that spring on what for most of them would be a one-way trip, great magazines had been established with supplies and equipment gathered in from all over the empire. Segur tells us of the great magazines which were formed in major strategic cities such as Danzig, Koenigsberg and Thorn. Supplies from here were sent by boat up the Baltic coast, then into the Pregel river to Vehlau and Insterburg, then by land again to Labiau on the River Niemen. From here the supplies were to be shipped eastwards along that river and the Vilia to Kowno and Vilna. Unfortunately, due to the drought of early 1812, the Vilia was no longer navigable. Another problem was that the wagons used by the French in the invasion of 1812 were far heavier than the local Lithuanian and Russian carts – this was to be a major factor in the disaster which was to come so very soon.

On the diplomatic front, Napoleon gave orders that the Ottoman empire should be encouraged to step up the war with Russia on their common borders. Unfortunately for him, Alexander's diplomats were more effective and concluded the Peace of Bucharest on 28 May 1812 with Turkey, thus freeing up Admiral Paul Vasilievich Tschitschagoff's 25,000 strong Army of the Moldau, which was sent north to attack the French later in the year.

Napoleon's proclamation to the German contingents went as follows:

> Soldiers, Russia has broken her oath. An inescapable fate drags her along. Let the will of fate be done. Forward then over the Niemen. The second Polish war will be as glorious for our arms as the first, and the following peace will put an end to Russia's meddling in European affairs.

Early in the campaign; foraging in the Grand Duchy of Warsaw. Albrecht Adam.

After reading this out to the Westphalians on 26 June, General Vandamme added his own little codicil:

> Napoleon crossed the Niemen on the 24th of this month and has pushed the Russians back. We will now advance and conquer; in two to three months this will all be over.
>
> He who lacks the heart and courage to fight with us can hang up his sword in his billet before evening and fly to where he will!

Czar Alexander also issued a proclamation to his people:

> The enemy, with unequalled perfidy, threatens the destruction of our country. Our brave soldiers want to throw themselves on his battalions and destroy them; but we will not sacrifice them on the altar of this Moloch. There must be a general uprising against this universal tyrant... He has come with treachery in his heart and loyalty on his lips to enslave us with the help of his legions of slaves. Let us drive this plague of locusts out! Let us carry the Cross in our hearts and steel in our hands! Let us pluck the fangs out of this lion's mouth, and overthrow the tyrant who would destroy the world!

At a dinner in Danzig, prior to crossing the Niemen, Berthier, Murat and Rapp were with him. The Emperor suddenly asked Rapp: 'How far is it from Danzig to Cadiz?' 'Too far, Sire!' Rapp replied. The Emperor retorted:

> I can see, gentlemen, that you no longer have any taste for fighting. The King of Naples would rather be back in his pretty kingdom; Berthier would like to be playing the sportsman in Grosbois; Rapp would fain be enjoying the sweets of Parisian life!

There was silence – Napoleon had put his finger on the spot; war weariness was infecting even his most senior commanders. He was a giant alone among mere mortals. Or a megalomaniac detached from reality?

Napoleon's plan for 1812 was to leap across the Russian border and fall upon the two enemy armies, before they could unite, and to defeat them in detail. It was the same plan that had worked so well in 1805, 1806 and 1809; success against the bumbling Russians seemed a foregone conclusion. Peace would then be dictated, the Continental System re-imposed and Britain strangled. But success depended upon the Russian armies obliging by staying put, divided and up against their western border.

There certainly was confusion and a lack of unity in the Czar's high command at this point. General of Infantry Prince Michael Andreas Barclay de Tolly, commanding the 1st Army of the West (100,000 men), wanted to adopt a strategy of falling back before the superior invaders, buying time with space, until campaign attrition reduced the *Grande Armée* to a suitable size for a successful battle to be fought. The commander of the smaller 2nd Army of the West (30,000 men), General of Infantry Prince Piotr Ivanovich Bagration, an aggressive and very competent general, hated Barclay and wished to dispute every inch of Mother Russia's holy soil. The Czar was bombarded by plans from his numerous advisers, many of them foreigners and unpopular with the native Russian officers. Luckily for him, Barclay won the day. The rest is history.

The supplies in the magazines, created by Napoleon's orders, were only available for the Imperial Guard and other guard troops during the invasion. All other formations were told to collect rations and forage from the countryside. The

Bavarian cavalry with the IV Corps cross the Niemen watched by Prince Eugene.

population of the Grand Duchy was about 3,600,000, and the state had been sucked dry financially since its creation in 1807. The harvest of 1811 had been far below average, and the extra supplies demanded by Napoleon for his 'Golden Horde' of over half a million extra mouths were just not to be had. So the unfortunate line troops, barred from the magazines, were faced with the stark choice: take what was needed by force – for the peasantry would not willingly surrender their few supplies, cows, sheep and poultry – or starve.

The resultant chaos was indescribable. Farms, villages and towns were repeatedly looted, houses were torn down to provide building materials for bivouacs and fuel for the fires. Anything that would burn went into the fires. The foraging parties from the leading regiments in the immense column of invaders returned loaded to excess with everything that they could find; perishables that were not rapidly consumed rotted and were thrown away. The following regiments found nothing near the line of march and were forced to send foragers ever further away to find enough to survive. The unfortunate inhabitants of the Grand Duchy were transformed into starving vagrants.

Apologists for Napoleon have accused only the foreigners of having looted; this was far from the truth. The German contingents were used to being supplied with rations and forage from magazines; they were now forced, *at his explicit orders,* to steal to survive. And they were still in 'friendly' territory. The cavalry were reduced to feeding their starving horses on green grain crops or even thatching straw; colic swept through the horse lines. And this was *before* the invasion had even begun.

The Westphalian, Giesse, tells us that:

> On 13 April King Jerome held a review of his troops in Kalisck; he was more concerned with their smart appearance than with their welfare... Morale was already very low and suicides were not unknown.
>
> In the Saxon Palace in Warsaw, in mid-May, Jerome held daily reviews and inspections of his army in the gardens of his palace. He concentrated on the rapid formation of battalion squares as a defence against the notorious Cossacks.

Jerome's odd attitude to military priorities will surface again.

The Württemberg Cavalry General Wilhelm von Woellwarth was caught up in this disaster and had to justify his contingent's actions in the following report to his monarch:

> On entry into Poland the magazines established there were closed to our cavalry; even in the remote staging posts no provision had been made for troops moving through. Also, our advancing army corps had already consumed most of the supplies that they had brought with them and to my cavalry division fell the unhappy lot of having to shift for themselves in a Poland already hostile to Germans.
>
> As is well known, the Polish peasants have little enough for themselves and that which they had they were forced to give to the French magazines long before our entry into their country. Here [in Pagosz] the French magazines in the area were closed to our troops. I sent Commissary Crais to the magazines many times which helped not a bit as he was told that these supplies were for the use of passing Guard and French troops only. Thus here also, supply on a self-help basis was necessary.

Officers of the Italian guard in bivouac. Faber du Four. Author's collection.

On 30 May I recieved a personal order from the Duke of Elchingen [Marshal Ney] in Thorn: on command of the French Emperor I was to collect enough slaughter cattle for the whole Wirtemberg army corps for 20 days and to arrange this with the Polish government. This requisition had to be completed by 2 July i.e. within 48 hours. I sent Commissary Crais to visit the Prefects of the districts to liaise with them as to the manner and execution of the requisition. Crais could find no Prefects as they had all gone to attend a reception of the French Emperor who was to pass through the area on his way to Thorn this day. Prior to this, the Over Prefect had informed Commissar Crais that he was not in a position to assist with the supply of food for the men and would have to give his district over to the discretion of the troops. The regiments now despatched whole squadrons with their Regimental Quartermasters and the necessary requisition orders to collect the 800 oxen in 48 hours. Apart from this, the regiments were instructed by me to maintain the strictest discipline. The unpleasant circumstances of this enforced requisition of cattle gave rise to a great lament by all the nobility and peasants of the area. None of them came to me however; they all ran to the Polish General Krasinski – who advised them to wait just a couple of hours when the Emperor would arrive and he would present their complaints to him. In a few hours the Emperor came to Iznoraslau, two posts before Thorn, where all the noblemen who had had their cattle taken were presented by General Krasinski with the explanation that the Wirtembergers were robbing and plundering the area which was in fact, nothing other than the execution of the order of the Emperor himself and Marshal Ney to collect 800 oxen within 48 hours, which certainly must have appeared as plundering if the cooperation of

July; the French cavalry wade through the grain crops that were to prove so fatal to their horses.
Albrecht Adam.

the civil authorities was withheld. Krasinski troubled himself to increase this impression to the Emperor...

During the Emperor's stay in Thorn, the requisition detachments of Lieutenant Colonels Palm and Harditsch... arrived with the necessary oxen to complete the requisition; they were no sooner sighted by the Guard than all the oxen and supplies which they collected were taken from them by force... We reached the area of Insterburg on 15 June and found the whole countryside full of Davout's corps and the entire Imperial Guard. As the II Corps had previously marched through the area, it had been so plundered that the colonels had the most extreme difficulty in providing for their regiments on the 16th which was a rest day.

I sent Commissar Crais into Insterburg, where a great magazine had been established, in order to get at least bread for us, which we had not seen since the Vistula, but even this was denied to us... No Wirtemberg soldiers went into Insterburg ; no reports of excesses (by our troops) in the whole area came to me... Prinz Neufchatel [Alexander Berthier, Napoleon's Chief of Staff] was supposed to have exclaimed: *'que la cavallerie wirtembergoise avait portée le désastre dans Insterburg'*. That this was brought into the area before our arrival by French troops is the truth; but that the Wirtembergers brought disaster into this area is not true.

Koenigsberg, 10 August 1812.
Woellwarth, Generallieutenant.

Up until the crossing of the Niemen on 23 June, the weather in the region had been extremely hot and dry. Streams and wells had run dry, and there was a serious shortage of clean, safe drinking water for the men and horses of the *Grande Armée*. This rapidly became so severe that many men were reduced to drinking their own urine; many cases of suicide among the troops were reported and the proportion of stragglers grew to frightening levels. Napoleon, faced with a huge logistical problem, which would destroy his plan if he did not solve it quickly and effectively, just turned his back on it – and it ceased to exist. 'They have no bread. Let them requisition cake!'

So was the Grand Duchy of Warsaw ruined: thousands of civilians and soldiers were dead. Yet no-one dared to tell the Emperor that he had committed a series of cardinal errors. On rolled the endless columns of troops, recalcitrant conscripts, guns, equipment, supplies, camp followers, remounts and workshops, eastwards across Europe towards the River Niemen. The weather was fine and warm, the columns were shrouded in great, choking clouds of dust from the light soil, and many of the young conscripts, unused to prolonged heavy physical strain, fell out to the sides of the roads. The regiments and the overworked horses and oxen began to dwindle away.

On 23 June, under strict security as to its intentions, the vanguard of the *Grande Armée* reached the bank of the fateful River Niemen a short distance above the town of Kowno; the construction of three bridges was ordered. Napoleon was at one of the sites and Chambray reports hearing him hum the then-popular tune, 'Marlborough'. '*S'en va-t-en guerre*,' run the words, then repeat, more than once, the line: '*Ne sait quand reviendra.*' (He went to war, I don't know when he'll be back)

Next day Napoleon, with the first of the fighting troops of Davout's I Corps, crossed the river and trod the soil of Holy Mother Russia. A lone Cossack asked what they wanted and then galloped off into the woods. This was going to be a piece of cake. The II and III Corps followed. There was only one of Barclay de Tolly's divisions in the area; the surprise had been complete and a major river obstacle had been overcome without (combat) loss.

So the vast horde poured into Lithuania in extreme confusion, dying, shaking itself to pieces as it went, and the Russian armies fell back before them in very good order. Kowno was abandoned to the invaders without resistance, as was Wilna, which the Emperor entered on 28 June. Lithuania had fallen.

The Imperial headquarters and the Guard drew their rations as before, while the rest of the army pressed on with their sufferings, their requisitions, their looting and their outrages – as before.

A sudden change of weather took place on 29 June; a period of unseasonal cold began, coupled with violent rainstorms, which lasted until 4 July. The roads of the area were not metalled; the soil was light and sandy. In hot weather the marching columns were permanently shrouded in clouds of dust. But as soon as it rained, these same 'roads' were quickly turned into knee-deep quagmires, which stalled progress, trapped all vehicles up to their axles in mud and exhausted men and horses. The heavy wagons from western Europe just sank into this morass. Some 10,000 of Napoleon's precious horses died in this brief wet spell. More were reduced to such a weakened state that they were non-effective as cavalry chargers of draught animals – and died some days or weeks later. The logistical theory of the invasion was that the supplies in the wagons would be eaten down, then the draught animals would be slaughtered and cooked on fires built from the vehicles. As it was, the horses died, the food rotted and the wagons remained mired, blocking the 'roads' of the advance.

How had the Russians managed to evade Napoleon's great leap forward at the start of the campaign? The *Grande Armée* was divided into three groups and confronted the weaker Russian defence forces as shown below:

The X Corps was at Tilsit to the north east, with the task of guarding the far northern flank of the main body.
TOTAL 32,500 men, 100 guns.

They were opposed initially by the Riga garrison.
TOTAL 10,000 men, 28 guns.

These would later be joined by the Army of Finland of Lieutenant-General Count F.F. Steinheil.
TOTAL 28,000 men and 78 guns.

The Emperor commanded the main body, which concentrated between Danzig and Thorn and consisted of the Imperial Guard, I, II and III Corps and the I and II Cavalry Corps.
TOTAL 180,986 men, 528 guns.

Prince Eugene commanded the IV and VI Corps and the III Cavalry Corps around Plock, to the south of Napoleon's main body.
TOTAL 85,850 men, 150 guns.

These two groups were opposed by Barclay's 1st Army of the West, between Grodno and Vilna, with Wittgenstein's independent corps to the north.
TOTAL 104,290 men, 488 guns

King Jerome of Westphalia was to the south east again around Warsaw and Lublin with the V, VII and VIII Corps and the IV Cavalry Corps.
TOTAL 75,155 men, 232 guns.

They were opposed by Bagration's 2nd Army of the West between Bialystock and Brest Litovsk.
TOTAL 47,910 men, 180 guns.

Far to the south, around the Pripet marshes, was Schwarzenberg with the Austrian corps (and the VII Corps) at Lemberg.
TOTAL 49,313 men, 130 guns.

They were facing General of Cavalry A. P. Tormasov's 3rd Army of the West at Lutsk.
TOTAL 45,850 men, 164 guns.

Readers will have noticed that the third largest of Napoleon's armies was commanded by his brother, Jerome, whose performance as a military commander of a much smaller force had been so clearly recognised and condemned by the Emperor as pathetic in 1809. Once again the question arises: why did the Emperor continue to tolerate the antics of his siblings, who distracted him so frequently and failed him so utterly? Not only was Jerome given four corps to toy with, he was also given *the* key role to play in the crucial initial phase of the invasion; his aim was to catch and destroy Bagration's 2nd Army.

For some reason, the position of Jerome's group, spread out from Warsaw in the north west to the area of the River Bug – 160 km to the south east – in order to facilitate foraging prior to advancing eastwards, was wrongly assessed by Napoleon in relation to the speed of the 'lunge' that they would have to make in order to catch and destroy Bagration's 2nd Army.

As the Westphalian General von Ochs's biographer, Leopold, Freiherr von Holzhausen, recorded on page 220 of his work:

> On 14 June the king received orders to cross the River Niemen at Grodno. As the right wing of the *Grande Armée* had previously been designated to operate against Wolhynia [the present-day Ukraine], most of the troops were located in this direction and needed several marches in order to reach their new line of operations.
>
> By 17/18 June the Westphalian Corps was concentrated around Pultusk [50 km north of Warsaw] and set off by forced marches behind V [*Polish*] Corps via Ostrolenka [on the River Narew], Sczyczyn and Augustowo towards Grodno.[2]
>
> Napoleon and the main body of the army crossed the River Niemen at Kowno on 23/24 June and the advanced guard entered Wilna on 28 June. Napoleon's aim was to prevent the unification of the 1st and 2nd Russian Armies – this gave the king of Westphalia the task of catching up with Bagration's 2nd Army and bringing him to battle while Davout, with 40,000 men, raced for Minsk, to turn Bagration's northern flank and cut him off from Barclay de Tolly's 1st Army.
>
> Jerome tried to fulfill the Emperor's wishes by pushing on at full speed by more forced marches but, despite all the efforts of his men, his advanced guard reached Grodno only on 28 June. The Russians had broken the bridges; General Allix had them rapidly rebuilt and the VIII Corps entered Grodno that same day. There was a minor brush with some of Platow's cossacks who lost about 100 men.
>
> King Jerome entered the town with his guard cavalry and a Polish division on 28 June; the Westfalian infantry [those that had not fallen out with exhaustion or died of fatigue] came in on 2 July.
>
> Napoleon made Jerome entirely responsible for Bagration's escape, forgetting that on 14 June his V and VIII Corps were still in cantonements on the Vistula and the Bug. Jerome now allowed his shattered troops two days' rest so that the stragglers could catch up.

If Napoleon's judgement of Jerome's martial skills in 1809 was correct – and it is quite clear that it was – then why on earth did he let him loose again in such a senior position only three years later? And why did he allocate such a key role to his bungling brother's command? Was he subconsciously ensuring that a suitable whipping boy would be available when he needed one?

Another Westphalian participant who left records of the epic disaster was von Lossberg, a battalion commander with the 3rd Line Infantry Regiment. His account of Jerome's 'Great Leap Forward' seems to throw some doubt on the king's comprehension of 'speed'. He wrote:

> 20 June. Near Sielun. The king's army is moving on Grodno; the VIII Corps marched for eight hours today. We lost a lot of time due to having to halt and

present arms each time the king passed, and we had to wait from 2 o'clock in the morning to 7 o'clock, in order to draw six days' rations of flour. We only reached our bivouac at 7 o'clock at night and were very tired.

21 June. The same nonsense with presenting arms all day. Many officers try to make names for themselves in this manner. I do not know why Vandamme and Tharreau[3] permit it. If the king knew that each man was carrying 50–60 pounds and that they are so exhausted by this continual parading, I am sure he would also forbid it.

There were violent rows and recriminations between General Dominique-Joseph Vandamme (commander, VIII Corps) and King Jerome in Grodno on 30 June; Jerome removed Vandamme from command. Both men wrote passionate letters of self-justification to the Emperor. Napoleon appointed General Junot, probably mentally unstable at this point, to take Vandamme's place as corps commander. Vandamme's going was deeply regretted by all members of his corps; they were less worried that the Merry Monarch would soon depart. Junot's erratic actions at the critical battles of Smolensk and Valutina Gora were to cost his men dear.

Already, in this early stage of the campaign, the Emperor was becoming very uneasy at the military conduct of his brother – and others.

To Jerome Napoleon, King of Westphalia
Wilna, 4th July 1812.
I have received your packet sent from Grodno, at four o'clock yesterday afternoon. I was exceedingly glad of its arrival, as I hoped you would have sent the Major-General[4] news of Bagration's Corps, of the direction in which Prince Poniatowski had pursued it, and of the movements of troops in Volhynia. What was my astonishment at learning that all the Major-General received, was a complaint of a General!

I can only express my dissatisfaction at the small amount of information I have from you. I neither know the number of Bagration's divisions, nor their names, nor where he was, nor what information you obtained at Grodno, nor what you are doing. I have five or six columns in motion, to intercept Bagration's march. I cannot think you have so neglected your duty, as not to have pursued him, the very next morning. I hope, at all events, that Prince Poniatowski has followed him, with the whole of the 5th Corps. My operations are stopped for want of information from Grodno. I have had none since the 30th. The Chief of your staff does not write; Prince Poniatowski does not write. It is impossible to make war in this fashion! You never think to speak of anything but trifles, and I am distressed to see how thoroughly small-minded you are. If General Vandamme has committed acts of brigandage, you did well to send him to the rear, but in present circumstances the question is such a secondary one, that I regret you have not sent me information which might have been of service to me, nor explained your position by your courier.

I do not know why Prince Poniatowski does not correspond with the Major-General twice a day. I certainly ordered him to do so.

Postscript. You are jeopardising the whole success of the campaign, on the right; it is not possible to carry on the war in this way.
Correspondence CCCCI.

About this time, General Vandamme was removed from command of the VIII Corps. Von Lossberg had this to say on the event:

> Something about which I as a soldier am very sorry, is that Vandamme is leaving the army due to disagreements with the king. It is said that he meddled in the internal affairs of the Westphalian army. I cannot confirm this, but if he complained about the general staff and the commissary officials, he certainly had just grounds for unease. Especially the commissary officials, whose qualifications are limited, it seems, only to a knowledge of the French language. Thus only Frenchmen and French-speaking Germans are found in this branch, and many of these *ex-patriate* Frenchmen have often been openly condemned by Vandamme as being totally incompetent. We shall only realise the full effects of his loss when we enter our first combat; this is his element, I believe.

So what was happening on the Russian side of the hill? We know that Prince Bagration chafed at being under the command of Barclay de Tolly and hated surrendering even a foot of Russian soil. This letter from Bagration to Araktchejev, received by the latter on 15 August, gives us some insight into his agony:

> ...It's not my fault; initially we stretched ourselves out like a piece of catgut until the enemy fell upon us. Without firing a shot we began to withdraw, I don't know why. In the army – as in all Russia – all think we have been betrayed. I cannot defend Russia alone. The 1st Army ought to advance to Wilna at once; what do we fear? I am completely surrounded and cannot yet say where I will break out. I am not inactive but my state of health has changed and I have been feeling unwell for some days. I ask you as a friend – ADVANCE! Russians must not flee. We are starting worse than the Prussians.
>
> I will find a point where I can break through, even with loss. For you it is insulting. You have a fortified camp in your rear, there are no enemy forces on your flanks and only a weak corps to your front. You must attack. The queue of my army has been fighting hand-to-hand for a whole day now... I cannot fall back on Minsk and Wilieka due to the forests, swamps and bad roads. I have no peace. As God is my witness, I am glad to do anything, but one must act with certainty and according to circumstances. You have withdrawn and I have to fight my way out. If I am not strong enough to carry out this task, it is better to relieve me of this burden and give the command to another; why sacrifice the troops to no purpose and without satisfaction? I advise you, attack at once. Don't listen to anyone. The bullet is a cowardly poltroon, the bayonet is bold. That's how I think. The wisdom of Phull!
>
> Lament for the Czar and for Russia! Why let the enemy dictate to us when we can beat him? It is very easy to give the order to advance; make strong reconnaissances with the cavalry and attack with the whole army. That is honour and fame! Also, I assure you, do not stay in the armed camp. The enemy won't attack you but outflank you. Attack for God's sake! The troops are brave! Orders were given for us to fight but now we always run away. Here you have my openness and dedication to the Czar and to my Fatherland. If you do not agree with me then let me go. I do not want to witness the destructive results. You can fall back 500 Wersts if our destruction threatens.

Now excuse me! I have spoken to you as one Russian to another. If you don't share my opinion then forgive me!

Between us, I have been extremely insulted by the 'Minister' [Bagration always referred to Barclay in this derogatory fashion] but he has considered things and asked me in writing for forgiveness. I have forgiven him too and treated him as a senior and not a junior commander. I do this – and will continue to do it out of dedication to my monarch.

Prince Peter Bagration, on the march at Katan village, 7 August.

Another letter from Bagration to Araktchejev was written on 10 August:

For heaven's sake, you may send me where you wish – even as a regimental commander – to Moldavia or the Caucasus, but I cannot stay here; the whole headquarters is so filled with Germans that it is impossible for a Russian to survive. You may send me on leave if only for a month. By God, I'm being driven mad by all this to-ing and fro-ing! The army has scarcely 40,000 men but it is stretched out like a thread and drags itself to flank and rear. You can split my army into two corps; give one to Rajewsky, the other to Gorchakov, but send me on leave! I thought I was serving the Czar and the Fatherland, but it seems that I'm serving Barclay. I confess, I don't want to.

On 16 July Marshal Davout arrived at Jerome's headquarters in Nieschwitz and, with great satisfaction, handed him a letter from the Emperor; it was to tell Jerome that he was sacked and should return to his seraglio in Kassel. Davout took command of the right wing of the *Grande Armée*. But this failure in the southern sector of the central front was not the only thing that went wrong in this Great Plan. Napoleon's personally-led main group of the *Grande Armée*, to the north of Jerome's, was also unable to bring its prey (Barclay) to battle when they rushed across the Niemen on 23 and 24 June 1812.

Jerome had failed his brother again, but so had all the other commanders in the *Grande Armée* in 1812. Perhaps the goals that the Emperor set them were simply unattainable given the weather, the distances to be covered, the state of the roads and the tactical agility of the Russian armies. The cost of the pursuit to Jerome's group had been high (and would continue to be so), despite the almost total lack of contact with the enemy, as can be seen from the parade statistics shown below:

Corps	23 June	20 July	28 July
V (Poles)	30,000	23,000	22,000
VII (Saxons)	17,000	14,000	12,500
VIII (Westfalians)	18,000	14,000	10,000
IV Cavalry Corps	10,000	6,500	5,000
Totals	75,000	57,500	50,000
Deficit		17,500	25,000

So, in less than a month, Jerome's army had lost one third of its strength, and the only action it had fought was on 9 July at Korelitchi, where their advanced guard had lost 356 casualties to Hetman Platov's Cossacks. These losses were reflected in the other

The crossing of the River Niemen at Pilony on 30 June, with grenadiers and a pontoon vehicle.
Faber du Four.

French armies of the central group as they straggled forwards. If the chase was to extend for any distance, it did not need a genius to calculate that the *Grande Armée* would evaporate from a raging torrent to a pathetic trickle, even without fighting any battles.

If Jerome was late at Grodno on 28 June, Prince Eugene's central group was even further behind. They reached the Niemen at the village of Preni (about 30 km south of Kowno) on 2 July, had advanced as far as Novi Troki by 12 July and were reviewed by Napoleon at Wilna two days later.

Even in early June, Captain Abraham Calkoen, a member of the 2nd (Dutch) Chevau-Leger-Lanciers of the Guard, had written to his father:

> You cannot imagine these countries, especially northern Poland. They are real deserts. You can march ten leagues over sandy heathland without even seeing a house. The villages that you find at the end of the day are just miserable little hamlets of 'Noah's Arks', where the host, his guests, his oxen, his pigs, his lice and his chickens all live in the same room. The pigs eat under the table, just like dogs. You can imagine what the beds are like – one is absolutely devoured by fleas. The food is of a similar standard; there is no wine, just a miserable, sour, black beer, and the high point is a disgusting sort of brandy. The crowning misfortune is a language that was invented by the devil, and a nation so stupid that they cannot even understand sign language. All this applies only to the country bumpkins – the inhabitants of Warsaw and Posen are very friendly and speak French very well.

The Emperor is in the neighbourhood and we await his arrival from Danzig. Tomorrow we are going to Braunsberg, and from there to Koenigsberg... We march 10 to 15 hours a day in suffocating heat, but then yesterday we had the first rain and hail, and it was very cold. I hope we have some decent weather at the bivouac, which cannot be far away.

Notes

1 The border between Hamburg and Denmark then ran close up to the city.

2 From Pultusk to Grodno was a distance of about 250 km; marching at a rate of 20 km per day – as in the Nijmegen Marches today – this would take about 12 days on good roads with healthy, well-nourished men. In Lithuania in 1812, none of these criteria applied, but despite this, his men – some of them – covered the distance in just ten days. It was not good enough for the Emperor.

3 Commander, 23rd Infantry Division.

4 Alexandre Berthier, Napoleon's invaluable Chief of Staff.

Chapter 3

Wilna – Tinseltown

On 28 June Napoleon had entered Wilna, capital of Lithuania, in triumph just after the Czar's headquarters had evacuated it. The town was decorated with the badges of Poland and Lithuania (the white eagle and the mounted warrior) and that evening a delegation of the local nobility approached him to beg for the confederation of the two states, which Napoleon was only too pleased to agree to. On 1 July, a solemn proclamation to this effect was read out in Wilna cathedral and two days later an imperial decree was published nominating a provisional government with Bignon as imperial commissaire. One of the first acts of this new government was to order the raising of five infantry and four cavalry regiments, which were integrated into the army of the Grand Duchy of Warsaw as the 18th–22nd Infantry and 17th–20th Lancer Regiments. Prince Ronauld Giedroyc was appointed Commander-in-Chief of this embryonic army and one of Napoleon's aides, the Dutch General Hogendorp, was given the task of supervising the raising and organization of the new troops. Fine words and titles indeed, but the tiny state had absolutely no funds with which to realise the scheme and its economy was in ruins due to the effects of the war so far. A large loan had to be granted from the imperial treasury for the purpose but men, weapons and equipment were extremely hard to find and many of the new units were never brought up to full establishment. His failure to galvanise the entire Lithuanian nation for his own purposes was a deep disappointment to Napoleon; only the upper aristocracy and the students rallied to his colours, while the mass of the populace remained passive. Another anticlimax was how few Lithuanians in Russian and Austrian service left their posts to return home and join these new regiments.

From the various accounts that have been consulted, there emerges a picture of Wilna in July of 1812 as being an island of sanity, order and plenty, worlds away from the grim, bitter struggle for existence that was consuming everyone else in the central sector of the Russian front. It was Hollywood in 1812.

Here was Napoleon, his Imperial court, etiquette, the splendid Imperial Guard, the glittering diplomatic corps, receptions, balls and parties, plays, dinners, grand parades and troop reviews. Outside the gates was a sea of desolation that stretched for scores of miles in every direction. Inside was civilisation on the Parisian level; outside were horror, hopelessness, destruction, starvation and want on a scale not seen since the worst days of the Thirty Years' War. And the invasion had only just begun.

So both main Russian armies escaped intact to the east to fight another day. True, their initial attempts to join up were frustrated at Mir on 10 July and at Saltanovka (Mogilev) on 23 July, but their critically important junction took place at Smolensk on 16 August.

Napoleon's plan had been over-ambitious and had misfired; once again, he had underestimated his enemy. What was he now to do? Even before the invasion he had been – not surprisingly – confused in his own mind about how to tackle the challenge of the immense Russian empire. At one point he explained that his initial aim was only to liberate Poland. But Poland had once been a vast kingdom, stretching down into south western Russia; so what did he mean?

On another occasion, he said that he would only go as far as Smolensk. 'There or in Minsk', he told a member of his entourage, 'the campaign will end. I shall winter in Wilna, organise Lithuania, and live at Russia's expense. If then peace cannot be secured, I shall, next year, advance into the centre of the enemy's land, and stay there until the Czar becomes pliable.'

When he was in Wilna, with the Russians still fleeing before his armies, he again appraised the strategic situation:

> If Monsieur Barclay imagines that I am going to run after him to the Volga, he is making a great mistake. We will follow him to Smolensk and the Dwina, where a good battle will provide us with quarters... It would certainly be destruction, were we to cross the Dwina this year. I shall go back to Vilna, spend the winter there, send for a troupe from the Théâtre Français, and another to play opera. We shall finish off the affair next May, unless peace is made during the winter.

He then wrote a conciliatory letter to Alexander, proposing negotiations; it was delivered, but never answered.

Prince Schwarzenberg was the commander of the Austrian corps operating together with the Saxons on the right flank of Napoleon's main thrust at Moscow. They started off from Bialystock and reached Lublin on 20 June. On 2 July his advanced guard under General Frehlich crossed the Bug river.

The young Austrian captain of Ulans, Joseph von Boehm, ADC to Schwarzenberg, described the state of the Austrian corps at that point:

> These were select troops; if they were not totally enthusiastic about this operation, they were full of the best military spirit and discipline. We were well supplied with everything and in the best condition. The enemy troops facing us had withdrawn and seemed to wish to avoid combat.

Austrian headquarters were now (4 July) in Pruzany and Prince Schwarzenberg decided to inform Napoleon of these facts and selected von Boehm to carry the despatches to Imperial HQ, which they knew to be in Wilna at this point. 'I knew the contents of the despatches,' wrote von Boehm, 'and I had been briefed to answer any questions the Emperor might ask. I also had some verbal messages for Marshal Berthier and the Foreign Minister, the Duke of Bassano, who was also in Wilna, where he had set up diplomatic headquarters.' Von Boehm set off on the night of 4/5 July and arrived in Grodno at King Jerome's headquarters from the south. He described Jerome's field headquarters:

> I arrived in Grodno on the morning of the 6th and found King Jerome just about to set off to Minsk (to support Davout) with his guards and Prince Poniatowsky's corps. The guards and most of the infantry were in Grodno and its suburbs, and the V Corps (mostly Polish cavalry) were placed in echelon,

by regiments, along the road to Minsk and ready to march off. It would be hard to find finer, or better mounted troops.

The King of Westphalia received me in his quarters; it was a formal court, everyone was in full dress uniforms. My audience was brief and I set off again in a Russian post chase for Lida.

Lida was supposed to have been full of Cossacks the day before, but as the road along the Niemen via Kowno seemed too long for me, and as an Italian cavalry division had already set off in that direction, I took the chance. Arriving in Lida at midday, I found it to be empty of friend or foe, although the townsfolk told me at the post office that 300 Cossacks had left only that morning and were supposed to be in the woods near the town. After a brief pause for thought, I decided to push on for Wilna by the most direct route.

Much to my relief, I met the first of the Chasseurs à cheval of General Claude-Raymond Guyot's division[1], cursing their way through the huge Bialowiczer Forest, in which they had lost their way from Lida. Generals Guyot and Ornano and their staff were sitting disconsolately in a little muddy clearing by the road, roundly cursing the country and everything in it.

As the chasseurs said that they had seen some Cossacks, I asked to be allowed to exchange my post chase for a horse, which the general graciously agreed to; he also gave me a small escort. I distributed my small store of rations among the escort and we set off. We rode through the night and arrived on the outskirts of Wilna at 7 o'clock on the morning of 7 July.

The entire area was devastated, every village thoroughly plundered; there was nothing to be found anywhere. Even some gensdarmes, usually held by the soldiery to be superior beings, had been wounded by a gang of marauders and were cursing the total breakdown of discipline.

Many regiments of IV Corps had absolutely nothing to eat. '*Nous sommes donc venus dans ce sacre pays pour manger des herbes commes les bêtes,*' [We have come to this bloody country to eat grass like the animals] they groaned.

Some regiments – luckier than others – drove entire herds of cattle, sheep and pigs, under heavy guard, with their rearguard.

The cavalry and artillery trains had been foolish enough to let their horses eat green grain; this, combined with the heavy rains and the violent swings in the temperature, meant that the roads and the camp sites were covered with the cadavers of thousands of horses, which no sooner collapsed and died than they began to rot. The air was full of the pestilential stench for miles.

The town and the extensive suburbs were packed with troops of the infantry and cavalry of the Imperial Guard. Imperial headquarters was in the Governor's palace, which Alexander had occupied shortly before. I dismounted, thanked my weary chasseurs and delivered my despatches.

Marshal Berthier, Colonel Count Flahaut (then an ADC to Berthier), Generals Lagrange, Girardin and others greeted me in friendly fashion; my long residence in Paris now paid off well.

Marshal Berthier took my despatches to the Emperor; I immediately fell fast asleep in a chair. Berthier had trouble waking me. '*Reveillez-vous, jeune homme, et suivez-moi; l'empereur desire vous parler a l'instant même; il avait de la peine à croire, que vous etiez par la route de Lida.*' [Wake up young man and follow me; the Emperor wants to know what you saw on the road from Lida.]

We crossed the courtyard to the Emperor's quarters in the palace proper. The reception rooms were full of generals, secretaries busily writing and other civil administrators.

The generals seemed to be quite happy to see an Austrian officer among them. No sooner were we announced than I was ushered in to the Emperor by the duty ADC – General Narbonne if I am not mistaken.

Von Boehm found the emperor in a room that opened onto the garden, and he described him in some detail, noting his uniform, medals (he wore the small crosses of the Order[2] of the Iron Crown and the *Legion d'Honneur)*, and the fact that his famous hat was close by on a side table. He contined his report:

In the centre of the room, several large tables had been pushed together and were covered with Rizzi Zanone's[3] map of Russia and several despatches, including mine. All the latest known positions of the army corps were marked on the map in different coloured pins, that of our Austrian and Saxon corps as well.

When he saw me enter, Napoleon took some steps towards me; his usually piercing glare was somewhat friendlier than usual; he smiled slightly. Speaking quickly, he said: '*Eh bien, vous êtes donc, à ce que Berthier me dit, venu par Lida?*' [Well, you are here, Berthier tells me that you came via Lida?] I answered: 'Yes Sire, via Grodno and Lida.'

'*Et les cosaques,*' he continued, '*on pretend, qu'ils étaient avant-hier à Lida, et n'avez-vous pas recontré de cavalerie italienne?*' [And the cossacks, they tell me that they are between here and Lida, and didn't you meet the Italian cavalry?]

'There were about 300 horses, but they left at dawn on the day of my arrival and I never saw any of them. As for the Italian cavalry, I found them in bivouac in the forest of Bialowicz, three leagues from Lida.'

'*Quand êtes-vous parti votre quartier-general? Et comment va le Prince de Schwarzenberg? N'a-t-il pas souffert de son erespiele jusqu'à présent?*' [When did you leave your headquarters? And how is Prince Schwarzenberg? Is he still suffering from erysipelas?[4]

'The prince is very well, Sire, since he left Paris he is always on horseback.'

'*Avez-vous trouvé de l'avoine dans le pays? Et peut-il fournier ce qu'il vous faut? Ici on n'en trouve qu'avec peine; nous sommes déjà depuis huit jours au vert et j'ai perdu de trois mille chevaux.*' [Have you found oats in this country? Have you been able to make up supplies? We have none here; we have been feeding green corn for eight days and I have lost over three thousand horses.][5]

'Up to now, your majesty, we want for nothing and have found plenty of forage for the subsistence of the cavalry and the train everywhere.'

'*Qu'est ce qui commande votre cavalerie?*' [Who is commanding your cavalry?]

I had to think quickly here, for our cavalry was not concentrated under a specific general as was the French. So I named the most senior cavalry general: 'Feldmarschall-Lieutenant Baron Frimont.'

'*Ah! C'est donc Frimont, du reste il s'appelle Fremont, et non pas Frimont, la famille est française. Et le general Wrede qui sert dans votre cavalerie, est-il parent du general bavarois?'* [Ah! So it is Frimont; there are some who say he should be called Fremont and not Frimont, it is a French family. And General Wrede, is that a relative of the Bavarian general?][6]

I was not sure, but I said that it was; in fact it was his brother. Napoleon now switched subjects: *'Combien de pontoons vous a-t-il fallu, pour passer le Bug? Et comment appelez-vous l'endroit ou vous l'avez passé?'* [How many pontoons did you need to cross the Bug? And what do you call the place at which you crossed?]

'We crossed at three or four spots around Drohyczin and we put twenty pontoons into the river.' I answered, but I was wrong, we used far fewer pontoons.

'Le Bug doit donc être bien large où vous l'avez passé.' [The Bug must be very wide where you crossed.'] responded the Emperor; I said nothing. He came back to Grodno: *'C'est donc le 6 de grand matin, que vous avez passé a Grodno? Il y avait encore des troupes du 5ème corps?'* [You passed through Grodno on the morning of the 6th? There must have been troops of the V Corps there?]

'I passed through Grodno on the morning of the 6th and I found there the king of Westphalia with his general headquarters and the Westphalian guard, and before Grodno all the cavalry of V Corps, echeloned along the road to Minsk, but all were waiting to march with general headquarters.'

'Bah!' interrupted the Emperor, *'Le roi de Westphalie le 6 encore à Grodno, mais çela n'est guère possible! En êtes-vous bien sur?'* [Bah! The King of Westphalia still in Grodno on the 6th! It's scarcely possible! Are you sure?]

I answered that I was certain; he uttered some words of displeasure and muttered to himself. I understood only: *'habits brodés'* [embroidered coats]. He walked up and down and then became friendly again: *'Vous disez au Prince, que je viens de faire écrire a Vienne, pour vous avoir auprès de moi. Vous allez marcher au centre. Vous êtes de braves gens et nous ferons la campagne ensemble.'* [Tell the Prince that I have written to Vienna, because I want you close to me. You will march in the centre. You are fine fellows and we will fight this campaign together.]

Somewhat surprised, I bowed deeply.

'Vous lui direz,' continued Napoleon, mixing up the names of the places, *'que le roi de Naples a enfin vu l'ennemi près de Pilwiskey vers Drissa,[7] il n'y avait que de la cavalerie legère et peu de canons, le roi de Naples les a fait charger, mais les Russes se sont assez mal battus – en general çela n'a pas été de longue durée. Les Russes ont comme d'ordinaire pris le systeme d'exagérer excessivement leurs forces et vous aurez de la peine, d'avoir de bons renseignements. Du reste, s'ils veulent tenir on tachera de les entamer sur la Duena.'* [You will say to him that the king of Naples finally caught the enemy at Pilwisky on the Drissa, they had only some light cavalry and a few cannon, the king of Naples charged them, but the Russians were easily beaten – in general these actions do not last long. The Russians adopt the system of exaggerating their forces and you will have trouble getting good intelligence. For the rest, we will cut the line of the Duena.

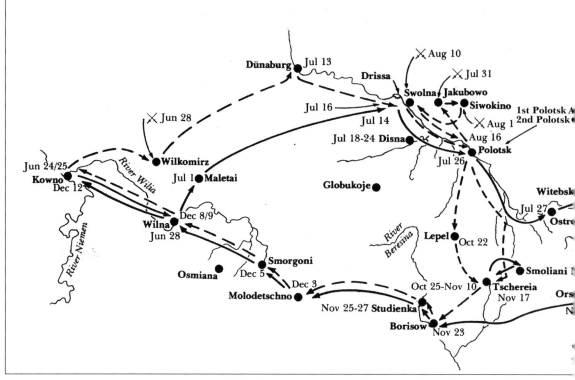

The central area of operations and Polotzk.

A short pause and then: '*C'est donc à Riasna où vous avez quitté le Prince Schwarzenberg?*' [It was at Riasna that you left Prince Schwarzenberg?]

'The Prince's general headquarters are at Pruzany.'[8]

'*Mais c'est Riasna d'après la carte.*' [But it is at Riasna according to the map] said the Emperor, leaning over the table. I pointed silently at Pruzany; he said nothing.

There followed some small talk about how many lancer regiments the Austrians had and whether they were organized by battalions or squadrons and how many. Boehm recalls that he had had the identical conversation with Napoleon in the Tuileries. The Foreign Minister, the Duke of Bassano (Maret) was the conduit through which all correspondence between Napoleon and Schwarzenberg passed – and was filtered. He loved to play the Great Commander and often 'advised' the generals. Boehm's report continued:

Marshal Berthier invited me to attend the review at 6 o'clock that evening and to dine at his table. The marshal's table was wonderfully supplied; all the nobility of the court were there. The problem was that it all went at a great pace, because Napoleon did not like to spend much time eating, and we were in his presence, for he sat at a table in an adjoining room with Berthier, Bassano, Daru and the General of the Day.

Near my quarters was a recruitment stand for the new Lithuanian regiments; brandy flowed in rivers and the patriots made an infernal din,

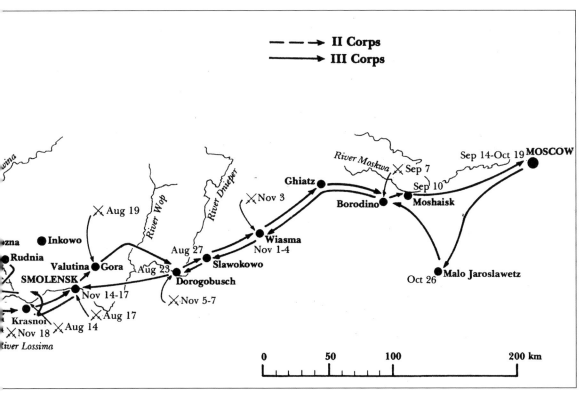

II Corps (dashed arrow legend)
III Corps (solid arrow legend)

Map labels:
MOSCOW — Sep 14-Oct 19
River Moskwa — X Sep 7
Sep 10
Moshaisk
Borodino — X Nov 3
Ghiatz
Malo Jaroslawetz — Oct 26
River Wop
River Dnieper
X Aug 19
X Nov 3
Wiasma — Nov 1-4
Aug 27
Slawokowo
Dorogobusch — X Nov 5-7
Inkowo
zna
Rudnia
Valutina Gora — Aug 23
SMOLENSK — Nov 14-17
X Aug 17
Krasnoi — X Nov 18 — X Aug 14
River Lossima
wina

Scale: 0 50 100 200 km

without much enrolling being done. General Krasinski[9] of the French lancers went to an awful lot of trouble for nothing.

At 6 o'clock that evening, the review took place; there were about 35,000 men of all arms (mainly from the Imperial Guard), all in full dress, arranged in many ranks. I was included in the Emperor's suite, which consisted of only a few people. I had been given a fine Limosine grey to ride, richly harnessed and with gilt stirrups and a red velvet saddle.

Napoleon was in an extremely bad mood and spoke sharply and briefly to Berthier and Caulaincourt. Many complaints were made to him by the local civil authorities about robbery and plundering; most of the corps commanders complained of the utter lack of supplies and of the difficulties of the march; things that he hated to hear about.

On the ride to the parade ground we met scores of looters that had been rounded up by the flying columns; they were threatened with death by shooting by the Emperor. '*Qu'est-ce-que c'est, que ces marauds là; je les mettrai a l'ordre, je les ferai fusiller par douzaines!*' [Who are these, they are maurauders; I will give orders that dozens are to be shot!] he shouted in great rage.

Finally he rode along the front of the parade; utter silence in the ranks. Every now and then a soldier stepped forward, his musket at the present in his left hand, and handed him a note with his right hand. The Emperor spoke to them in a friendly and confidential manner to them. Then he would hand the note to Berthier; once or twice he ripped the supplicants off a strip.

Finally the review was over and the Emperor positioned himself in the centre of the front of the troops... they began to march past him with bands playing. A heavy storm was blowing up fast in the oppressive heat, but none dared to mention it to the Emperor.

Right at the end of the parade Napoleon criticised the commander of a newly-raised battalion of Chasseurs (the men were all the sons of foresters[10]) for the sloppy stance of his men. The unfortunate tried to excuse himself; this enraged the Emperor. '*Laissez-vous, Monsieur, point d'excuses, si vous aviez fait en route, ce que vous auriez dû faire, le bataillon aurait meilleure tenue et il vous serait rester encore assez de temps pour dormir.*' [Quiet Sir, no more excuses. If you had done on the way here what you should have done, your men would have looked much better, and you would have had an opportunity for some sleep.]

The march past was concluded in the pouring rain, and then we all raced back to the palace in Wilna through the mud. Napoleon was sopping wet – as were we all – and the points of his hat were drooping down to his shoulders.

It was now night and several of the staff had gathered around Marshal Berthier. There was bad news from Marshal Davout;[11] it did not remain a secret very long. The Marshal reported that due to the absolute absence of food in the devastated country, and the exhaustion of the troops, who had lost touch with the pitifully few supplies crawling along behind them, that he had been unable to reach Minsk in time to head off Russian Prince Bagration in his attempt to join up with Barclay de Tolly.

Davout's advanced guard had tried, at cost of great losses, to push them off the road from Borisow and into the marshes of Bobruisk, but had failed.

The ingenious plan of the Emperor's had been foiled by local difficulties, and Prince Bagration's march on Smolensk was now unstoppable. His junction with Barclay took place there a few days later.

Next day more bad news arrived by courier; Sebastiani's [2nd Cavalry Division, II Cavalry Corps] cavalry division, in an advanced position near Drissa, was attacked in the night of 6/7 [July] by the Russians. The French sentries were sloppy – it often happened – and 6,000 of the enemy had burst into their camp and taken many prisoners. The 8e Dragoons had been utterly destroyed and some guns had been lost.

This report is a mystery: von Boehm must have misunderstood something. According to Six, Sebastiani was beaten by Wittgenstein at Drissa on 15 July and surprised by Platow at Inkowo on 8 August. For these blunders, he was replaced by Pajol next day. Also, there was no 8e Dragoons in 1812; that regiment had been converted to the 3e Chevau-legers on 18 June 1811. Talleyrand-Perigord was colonel of the 8e Chasseurs à cheval, which was in the 3rd Light Cavalry Division, III Cavalry Corps. Von Boehm continues:

> The colonel of this regiment, Talleyrand-Perigord, a nephew of the minister, appeared shortly afterwards in Wilna with more details of the action.
>
> The poor colonel was one of the first dandys and Beaus of Paris and now he had only that which he stood up in. His horses, his baggage – all had been lost. His many friends chipped in and soon re-equipped him, but the robust military humour (which the French are never short of) was in plentiful supply and there was much to laugh over.
>
> On the morning of 10 July the regiments of the Guard started to move out in the direction of Drissa and Witebsk; these troops were well-supplied with

everything, except forage, of which there was none. Some of the Old Guard remained at Wilna.

They were keen to meet the enemy and all hopes were fixed on their leader [Napoleon] who would be able to solve any difficulties.

For my part, judging by what I had seen here, I could not suppress an ominous feeling of impending doom as I saw them march off. With very few exceptions, they were all dead men! Eight months later, in the headquarters of the Viceroy of Italy (who was in command of the remnants of the army after the great catastrophe) in Frankfurt on the Oder, there were scarcely 500 men fit for duty!

On that same day, the deputations of the councils of the Duchy of Warsaw – and some from Lithuania – went to see the Emperor; the exact content of his speech became known only later, but they all came away with long faces. These delegates had been ambushed and even their leader, Senator Wibicki, and many others, had been robbed by French maurauders.

On 11 July the Reserve Artillery Park was reviewed; some 90 guns and over 300 ammunition wagons had to be abandoned in Wilna due to lack of horses.

There was talk that the great Imperial headquarters would soon move; I thus tried to organize my return trip, but had no luck until the next day.

Post horses were just not available, either in Wilna or the surrounding area. At the Emperor's order, I was issued with a courier's pass by the Major-General [Berthier]. This document required all military and civil authorities to support my journey and to supply me with post horses. I was also able to commandeer ADC's mounts.

The Major-General handed me my despatches, which contained our new orders. He embraced me and asked me to carry his warmest regards to the Prince, whom he hoped to see again soon and to tell him some new secrets.

Under this term, I understood him to mean the general advance of the central army against Barclay's army and the advance against Drissa. [Which failed to materialise, as the Russians abandoned the place.]

Most of Berthier's officers were sent off with despatches that day; the few that were left pitched in to make the best of my farewell party.

The eternal problem was horses; it was impossible to dream of finding any replacements for 20 Meils [150 km] around.

The horses that I took would have to be good for days. I was given a veteran Gensdarme, who led me to a walled enclosure in one of the suburbs, where, under heavy guard, some hundred horses were held, exclusively for use by Imperial Headquarters. They had mainly been requisitioned from Jews and no-one else was allowed to use them.

When Napoleon left Wilna on the night of 16/17 July, Hogendorp was appointed Governor General of Lithuania. Shortly after this, as von Boehm mentioned above, a deputation from the Polish parliament arrived at imperial headquarters to ask Napoleon to declare that Poland had been reconstituted as a political entity; this he refused to do as it might have precipitated a rupture with Austria, and this created a profoundly bad impression among the Poles.

We shall meet young von Boehm again later on in the campaign.

Notes

1 In fact, the 12th Light Cavalry Brigade, IV Corps.

2 Napoleon founded this Order on 5 June 1805, following his coronation as King of Italy on the previous 20 May. The badge of the Order was the ancient crown of old Langobard kings, with the imperial eagle in the centre. The obverse showed Napoleon's bust. The Order ended with the fall of the Kingdom of Italy, but Kaiser Franz I re-established it in its current form [1894] on 12 February 1816.

3 Rizzi Zanone was a member of Goettingen's Academy of Sciences and cartographer to the French navy.

4 A red rash.

5 He was to lose over 10,000.

6 General of Cavalry Karl Philipp von Wrede commanded the 2nd Bavarian Division, VI Corps at Polotzk. In 1813 he would be defeated by Napoleon at the battle of Hanau.

7 On the River Duena.

8 Pruzany is about 45 km further south west from Slonim than Riasna (now Ruzany).

9 General Count Vincent Krasinski commanded the 1st Polish Lancers of the Imperial Guard. After Napoleon's first abdication, he entered the army of the new Kingdom of Poland and later became viceroy of that state.

10 This unit may have been the Polish Jaegers of the Bug.

11 Commander, I Corps.

Chapter 4

After Tinseltown – reality

Meanwhile the starving troops of the *Grande Armée*, lashed ever forward, ever faster by their master, had outrun the surviving, lumbering, wallowing supply vehicles. On 29 June, von Lossberg reflected on the state of supplies:

> Near Jastrzeben. We have had no magazine supplies since Pultusk. Each regiment has now equipped itself with herds of cattle, which march behind it. The Poles, who march in front of us, strip their own country bare in order to be able to feed themselves; the French in East Prussia are supposed to be much worse.

And on 3 July: 'At Lipsk... the king has directed that the troops must limit their food consumption to their issued rations (If only they were issued!)...'

If the logistics of the *Grande Armée* had collapsed at the first fence, the Russians had established an extensive system of ration and forage magazines – and the system worked. At Riga and Duenaburg were stockpiled supplies for eight infantry and four cavalry divisions each for one month; at Drissa were four days' rations, in Disna were thirteen days' rations and ten days' oats. Other depots were established as follows.

Location	Supplies for (weeks)	Infantry division	Cavalry division
Weliki Luki	1	8	4
Novgorod	1	8	4
Bobruisk	4	2	1
Mogilev	8	2	1
Kiev	4	9	4
Sossniza	8	9	4★
Swenziani	4	8	4
★ not complete			

In Grodno, Brest, Slonim, Sluzk, Pinsk and Mosir were each one month's supplies for two infantry and one cavalry divisions, and in Lutzk were two month's supplies for nine infantry and four cavalry divisions.

As events (and the adoption of Phull's plan) proved, these magazines were too large and sited too far to the west, but most of them were eaten down before

Artillery train wagons ford a stream. Albrecht Adam. Author's collection.

French troops on the march; note the water wagon. Albrecht Adam. Author's collection.

The story of Napoleon's logistics in Russia in 1812, encapsulated in one picture. About 10,000 horses died within a few days in July. Faber du Four. Author's collection.

falling into enemy hands, or were burned. There were insufficient bakeries and, when requisitioning was introduced, it failed due to the rapid enemy advance and the scarcity of local produce. The Russian army suffered much hardship during the retreat along the upper reaches of the River Dwina (after abandoning the Drissa camp), as their strategic plans had not foreseen operations in this area and no magazines had been established there. The difficulties which faced the *Grande Armée* during their advance, through a devastated countryside and with no effective supply system of their own, have been graphically recorded by many of the unfortunates who survived the campaign.

In August, the Czar introduced a Grocery Tax on the populace in the area of operations; it was paid in black bread, barley and oats and worked very well after Borodino. During the pursuit of the beaten invaders in November, the supply situation of the Russians was helped immensely by their capture of Napoleon's great depot in Minsk, on 17 November, and of that in Wilna on 8 December.

The retreating Russians applied the scorched earth policy to the land that they left for the invaders; stocks of forage and food were eaten down, evacuated or burned, as were the towns and villages. Wells and streams were defiled with dead animals and refuse.

The 2nd Lancers of the Imperial Guard arrived at Wilna on the evening of 28 June in pouring rain, to find that all the Russian army magazines in the city were ablaze. Albert de Watteville of the regiment wrote to his parents:

> Our reconnaissance tells us that the Russians are still withdrawing. Their
> main body has already crossed the Duena. A small part of Bagration's corps

Supply wagons of the IV Corps, early in the advance. Albrecht Adam. Author's collection.

Bavarian cavalry on the march in July 1812. Albrecht Adam. Author's collection.

has joined the corps which is falling back on Wilna after being defeated at Swenziani.[1] We are told that Counts Orloff and Roumantzieff have already been sent to parley with us. All the information we are gathering and the reports which reach us seem to correspond: the Russians have suffered a disaster and their army has been dispersed. Napoleon is reorganizing Poland, appointing a prefect and sub-prefect at Wilna and setting up units of Gendarmes. Everyone is coming to General Colbert, asking him for passports to take up service at Wilna; Polish deserters from the Russian army are flooding in here every day. We have found some Russian magazines with provisions of all kinds and hospital stores, as well as a tax chest… the countryside is very good, but we are eaten up by insects of all kinds and overwhelmed by the extreme heat. Luckily storms come to refresh us every night.

Bavarian Captain Maillinger[2] described the conditions of the *Grande Armée* on 5 July at Ganuschischki, just east of the River Niemen crossing:

> The shortage of bread began as soon as we touched enemy soil. There was no forage either; we were forced to cut the half-ripened grain for the horses or to drive them into the fields and let them graze. This caused colic, bloat and often the death of the horses. By the bridge of Pilony and at each camp site, we saw hundreds of dead horses, many of them had burst open. On the right bank [of the Niemen] we found dozens of overturned and looted wagons, even from the French and Italian guards. The finest coaches and pack-wagons lay there, each surrounded by a group of dead horses. The impression was that of following a defeated army rather than an advancing one.
>
> In every village and town that we passed through, we found all the houses burned down; the inhabitants had left and taken everything that they could with them, destroying all that they left behind.
>
> On 14 July, at 10 o'clock, Napoleon mustered the Bavarian corps.[3] Despite the difficult marches and the lack of bread, the corps still had over 25,000 men and was in good condition.

At this parade, some of those in the Emperor's retinue said that the VI Corps was even finer than the Imperial Guard. The Westphalian von Lossberg recorded on 6 July:

> Near Jesiory. We left bivouac at Grodno at 2 o'clock in the morning, marched for eight hours and were on the road until midday. We marched in double column with the Poles in the direction of Minsk. Latour-Moubourg is one day's march ahead with eighteen cavalry regiments.
>
> It was so hot that all regiments lost men through exhaustion. In our regiment one officer collapsed and died on the spot. Some hours after reaching the bivouac area, I was told by the officer in charge of the baggage train, that a wagon of the regiment, which had fallen out of the column due to a breakdown, had been attacked by Polish marauders and the NCO and the two drivers who were with the vehicle had been very badly mishandled. Among the items stolen were my best uniform, epaulettes and underwear.
>
> 9 July; near Bjeliza. Again, a heat today such as is unknown in our region. As we entered our bivouac site a number of Polish officers came to meet us with drinks to refresh us. Just as I dismissed the battalion, a mounted Polish

officer rode up to me, presented me with a bottle of red wine and a glass and said: 'Allow me comrade! Very hot! A glass of wine – do you good!'

He then took my servant with him to the sutleress where he could buy more such bottles.

In a manor nearby, which had already been plundered by the Poles, I found some ice, which enabled me to cool my drinks.

The Russian rearguard of the 1st Army of the West was Hetman Platow's Cossack Corps. Withdrawing in good order, defending their homeland with skill and determination, these light horse regiments laid some excellent ambushes for the vanguard cavalry of the *Grande Armée*. On three occasions within a week they gave their pursuers of King Jerome's army (the V Corps and part of Latour-Maubourg's IV Cavalry Corps) a bloody nose.

The clash at Korelitchi, 9 July

A village on the Minsk–Wolkowysk road; a Russian victory of Hetman Platow's Don Cossacks of the 1st Army of the West over General Turno's brigade of the 4th Light Cavalry Division, IV Cavalry Corps. **This was the first action of any size in the invasion.**

The Polish units involved were three squadrons each of the 3rd, 15th and 16th Lancers, some 900 men. Platow's Cossacks were the Pulks of Grekow VIII, Ilovaiski V, Ilovaiski IX, Ilovaiski XI, Ilowaiski XII, Karpov II, Sysojev III and a battery of horse artillery. They totalled about 4,500 men.

Platow deployed most of his force in the wood of Jablonovitchina, south of Mir, with three Sotnia (squadrons) at the village of Piasotchna. The French held Korelitchi; then advanced with the 3rd Polish Lancers of Turno's Light Cavalry Brigade in the lead. This regiment dashed past the Cossacks at Piasotchna and clashed with Sysoyew III's Cossacks. During the mêlée more Cossacks took the 3rd Lancers in rear; only with great difficulty did any of that unfortunate regiment escape. Turno's other regiments advanced on Piasotchna but were driven off.

The Poles lost 356 killed, wounded and captured in this very successful rearguard ambush; Russian losses are not known exactly, but were very light.

Mir, 10 July

The Polish units involved were three squadrons each of the 3rd, 15th and 16th Lancers, some 900 men. Platow's Cossacks were the Pulk of Ilovaiski V, Achtyrski Hussars, Kiev Dragoons and the 2nd Battery of horse artillery of the Don Host. General Kuteinikov's force included the Cossack Pulks of Balabin II, Grekow XVIII, Kharitonov VII, five Sotnias of the Ataman Pulk and the Simpheropolski Tartars. They totalled about 4,500 men and in part were hidden in an ambush trap on the road south from Mir. General Rozniecki, with the 4th Light Cavalry Division, IV Cavalry Corps, advanced recklessly out of the town and sent the 7th Polish Lancers cantering off ahead. They fell into the ambush and were thrown back to Simakowo. General Kaminski's 16th Division, V Corps came up to Mir and there followed a combat which went on until 9 o'clock at night

The clash at Mir, 11 July

Again in the central sector. A village further east from Korelitchi, on the same road, about 180 km south west of Minsk. Almost the same participants as at

continued...

Korelitchi; this time it was Rozniecki's 4th Light Cavalry Division of the IV Cavalry Corps, the 3rd, 9th, 11th, 15th and 16th Lancers. A total of about 1,600 men, probing forward, eager to avenge their defeat of the previous day. Platow's forces were three Cossack Pulks of the Ilovaiskis, the Kiev Dragoons, Achtyrski Hussars, a battery of horse artillery and General Kuteinikov's infantry brigade of three battalions. Russian total was some 5,000 men. Polish losses were about 600 men; the Russians lost 180 killed and wounded. Following their tactical success, Platow continued his withdrawal as he was too weak to think of standing against the vastly superior forces that were bearing down on him.

The clash at Romanowo, 15 July

In the central sector, another village on the Minsk–Wolkowysk road. The Polish pursuit continued; this time the cavalry of the V Polish Corps (General Dziewanovski's 19th Light Cavalry Brigade: 1st Chasseurs and 12th Lancers) some 700 men. Hetman Platow's Cossacks were two Pulks of Ilowaiski, two of Karpov, three of Kuteinikov and that of the Ataman. There were also the Achtyrski Hussars, Kiev Dragoons, the Litowski Ulans, the 5th Jaegers and the 2nd horse artillery battery of the Don Host; some 12,000 men. Platow's task was to slow down the allied advance. Again, the Poles drew the short straw; confronted with a larger Russian force, they began to withdraw. Latour-Maubourg indignantly ordered them to advance again. They were overwhelmed and lost 279 men killed, wounded and captured. Russian losses were light, but not exactly known. The next action would be at Saltanovka, on 23 July.

Four days before this latter action, von Lossberg's fortunes seemed to have been looking up:

> 11 July; near Novogrodek. Novogrodek has been plundered by the Poles – and the Westphalian corps headquarters which followed them also did reasonably well! Our sutleress has also been able to buy supplies, especially beer and brandy, from the numerous marodeurs. This is important, as, in view of the very irregular supplies of food which we receive, the troops have to be self-reliant. Today, as an exception, we have been issued with bread and brandy, and, as our regiment has its own herd of cattle, everyone is eating and drinking at the moment.

On 14 July von Lossberg recorded how bending the army's marching regulations, life could be made much easier:

> Near Nieschwitz. We marched for eight hours and caught up with the Poles again. The king has set up his headquarters in a palace outside the town. This area is a rich grain growing area and one of the best regions of Lithuania for cattle-raising.
>
> The herds of cattle and other domestic animals, which the regiments carry along with them, have grown considerably since the beginning of the campaign. In our regiment we even have two oxen. This herd, under a guard commanded by a reliable NCO, follows the corps and each evening it is turned out to graze near the regimental bivouac. The NCO in charge sends the cattle to be slaughtered to the bivouac and also informs the regiment of his location. The meat from the beasts is distributed to the men for use the next day, so that

they can start cooking as soon as they reach their bivouac place.

Our colonel has also arranged that as soon as we get near to the bivouac area, men from each company are sent out to bring in water and wood. These fatigue parties usually rejoin the regiment before it is dismissed to set up camp, thus much time is saved and within two hours of reaching the camp, the men are eating, while in the other regiments, which stick to the rules, the cooking pots are only just being put over the fires. Our men can thus get to sleep two hours earlier and are better refreshed next morning.

Eight pm. I heard at five pm that the king has been ordered back to Kassel by the emperor for refusing to be ordered about by Davoust. [sic]

And so it was. The day after the clash at Romanowo, Marshal Davout (an old enemy of King Jerome) arrived in the king's headquarters in Nieswitsch, carrying orders from the emperor handing Jerome's command over to him. With no little glee, Davout presented his despatch. The much-humiliated King Jerome at once left the army and headed back to Westphalia, taking the entire guard with him. They were – quite naturally – overjoyed to turn their backs on Russia.

Davout reported this to Napoleon; as soon as Napoleon heard of this, he ordered Jerome to send all but his garde du corps back to Davout. The unhappy troops set off on 21 July, but did not catch up with their corps again until 1 August at Orscha. Jerome and his garde du corps reached Kassel in August – in a sorry state.

The VIII Corps marched for Minsk on 16 July. On 27 July their advanced guard under General Hammerstein reached Orscha on the River Dniester and it was here that General Junot finally caught up with them three days later and took command. The corps stayed in Orscha for fourteen days, allowing many stragglers to

Marshal Mortier, Duke of Treviso, commander of the Young Guard in 1812.

catch up. So far, they had not even seen any live enemy, but had already lost over 2,000 men.

Justice in Russia was rough and rapid. Von Lossberg noted:

> 25 July; near Toloschin. At the little village of Bobre on the River Drujek, we saw some French soldiers of Davoust's [sic] corps shoot a commissary official who had been condemned to death for accepting a bribe of 200 Thalers, to allow food, which should have been collected for the troops, to go to the natives. The low fellow deserved the noose and not a bullet!

On 29 July the Westphalians reached the River Dniepr; on the opposite bank was the village of Kopys. Marshal Davout ordered that they cross the river and occupy the area and the nearby palace. General von Borstel gave the task to von Lossberg:

> I took four companies and crossed to the right bank. The ferry, which I used, could hold two companies, and as soon as they landed on the far bank, the few Cossacks who were in the town left.

With a Polish field officer of Davoust's [sic] staff, I rode through the river beside the ferry; in front of us was a lancer, testing the depth of the water with his lance. Our horses had to swim about six or eight paces. Although my horse had not swum before, it seemed to enjoy it; perhaps because it was in the company of other horses.

Kopys has about 500 houses and 1,500–1,600 inhabitants. The authorities are co-operative and thus I have seen to it that my soldiers will keep out all the stragglers who may come here in the hope of loot. I have already received bread, brandy and fruit for all the troops for one day and have ordered 12,000 rations of bread for tomorrow.

In the town hall here, I found six oxheads of brandy and two hundred flagons of vodka, that were destined for the Russian army. I will not issue this latter item, but take it with us and give it out gradually, so that they can use it to improve the quality of the brandy. The spirit is so strong that only Russian stomachs can take it.

Despite the checks suffered by the Poles, Napoleon was still in an aggressive mood. He was forced to allow the tired troops some rest however, as his generals were increasingly concerned at the rapidly dwindling numbers of men still able to keep up with their eagles.

On 4 August Junot held a review of his corps; eight days later they set off for Smolensk, together with the other corps of the main body of the army. The Westphalians formed the right wing, with I Corps to their left. A reinforcement draft of 300 cavalry and 1,200 infantry had joined the Westphalians in Orscha.

Notes

1 A minor skirmish.
2 Of the Infantry Regiment Koenig, 19th Division, VI Corps.
3 At Sakret, outside Wilna.

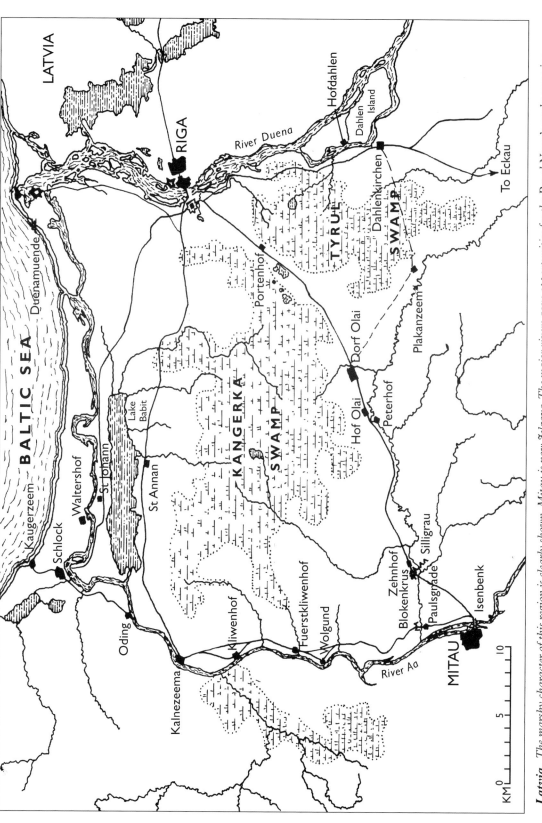

Latvia. The marshy character of this region is clearly shown. Mitau is now Jelgava. The major rivers gave opportunities for the Royal Navy's gunboats to intervene in the conflict on the Russian side.

Chapter 5

Latvia – a world away

In March 1812, France and Prussia signed the Treaty of Paris, in which Prussia was to furnish a corps of 14,000 infantry, 4,000 cavalry, 2,000 gunners and 60 guns to act with the left flank guard up in Latvia and to take the Baltic port of Riga.

The Prussian king was more or less forced to join Napoleon; if he had sided with Russia, his country – and the House of Hohenzollern – would have been destroyed. Prussia was still partially under French occupation and infested with French spies; the surrounding states were awash with troops; the choice was simple. Even if the unbelievable happened, and Napoleon were to be defeated, Friedrich Wilhelm could always expect sympathetic treatment from Alexander.

This move, dictated by sheer necessity, was too much for about thirty senior officers of the Prussian army. Scharnhorst, Gneisenau, Boyen and Clausewitz were among those who left rather than soldier alongside the hated French. Yorck was only persuaded to take part in the expedition by a most persuasive and flattering letter from the king, in his own handwriting, promising rich rewards for his alliegance.

On 9 March General von Grawert was appointed to command the Prussian corps, with General von Yorck as his second-in-command. Napoleon had insisted that Blücher be removed from his command and would not countenance his

Johann David Ludwig von Yorck,
Commander of the Prussian Corps
Born on 26 September 1759 in Potsdam to David Jonathan von Yorck, a captain in a grenadier battalion, Yorck entered military service on 1 December 1772 as an officer cadet. In January 1780 he was cashiered for insubordination to a captain whom he accused of looting and was sentenced to one year's fortress arrest in Friedrichsburg. In June 1781 he entered the Dutch service, and from 1783–84 he served together with the French Admiral Suffren against the British at the Cape of Good Hope and in the East Indies. In 1786 he returned to Berlin and asked Frederic the Great to reinstate him in the Prussian army. The king noted on his letter of application: 'At his own admission, he served in the French fleet under Admiral Suffren. He may be familiar with naval service, but that is no reason to suppose that he would understand land warfare in one of my newly raised regiments.' Next day, Frederic noted: 'After his last service I would be silly

to employ him in the infantry; that would be just like a cook wanting to be a dancing master.'

Yorck persuaded the new king, Freidrich Wilhelm II, to take him back into Prussian service in 1787. He proved to be an excellent regimental officer. In November 1799 he became the commander of the Feldjaeger Regiment, which he found in a neglected state; the officers were brawling drunks and gamblers. The men were indisciplined and spent their time poaching. Yorck improved matters and reaped the king's praise at the 1800 army review. On 11 June 1800 he was promoted to lieutenant-colonel.

Prussian General von Yorck, commander of the Prussian contingent in Latvia in 1812. He was to conclude an armistice with the Russians on 31 December of that year, which saved the Prussians many casualties and gave them a kernel of battle-hardened troops for the 1813 campaign. It also forced the hand of his king, Friedrich Wilhelm III, to come over to the allied side.

In the war of 1806 Yorck was in the Duke of Weimar's corps; after the lost battle of Jena he commanded the rearguard and marched through the Harz mountains to join Blücher's corps. He was wounded and captured at Lübeck. Most of his Jaegers evaded capture and rejoined the colours; they were an example to the entire army. Yorck was exchanged in January 1807 but was still sick from his wound. The defeat of 1806 had hardened and embittered him; he was known as 'the man carved from iron'. He was awarded the Pour le Mérite in 1807.

In November 1811 Yorck was appointed Governor General of Prussia and prepared plans to resist a British invasion. Yorck hated the French and took steps to move all state property out of their clutches. During the campaign in Russia in 1812, Major von Wrangel – ADC to king Friedrich Wilhelm III – was sent by the king as special attaché to General von Grawert, the first commander of the Prussian corps in the invasion. He carried the following verbal orders from the king:

1. Avoid all bloodshed as far as the honour of the troops will allow.
2. In the case of a general withdrawal, part from the French and concentrate the Prussian corps in Graudenz without letting either French or Russians into the fortress.
3. Await further orders from the king there.

When von Wrangel reached the HQ of the Prussian corps in the field Yorck had assumed command, so he delivered his message to him, which must have had great influence on Yorck's conduct in concluding the Convention of Tauroggen with the Russians in December 1812.

From 1813 to 1815 von Yorck commanded the I Corps. Before he left Berlin on 27 March 1813, he attended church service and, kneeling before the altar, said: 'From this moment on, none of us now owns his own life, none of us must count on seeing the end of the war, everyone must be ready and willing to give his life for king and fatherland. Now we go off to war. I swear, an unhappy fatherland will never see me again!'

Yorck was the first to be decorated with the Iron Cross (II Class). At Lützen on 2 May, as he led his corps past the Prussian king, Friedrich Wilhelm asked him: 'Where's the Iron Cross I gave you?' Yorck responded: 'Your Majesty, I won't wear it until those I recommended for it get theirs.' 'You recommended a lot,' said the king. 'Only those who deserved it for bravery!' retorted Yorck.

For his efforts in the 1813 campaign, when he was placed under Blücher's command, Yorck was ennobled as Graf Yorck von Wartenburg. But his greatest test was yet to come. On 16 October von Yorck's I Corps fought and won the battle of Moeckern, outside Leipzig. For this he received the Russian Order of St George 1st Class. On 8 December he was promoted to General of Infantry.

In the 1814 campaign von Yorck fought at Chalons, Montmirail (he was rightly criticised for not joining the fight soon enough), Laon, where he had a blazing row with Gneisenau because the latter forbade him to exploit his initial surprise, and Paris. He was awarded the Grand Cross to the Iron Cross. On 30 May he was in the delegation of the allied monarchs, which went to London.

In April 1815 von Yorck was given command of V Corps, but the war was over before he reached the front. His eldest son was killed at Versailles on 1 July 1815. He retired on 26 December 1815 and died on 4 October 1833 in Klein-Oels, Silesia.

employment in the expedition. Early in the campaign von Grawert fell ill and von Yorck took command.

The Emperor further directed that the Prussians be incorporated into Macdonald's X Corps. Part of the Prussian contingent (three battalions, a troop of dragoons and a battery of artillery) were detached to Memel and a flotilla of six gunboats, with Prussian crews, but under French command, was also stationed there. French General of Engineers, Baron Jacques-David Campredon, commanded the town initially. He later joined Macdonald to command the engineering operations of the siege of Riga.

When X Corps moved forward on Russia on 16 June, the 1st Combined Prussian Hussars were detached to the 7th Division, which had no cavalry of its own.

Etienne-Jacques-Joseph-Alexandre Macdonald, Duc de Tarente, Commander X Corps

Born on 17 November 1765 in Sedan (Ardennes), the son of a Scottish Jacobite, Macdonald entered military service in 1784 in the *Legion Irlandaise*. He had a long and active career, seeing action and being promoted by degrees. He retired from his position as *General de Division* commanding the 3rd Division of the *Armée du Nord* in Zeeland due to ill health in October 1795, but later returned to command the division. In November 1798 he became Governor of Rome and commander of the 1st Division of the *Armée de Rome*. He was victorious at Faventino, Civita Castellana and Otricoli; and at the taking of Calvi. He assaulted Capua without success on 3 January 1799 and was later removed from command due to differences with Championnet.

Throughout 1799 Macdonald saw further action, but, having been sent on sick leave in July, he was relieved of his duties on 13 November. In April 1801 he was appointed ambassador to Denmark until the end of January 1802. He then fell into disfavour with Napoleon in 1804 for his defence of Moreau, who was implicated in a plot to kill the Emperor.

Macdonald went into the service of the Kingdom of Naples in February 1807, a post he held for almost two years, until transferred to the *Armée d'Italie* as commander of the V Corps. On 6 July 1809 he broke the Austrian centre in the battle of Wagram. For this he was made marshal six days later, although he received his baton on the field on the day of the battle. On 14 August 1809 he was created *Grande Aigle* of the *Legion d'Honneur* annd next day he received an annuity of 60,000 francs from Naples. On 9 December 1809 Macdonald was created Duc de Tarente.

On 3 June 1812, Macdonald was appointed to command X Corps in Russia. He crossed the Niemen on 24 June and operated against Riga together with the Prussian corps until 30 December, when Yorck's Prussian corps reached a separate peace with the Russians. This, and the destruction of the *Grande Armée*, forced him to withdraw south-west. He reached Koenigsberg on 3 January 1813 and Danzig seven days later. Here he handed over the X Corps to General Rapp and was placed *à la suite* of the imperial general staff.

He went on to command the right wing of the army at Lützen and at Bautzen, before being appointed commander of the *Armée de la Bober* and being heavily defeated at the Katzbach by Blücher. He fought at Wachau on 16 October and at Leipzig two days later; escaping capture by swimming the River Elster

In the 1814 campaign he fought in various actions and was charged by Napoleon, together with Ney and Caulaincourt, with negotiating peace with the allied monarchs on 4 April. On 6 May he became a member of the council of war under Louis XVIII and on 4 June he was created a Peer of France.

As commander of the *Armée du Gard* Macdonald accompanied Louis XVIII to the Belgian frontier in 1815, then returned to Paris to serve as a grenadier in the National Guard. After Napoleon's second abdication he was created *Grande Chancelier of the Legion d'Honneur*. In September 1815 he became Minister of State and a member of the privy council. Further honours followed: the Grand Cross of the Order of St Louis in January 1816 and Knight Commander of the Order of St Esprit in 1820. Due to his frankness in dealing with the king, Louis dubbed him 'His Outspokenness'. Macdonald was bald in 1812 and very embarrassed about it; hence his pleasure at the arrival of his wig. He died on 25 September 1840 in the castle of Courcelles-le-Roi (Loiret).

The effects of Napoleon's mad invasion were to be seen even in early May, as Lieutenant Julius Hartwich of the Prussian Leib-Infanterie-Regiment reported from the Marienburg-Dirschau area on the Vistula on 3 May:

> We had now reached the Military Road – a concept of horror at this time – along which the army had been advancing for some weeks. The banks of the Vistula had been like the promised land; but what a state they were now in! Robbed bare, stripped of supplies, the cattle laying dead all over the place. For

the supply trains and artillery parks, which passed through on the soft, dirt roads, demanded draught animals from the farmers, to replace their own starving nags that could no longer pull their loads. The first ones took all the horses; when all of these were gone, they took cows and even calves, which were rapidly driven to death. So the cadavers littered the sides of the road, in which the vehicles remained, stuck up to their axles in mud, while the drivers quartered themselves on the unfortunate peasants. The scenes of devastation were indescribable.

Along the road were splendid manor farms, with gilded domes on the gables, over two or three floors of windows, glittering in the sun. These were the homes of the old Prussian colonists, the Mennonites, whom Frederick the Great had urged to settle these once-empty lands.

In Czarlin were still 20 men and 70 horses from the artillery train of the Prince of Eckmühl.[1]

Apart from the mayor's house, there were only seven workers' cottages in the place. In order to give the men of the regiment straw for their bivouacs, most of these roofs had been stripped.

The local supplies have already been exhausted; luckily, we get a daily ration of $\frac{1}{2}$ lb of bread, $\frac{1}{8}$ Metzen[2] peas, $\frac{1}{8}$ quart of brandy and, on each third day, a 6 lb loaf. The Administrator here is rich; he hosts us four officers, Dr Khiel from the company, the son of the glass merchant from Brandenburg and the sergeant major, as well as finding a camping site for 75 men.

The Prussians now marched on to cross the River Vistula by the bridge of boats built by the French at Dirschau. Although the distance they had to cover was only two Meilen (15 km) it took eight hours due to the washed-out state of the roads. Dirschau had been entrenched to form an armed bridgehead.

Hartwich continued: 'On 6th May we marched on through verdant cornfields and over wooded hills, some 20 km to Mühlhausen; we marched together with the 25e French Regiment.'[3]

On 9 May Hartwich passed Heiligenbeil and two days later the Prussians entered Koenigsberg, where they passed in review before generals von Grawert, von Yorck and von Heister. By 29 May, Hartwich's regiment was downstream from Tilsit on the lower River Niemen; the weather was fine and he had time to record his impressions of the fisherfolk of the area:

... these fisherfolk are amongst the poorest here. They live under the sky, nine families in all, each family protected only by a canvas sheet stretched diagonally over them. The able men and women go fishing every day and only come back in the evenings. Old folk of both sexes weave nets and care for the dozens of children playing in the sand. Some evenings I went back to their camp and watched them eat supper. They would scatter salt on their slice of bread, then place small, boiled fish on it; then they would take some soup with a large, wooden ladle and drink it. They bartered the bigger fish for thread, bread and their insignificant clothing. It was heart-breaking to see.

Even here, the inevitable effects of the sudden, great increase of population, which this area had to support, were all too soon evident.

The Georgian General Prince Peter Bagration, commander of the 2nd Russian Army of the West in 1812. Despite being on very poor relations with his commander, Barclay de Tolly, he served loyally under him and extracted his army from the jaws of Napoleon's trap at the start of the campaign. He was mortally wounded at Borodino on 7 September and is buried on the battlefield.

The hardships were rapidly increased; the prices of all foodstuffs shot up and rationing was introduced. Meat was almost too dear to think of, so we cooked in our billets. Had it not been for the cheap fish, I don't know what would have become of us.

On 12th June, Marshal Macdonald entered Labiau ... On this day a corps of 20,000 Frenchmen were in the area of Tapiau; they devastated the entire area, because there was no forage for their horses.

On 15th June, Napoleon reviewed 40,000 French (?) troops at Wehlau ... he then went on to Gumbinnen to review all the other French troops.

Our [Prussian] headquarters was in Tilsit. On 22nd June we began to build a bridge of boats over the River Memel, which was not finished until the evening of the 23rd. Marshal Macdonald, Duke of Tarento, was also here. On 28th June we marched for Tauroggen, crossing the Russian border at Kutturen, and went on to Mordel, the first Russian village; we then went on to Tauroggen itself.

This was the first time that I had been in a foreign country in my life; I could not understand the language, and even in the heat of summer, the local people were wearing fur coats and long skirts.

By 1st July we were in Rossiena, a pretty and clean little town of straw-thatched wooden houses. There was also a fine (Fransiscan) abbey, with a tiled roof, in which Marshal Macdonald set up his headquarters. Next day, we discovered a 'Colonial Shop' with lots of cheap goods; we bought plenty for our mess kitchen. This was well-advised, as yesterday, we heard that the corps paymaster had no more money with which to pay our wages. We were, however, issued with our usual rations of 1lb of meat, 6oz rice, or 8oz of pearl barley, tobacco, brandy and butter. We have also bought an ox, a sheep and eight chickens, who march with us.

On 7th July we marched on to Telsche, where we built a hutted camp. This was a sizeable Russian town.

On 10th July I was witness to an odd ceremony. In the presence of the local aristocracy, the local councils and our officer corps, the Prince Bishop Zandrowitsch of Samogitie dissolved the oath of loyalty to Russia and the people thus joined the insurrection. The County Councils swore alliegance to Napoleon. As part of this celebration, the County Councils had to provide each officer with his normal rations plus a bottle of wine, a pound of white bread, four ounces of butter, an ounce of coffee, two ounces of sugar and three eggs.

Latvia was being born.

Far off to the north west of the main theatre of operations, Marshal Macdonald's

X Corps (including most of the Prussian contingent) pushed up to blockade the port city of Riga from 24 July to 18 December.

This operation was very much a side-show in this dramatic campaign; the corps consisted of the 7th and 28th (Prussian) Divisions, about 32,500 men in all. There was not yet a siege train available, so no serious attempt would be made to capture the city. Riga was also low on the list of Russian priorities and it took months for the defence forces to gain in quality and quantity. But the Russians did have an advantage; the Royal Navy, under the diplomatic Admiral James Saumarez, escorted convoys of merchantmen into Riga and cooperated with the defence forces in mounting coastal raids behind French lines. Hartwich's diaries continue:

> On 17th July we reached Memel... Next day we crossed the 'holy' River Aa, then the force split into two halves; one going to Mitau, the other to Liebau. Each detachment had two guns.
>
> That evening, Liebau was found to be free of the enemy. It is a pretty, rich little town on the Baltic coast, with about 6,000 inhabitants and a fine harbour. Most of the houses are of wood, but very finely decorated. The windows are glazed and the benches in front of the doors are painted with red or green oil paint. The town has five churches and a synagogue. The main church is Lutheran and is sited in the best quarter of the town. It is built in the new style, white, with golden decoration inside. It is the most beautiful church that I have yet seen.

Macdonald's advance, in contrast to the mad race forward which took place in the central section, was slow, deliberate and cautious. This gave the Russians in Riga time to prepare their defences and to call up and train a force of militia. The discipline of the polyglot 7th Division was so bad and their depredations on the countryside through which they passed so terrible, that Macdonald finally appointed the Intendant of the Prussian division, Staatsrat Ribbentropp, to manage the collection and distribution of rations and forage for the whole corps.

The men carried three days' rations in their haversacks. This amounted to four pounds of bread, and one each of biscuit and rice. Each company had a ration wagon with five days' worth of bread and biscuit and the three train companies of the corps carried a further twelve days' worth. Two days' worth of forage were also carried.

In great contrast to the heavy and bitter fighting, which took place at Polotzk and in the 'Moscow corridor' – and even at times in the southern sector – the fighting around Riga in Latvia was amazingly low-key and the deprivations suffered by the invaders by no means as harsh or prolonged as in the other sectors. Prussian veterans of combats with the Russians explained their low casualties (despite the heavy volumes of hostile musketry) by saying that the Russians often fired from the hip, only rarely putting the musket to the shoulder. Thus, most of the balls went over the enemies' heads. This harks back to the doctrine of the 'sainted' Suvorov; whose favourite saying was: 'The bayonet is a fine fellow, the bullet is a fool.'

Russian General Essen I commanded the defence forces of Riga and all of Latvia; he was supported by eighteen British and twenty-one Russian gunboats. His chief of staff was Lieutenant Colonel von Tiedemann, who had transferred from Prussian service shortly before the outbreak of war.

Part of the epic cavalry battle, which preceded the final capture of the Grand Battery at Borodino. Russian cuirassiers clash with the Saxon Garde du Corps.

A strong force of Russians under General Weljaminov was busy scouring the countryside before Riga, gathering up or destroying all the stocks of food and fodder that they could find. On 5 July elements of the Prussians and the 7th Division captured a magazine of supplies and a chest of 9,000 Roubels at Ponawesch. The Russians they surprised here belonged to Weljaminov's force.

1st clash at Eckau, 19 July

A village 12 km east of Mitau (now Jelgava), 40 km south of Riga in Latvia. Victory of Prussian Colonel von Horn's 2nd Brigade over General Lœwis's Russian militia. This was the opening action in Latvia.

The Prussian troops involved were the 3rd and 4th Combined Infantry Regiments, 2nd and 6th Fusilier Battalions, the East Prussian Jaeger Battalion, two squadrons of the 3rd Hussars, two of dragoons, two and a half horse batteries and one and a half foot batteries, some 6,585 men. They lost ten killed, sixty-eight wounded and fifteen missing, as well as 116 horses.

The Russian militia and depot troops – scratch units – were eight battalions, eight squadrons of regular cavalry and a Pulk of Cossacks. They totalled 4,200 infantry, 1,200 cavalry and twelve guns. Losses of killed and wounded were not known; 319 were captured as was a colour (by the dragoons) and three ammunition wagons. They were pushed out of Eckau as darkness fell.

The new tactics of the Prussian army (much greater use of skirmishing and

---

continued...

open-order combat) had certainly proved themselves.

This action secured the left flank of the 7th Division and cleared the way for Macdonald to cross the River Duena. On 23 July allied patrols appeared before the walls of Riga; General Essen panicked and set fire to a suburb of the town on the glacis. The strong winds fanned the flames and much of the town was soon destroyed. Damage was estimated at sixteen million Roubels. Essen was sacked.

The first clash at Schlock, 5 August

A coastal village, on an island in the mouth of the River Aa, 18 km west of Riga. A minor Anglo-Russian victory over the Prussians. Russian General Loewis, with part of the Riga garrison (eight battalions and some cavalry) and thirteen British gunboats (with a battalion of infantry on board), against part of the 1st Prussian Brigade (1st Fusilier Battalion, 30 men of the East Prussian Jaeger Battalion and two squadrons of the 3rd Hussars).

The gunboats bombarded the 620 Prussians who fled into a swamp, where they hid all night after losing ten killed and wounded and fifty captured.

The clash at Wolgund, 7 August

A small Latvian village, some 20 km south-west of Riga. A minor Prussian victory (General von Kleist, with the 2nd Brigade) over the Russians of General Loewis.

Prussian units involved were the 3rd Combined Infantry Regiment, three companies of the 6th, the 1st Fusilier Battalion, two squadrons of the 3rd Hussars, two of the 2nd Dragoons and five guns.

General Loewis had eight battalions of militia and grenadier depot troops, 200 cavalry, six guns and six gunboats.

The Russians lost 140 men, the Prussians some sixty-five.

Napoleon demanded more aggressive action of Macdonald and pointed out the possibilities of cooperation with Oudinot at Polotzk, but Macdonald preferred to remain in Latvia, his corps spread out in an arc of about 150 km from Mitau in the west to Jakobstadt on the River Dueina in the east. Perhaps this was a wise decision.

Notes

1 Marshal Davout.

2 1 Metzen = $3/43$ of a litre.

3 The 25e Ligne was in Compans' 5th Division, I Corps.

Chapter 6

The southern sector

We turn now to the southern sector of the war, where the Saxons of the VII Corps and Austrians were operating. This theatre of operations is geographically dominated by the vast Pripet marshes, also known as the Roknito swamps, running eastwards from the area of Kobryn, along the upper reaches of the river of the same name, some 340 km to the town of Mozyr. In places these swamps are 150 km wide. They were – and are – the largest swamps in Europe and a major obstacle to all movement; roads through them are extremely few and far between. They are also extremely dangerous. Austrian accounts of operations there in 1812 talk of men and horses disappearing within seconds, never to be seen again, if they strayed from the track.

The few roads that crossed or entered this marshland were built of tree trunks and were of very limited military use. Running repairs of these fragile tracks was a daily task. Another aspect of life in this region was the mosquito. Men and animals were subject to a constant offensive barrage by thousands of these rapacious insects, which must have made life extremely difficult. There were very few towns or villages within the area of these swamps.

Tha Saxon bridging train company was called upon five times to deploy their pontoon bridges. Despite all the difficulties of the terrain, they returned to Saxony at the end of the campaign with all their vehicles and were missing only ten pontoons that had been damaged and abandoned. Each battalion and squadron of the Saxon corps had a ration wagon. Logistics personnel were attached to the advanced guard and were responsible for requisitioning rations as the corps advanced.

As there were insufficient train vehicles at the start of 1812, Saxony paid for 300 to be made for transporting biscuit. Due to the impassability of the roads, replacement stocks of uniforms, equipment and shoes were sent by river barge from Saxony to the area of operations, along the Vistula and the Bug. Unfortunately, they either never arrived, or came up very late, and most of the items were mouldy. Away from the marshes, the ground was fruitful and the Austrians and Saxons suffered few of the desperate, long-term shortages that so afflicted Napoleon's central group.

The Austrians fielded 26,830 infantry, 7,318 cavalry and 60 guns; while the Saxons, still under Jerome's command at this point, had some 21,000 men and 56 guns, as well as 20 regimental pieces. The allies in this sector were opposed at the end of June by General Tormassow's Third Army of the West, some 46,000 men. It was spread along a front of 275 km facing the River Bug, with its headquarters at Lutzk, on the River Styr; the right wing was at Kowel, the left on the border with Podolien. Off

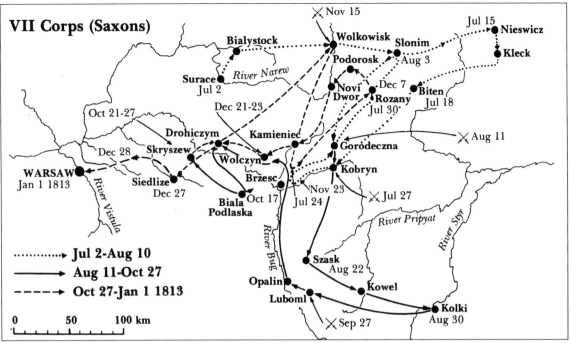

VII Corps (Saxons)

Nov 15
Jul 15 · Nieswicz
Bialystock · Wolkowisk · Slonim
Podorosk · Aug 3 · Kleck
Surace · River Narew
Jul 2
Oct 21-27 · Dec 21-23 · Novi · Dec 7 · Biten
Dwor · Rozany · Jul 18
Drohiczym · Kamieniec · Jul 30
Skryszew · Gorodeczna · × Aug 11
Dec 28 · Wolczyn
WARSAW · Kobryn
Jan 1 1813 · Brzesc
Siedlize · Nov 23
Dec 27 · Biala Oct 17 · Jul 24 · × Jul 27
Podlaska · River Pripyat
River Bug · River Styr

···········▶ Jul 2-Aug 10
———▶ Aug 11-Oct 27
---- ▶ Oct 27-Jan 1 1813

Szask
Aug 22
Opalin · Kowel
Luboml · Kolki
Aug 30
× Sep 27

0   50   100 km

The southern flank; the area of operations of the Austro-Saxons and Tormassow's 3rd Army of the West.

to the east, at Mozyr, was General Ertell's corps of one cavalry and two infantry divisions. This would later be expanded to five infantry divisions.

The young Austrian Captain of Ulans, von Boehm, returning from Imperial headquarters in Wilna to Prince Schwarzenberg's in Pruzany in July, had been given a courier's transport requisition by Marshal Berthier and had managed to acquire 'a very miserable Jew with a Droshki and three good horses.' His account of his adventures continued:

> I took possession of my Jew and set off that evening. Scarcely had we left the town, than he asked me if we might leave the main road and use some shortcuts. He spoke fluent German and had been requisitioned in Kowno. We travelled on for two full days[1] in the direction of Slonim, resting in the woods only in the heat of the day and feeding the horses as well as we could. We changed horses in Slonim, and in the late evening of 15 [July] I reached our headquarters, which was still in Pruzany. [Pruzany was about 50 km north of Kobryn and to the north of the Pripet marshes.]
>
> The Prince was eagerly awaiting the despatches and my report. With his keen sense of the strategic situation, he seemed to be rather worried by our new task of 'marching on the centre', but there was much to be expected from the impending action at Drissa.[2] At all events, there was nothing else for us to do but to set off [north east] in the direction of Borisow.
>
> Our advanced guard had reached Minsk, and our headquarters Neswiecz, on 27 July, when a brigade of Reynier's VII (Saxon) Corps was attacked at Kobryn by Tormassow[3] and mostly captured. Reynier, naturally, called upon the Prince for aid, and this was the turning point of our

campaign, for in turning back to help Reynier, we abandoned the march on Moscow, the horrors of the retreat and of the Beresina, and the almost certain destruction which would have accompanied that.

Napoleon approved of the Prince's decision; the VII Corps was placed under the Prince's command, and the aim of the two corps was now: '*de porter la guerre en Volhynie, de couvrir le duche de Varsovie et la droite de la Grande Armée.*' [… to carry the war into Volhynia, to cover the Duchy of Warsaw and the right of the *Grande Armée*]

Lieutenant von Wolffersdorff, of the Saxon Infantry Regiment Prinz Clemens, relates how the corps, in the best of spirits and well equipped as they marched out of Saxony on 28 March to make for Kalisch, was soon very depressed by marching on muddy tracks in the pouring rain for days on end. As their own draught animals died of exhaustion, there were great difficulties finding replacements, as the natives drove all their stock off into the forests.

The same difficulties were experienced by the Austrians in this difficult terrain. To resolve the problem, Prince Schwarzenberg appointed a general to organize local supplies as they moved. This meant requisitioning from the natives, but great care was taken to prevent violence and it seems that the Austrians suffered little from starvation. In view of the lack of pay – for the agreed funds were not forthcoming from the French authorities – Schwarzenberg organized the issue of wine, brandy and tobacco to the troops in lieu.

At the Polish border, on 5 April, an imperial order detached General von Thielmann's cavalry brigade from the corps and sent it off to join Latour-Maubourg's IV Cavalry Corps. The Saxon Garde du Corps and the von Zastrow Kuerassiers would storm the grand battery at Borodino on 7 September with the 7th Heavy Cavalry Division.

Von Wolffersdorff tells us that on 6 April:

> …we reached Gostyn, which had been partially burned down. I was billeted in one of the outhouses of the abbey and the monks provided for us well. For the first time, I tasted mead, which is common in Poland and is prepared from honey.
>
> On 8 April we were quartered in a run-down old castle of the Graf Rublow. Some of the rooms were well maintained and I shared one with Lieutenant von Neitschitz. It was a great pleasure to sleep in a bed again – the first time since we crossed the Polish border.
>
> On 11 April I was billeted on some poor nobleman who didn't even have any bread.

From 25 April to 12 May VII Corps was in the area of Radom, in eastern Poland. The weather improved, but von Wolffersdorff relates that even then, there was very little food left in the area due to the continual requisitioning by passing troops.

> On 1 June King Jerome of Westphalia reviewed all the troops in the area at Gniewaszow, on the left bank of the Vistula. The king was a very mediocre rider; he rode a very fine English thoroughbred, which was much too fast and spirited for him. As he had come from Warsaw, the Saxon train department had to station 40 horses for his use at each station. He also demanded twelve riding horses for his ADCs.

The Saxon cavalry mounts were used to light bridles and bits; when they were fitted with the heavy Westphalian items, with their gilt fittings and clumsy bits, the horses went mad and threw their riders off. In vain the Saxon grooms tried to explain that the bridles were the trouble; the Westphalians refused to mount the horses again and made do with the peasant horses of the Polish guides, much to the amusement of the onlookers.

In order to reach out to the Austrian corps near Lemberg, the VII Corps extended itself from Lublin, all the way back[4] to Gora near Warsaw.

In the night of 15/16 June my regiment had to march off to Praga, a suburb of Warsaw, on the orders of King Jerome, to relieve his troops there... We stayed in Praga until 19 June and had plenty of time to see the city, which was full of Westphalian troops. I saw a detachment of Italian Horse Guards in wonderfully rich uniforms, with brass helmets and cuirasses...

From now on we bivouacked everywhere, except in rare instances, and we had to subsist just on our field rations, which our servants tried to make appetising; but hunger is the best cook and practice makes perfect. We often changed our march route and the ration wagons had great problems to find us, so we had to allow the men to forage for their food; a very negative step as far as the maintenance of discipline was concerned. The area we were in was very thinly populated; the villages far apart and most of the inhabitants had fled into the forest with their stock before we arrived.

Von Wolffersdorff then described the existing social system in that part of Russian Poland, which shocked him and seems to have been absolute feudalism. There were numerous – but poor – aristocrats who paid no taxes, servile peasant serfs, the property of their lords, who paid taxes and existed on the verges of starvation, and numerous Jews who flourished by holding the monopoly on trade and moneylending, making them despised but essential to the other social groups. They also ran all the inns and shops and functioned as brokers in all major transactions. Once a peasant had fallen into debt with a moneylender, he would never be free again.

The aristocrats were the only class allowed to hold civil offices. The agricultural methods were primitive; land rotation was practised and most of the soil could have produced much more, had it been properly managed. Spreading of manure on the fields was unknown.

The native cattle were small and produced little meat. Oxen were rarely seen. The horses were excellent, but had limited staying power. The ploughs were usually pulled by teams of four of them; often at a trot, with the ploughman running behind. There were plenty of pigs, which seemed to flourish. The meagre harvests seem only to have lasted until the new year, as much of it was rendered as rent or traded for other necessities. The diet of the peasants consisted of pickled beetroot and pickled cabbage, sour

Kaiser Franz I of Austria, Napoleon's father-in-law and reluctant ally in the 1812 campaign. In the 1813 campaign, Austria's decision to come over to the allied side during the armistice sealed the fate of the resurrected Grande Armée in the gigantic battle of Leipzig.

milk, potatoes, gruel and black bread, which was rock-hard and looked like a clump of earth. 'No dog in Saxony would eat it!' Brandy was drunk by young and old every day. Maize was the main winter feed of the cattle and pigs.

Von Wolffersdorff's account moves on to the crossing of the Russian border:

> Our advanced guard reached Poswienko[5] on the road to Suraz on 1 July; we followed today and crossed the border into Russia. The Russian troops had left the place shortly before and had destroyed the bridge over the River Narew. The area is rich and very fruitful... Next day we reached Bialystock. Our whole brigade and the Regiment Prinz Anton, was billeted in the town... which is famous for its breweries; the beer is very strong. Magazines and a hospital have been established here. Cossack patrols are seen every day.

The march eastwards went on; on 7 July the Saxons reached Wolkowysk, near Slonim. The weather was very hot, drinking water was not to be had and many men and horses dropped out of the columns from exhaustion. The Russians opposing them fell back without fighting to Minsk. The Austrians had now reached Ruzany and the V and VIII allied corps, with King Jerome, were in Nowogrudok.

The small Polish ponies could not move the supply wagons fast enough, so the troops existed on their rations of biscuits. The horses began to die from eating green fodder. Despite the heat, in every village the Saxons found cellars full of ice – regrettably the quantities were very small.

By 15 July the Saxons were in Nieswicz, about 90 km south west of Minsk. It was about this time that King Jerome was sent back to Westphalia; Napoleon ordered Reynier to take VII Corps back south west to Slonim to be closer to the Austrians. This was also done at high speed. From Bialystock to Bitin[6] was 330 km and had been covered in 16 days. The men and horses were exhausted.

Sergeant Vollborn, of the Saxon infantry Regiment Prinz Clemens, takes up the story:

> The weapons and equipment used by the Saxons in the 1812 campaign were praised in all official reports. It soon became clear, however, that the Russian weapons, especially the 12 and 8 pound guns, were better than the Saxon 6 and 4 pounders, as were the muskets, especially those of the Russian Jaegers, which had greater range and accuracy than the Saxon weapons.
>
> Our muskets, 'Vienna pattern' of 1811, had many defects; many of the men were terrified of them, as several barrels had burst during live-firing practice. Also, the 'Capots' or greatcoats, many dating from 1807 and used in the 1809 campaign, were worn out, and the French linen camping bags were very unpopular.

On 19 August, Colonel von Mellentin of the Prinz Clemens Regiment felt forced to issue an order to his regiment:

> Certain soldiers – particularly quartermasters – have been tempted by the disgusting example of other troops to mishandle the unfortunate natives by making demands, which their poverty does not allow them to fulfil. The company commanders are herewith required by me to make known to their men – especially the quartermasters – that any man who mishandles a native, no matter what the excuse, will be punished by being placed in staff arrest four days on bread and water, and will be chained to a wagon for four hours daily.

Vollborn wrote of the deadly rush that the VII Corps was forced to make:

> In the period from 5 to 19 July we had to carry out long marches in great heat. On one such march, I think it was the 9 July, 19 men died of exhaustion. The route led through a great pine forest, at the end of which was a little stream, in which were the rotting cadavers of several horses. Everyone rushed to the stream to drink; some drank themselves to death. Duty on the flanking patrols was the worst; there were often no paths and it was cross-country all day.
>
> In the bivouac at Slonim on 10 July, we had the first and most severe court-martial of the campaign. A quartermaster NCO of the 1st Light Infantry Regiment had taken a silver spoon from a manor farm. He was condemned to death and shot at 11 o'clock at night. If one considers that the reduction of the discipline, which gradually occurred, was the outcome of the breakdown of the food supply system, one would have to agree that hundreds of others should also have been shot.
>
> If one of our flank patrols found some of the farmers in the woods, with their animals and their supplies, then they just took what they needed. Opportunity makes a thief.

Premierleutnant Blassmann, of the Prinz Clemens Infantry Regiment, recorded the execution of the NCO:

> The NCO showed great courage at his execution. He selected the comrades that were to shoot him, and made a short final speech. The general had no alternative but to make an example of him, in order to maintain discipline. Then he knelt down on the heap of sand; he died at the first shot, without giving any sign of pain.

Sergeant Vollborn records that during one, well-earned rest at night during this march, there was a great panic when one of the men stuffed his pipe into his cartridge box and then set off his cartridges.

The complete breakdown of the food supply system meant that it was every man for himself. As there was a profusion of wild strawberries in the woods, the men gorged themselves on these – and then were hit by dysentery.

The clash at Kobryn, 27 July.
A town in Grodno province, in the southern sector, 47 km east of Brest-Litowsk. A victory of Russian General Cherbatov's 18th Infantry Division, 3rd Army of the West, over the Saxon General von Klengel's brigade. **This was the opening action in the southern sector.**

In mid-July, Tormassow was ordered to attack the enemy troops to his front. He moved north against VII Corps. General Reynier, aware of Tormassow's advance, still ordered General von Klengel to hold Kobryn (an isolated advanced post) until 28 July. The town lay at the western end of the Pripet marshes, was built of wood and contained a redoubt built by the Swedes during their invasion of 1709.

Adhering to his orders, von Klengel held on, reporting back the various Russian advances to Reynier as they occurred, although he did send off his train vehicles and

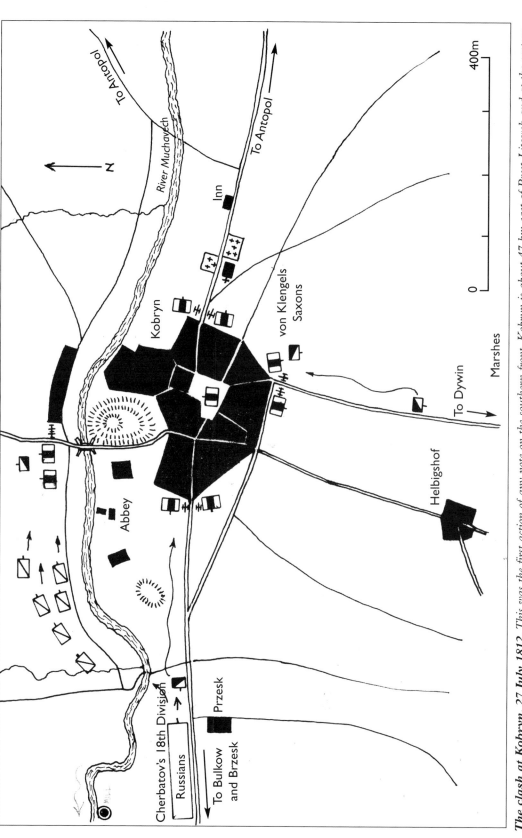

The clash at Kobryn, 27 July 1812. *This was the first action of any note on the southern front. Kobryn is about 47 km east of Brest-Litovsk and at the eastern edge of the Pripet marshes. Saxon General von Klengel, isolated with two infantry regiments, three squadrons of lancers and eight guns, was surprised, overwhelmed and captured in this village by General Cherbatov's 18th Infantry Division of Tormassov's 3rd Army of the West. The earthwork by the bridge dates from the time of the invasion of King Charles XII of Sweden. Author's collection.*

Labels within the map:

To Antopol

River Muchavech

N

Inn

Kobryn

von Klengels Saxons

To Antopol

To Dywin

Marshes

Helbigshof

Abbey

Cherbatov's 18th Division

Russians

Przesk

To Bulkow and Brzesk

MILL

0   400m

an escort of 300 Ulans to safety. On 27 July he was attacked by Cherbatow from Ratno and Mokrany in the south east, while Count Lambert's cavalry corps took Brest-Litowsk along the Bug from the south.

Tormassow's main body of 12,000 men and 22 guns advanced rapidly on Kobryn from the east, from Drohyczin. Klengel's brigade, Infantry Regiments Koenig and von Niesemüschel and Ulan Regiment Prinz Clemens, 3,300 men, did not stand a chance.

Early that day, the Saxon outposts on the roads to Brzesk and Dywin were pushed back on the town by heavy masses of Russian cavalry. At the same time, six other squadrons of Russian cavalry crossed the River Muchawiez by a ford below Kobryn and formed across the road to Pruczany. Russian batteries were placed on the western, southern and eastern sides of the town and opened up a heavy fire. Even though von Klengel might still have been able to slip away, he stuck to his orders to hold on until the next day.

By half-past ten the town was burning fiercely and completely encircled by Russian troops. Two hours of hard fighting followed, in which the Saxons began to run out of ammunition. They withdrew to two points; the market square and the old Swedish earthwork by the river (the Regiment Koenig). Here they held out doggedly for another seven hours, but the situation was clearly hopeless and von Klengel capitulated.

Saxon losses were 108 killed, the rest captured, together with eight guns and four colours. A squadron of eighty Saxon Ulans in Brest was also captured. Russian losses were light. General Tormassow was so impressed at the bravery of the Saxons that he gave the officers back their swords. The prisoners were marched off to Kiev, returning to Saxony only in July 1813; about half of the men died in captivity.

This loss shocked Reynier into calling for help from Schwarzenberg, now marching away from him towards Minsk. Reynier also pulled his corps back, north east, to Ruzany near Slonim, to await the arrival of the Austrians. Due to the difficulties of moving food forward through the swamps, Tormassow's advance came to a halt, but he did send Cossack bands forward into the Grand Duchy of Warsaw to disrupt recruitment and to spread terror.

So at last the Austrians arrived at Ruzany and the Saxons saw their first Russian prisoners. These were Baschkirs, armed with bows and arrows. They had to put on demonstration shoots for their hosts. Austrian sutlers bartered their wares among the Saxons; Hungarian wine and three-grain bread. Sergeant Vollborn regretfully traded his Lithuanian pony for a loaf of bread and a bottle of red wine – to cure his dysentery.

By now, the VII Corps had marched more than 600 km (200 km more than the main body of Napoleon's army) and had lost 4,500 men, including 2,089 in combat. This was about 20 per cent against 33 per cent in the main body over the same time, and combat losses in the main body were only one-tenth of their total losses. The VI (Bavarian) Corps, for example, had now lost 12,000 of their original 25,000 men.

Notes

1 South, through Lida.
2 The Russians evacuated this fortified camp, so the action did not take place.
3 3rd Army of the West.
4 163 km north west along the Vistula.
5 About 50 km south west of Bialystock.
6 Now Bycen, south of Slonim, which the Saxons reached on 19 July.

Chapter 7

The centre – Witebsk

Witebsk was a town on the River Dwina, about 130 km north west of Smolensk. One of the less realistic plans suggested to the Czar had been to construct a domestic version of Wellington's famous Lines of Torres Vedras, within which the Russian army would shelter if needed. Unfortunately, the vast plains of western Russia offer but few convincing obstacles. The only ones are the rivers, but these are all shallow, mainly with low banks, and easily forded. However, General von Phull – a German adviser of Czar Alexander – designed an armed camp to be built at Drissa.

Von Phull calculated that the camp would need 130,000 men to defend it, but in fact the 1st Army (to whom this task would fall) could only be brought up to 100,000. Apart from inadequate forces, the fortified camp was constructed on the western side

An Italian officer carries the packs of two exhausted soldiers during the early part of the advance.
Faber du Four. Author's collection.

General F.P. Uwarow, Russian commander of the I Cavalry Corps, who, together with Platow, mounted the raid on the northern French flank at Borodino.

of the river (it was in fact a bridgehead), the river was fordable at several points both up and downstream of it, and no provision had been made to fortify the eastern bank, or to ensure that adequate forces would be available to man these works if they were to be built. Many Russian officers were aware of these grave shortcomings, but the project went ahead and much time, effort and money was expended upon it. Meanwhile the hectic race to catch the elusive Russians – extremely destructive to the *Grande Armée* – went on.

On 28 June in Wilna, the II and VI Corps were detached together, under command of Marshal Oudinot, with General Gouvion St-Cyr commanding VI Corps, from the main body of the *Grande Armée* and sent off to the north east to Duenaburg, Swolna and Polotzk on the River Duena. Here they acted as flank guard, holding in check the I Russian Corps of General Wittgenstein until after the second battle of Polotzk on 20 October. They then fell back south to rejoin their comrades for the Beresina crossing. To the south, the VII (Saxon) Corps was also detached from the main body. On 2 July they crossed the River Narew at Surace to join up with Prince Schwarzenberg's Austrian corps to form the south flank guard.

On 21 July, Captain Abraham Colkoen, of the 2nd 'Red' Lancers, wrote to his father from Orscha:

> Here we are at Orscha on the Dniepr, a little above Smolensk.[1] Since Koenigsberg I have not taken off my boots; we have always been in the vanguard, always at the Russians' heels without ever being able to catch them. They retreat at an unbelievable speed, and all we have been able to capture so

far are several depots just as they were about to set them on fire, and a number of wagons loaded with powder, arms and baggage which were following their army. We have not given them a single sabre cut yet and we do not understand it... Their army seems to be split up by our forces, one part of it at Riga and all along the Dwina, and the other towards the Ukraine, and both are retreating... It is quite impossible that this campaign should last less than a year, and spending the winter in this country of bears and wolves is quite a prospect... I have lost all my belongings but what I stand up in... We have taken a convoy of 14 wagons loaded with sugar, coffee, pepper and ginger going from Riga to Moscow and have shared it out among the troops, so we are all drinking coffee day and night.

The 2nd Russian Army of the West, hurrying eastwards along the southern side of the central corridor, was attempting to join up with Barclay de Tolly's 1st Army (now at Witebsk, 160 km north of his location), but Davout's I Corps was able to frustrate this junction at Mohilev.

The clash at Saltanowka (Mohilev), 23 July. A village in the central sector, 10 km west of Mohilev. A French victory of Davout's I Corps: General Dessaix's 4th Division (85e Ligne) and Compans's 5th Division (61e and 108e Ligne) with Bourdesoulle's 2nd Light Cavalry Brigade (3e Chasseurs) over General Rajevsky's VII Corps. This formation consisted of General Paskievich's 26th Division (infantry regiments Ladoga, Nishegorod, Orel, Poltava, 5th and 42nd Jaegers).

Rajevsky had been ordered to hold Mohilew with his 16,000 men and 72 guns; he put the town into a state of defence. At the start of the action, the Russian 26th Division advanced to the south of Fatova, not knowing that all of Davout's corps was closing in on it. Rajevsky was forced to turn away to the south east and run for his life.

Davout lost some 4,134 casualties, Rajevsky lost 2,548. Off to the north Murat's cavalry, lashed forward with imperial fury, was about to catch up with the 1st Russian Army of the West.

The clash at Ostrowno, 25–27 July. A village in the central sector. on the left bank of the River Dwina, 20 km west of Witebsk. Victory of the French General Bruyère's 1st Light Cavalry Division, Niemoiewski's 15th Light Cavalry Brigade on I Cavalry Corps and Delzon's 13th Infantry Division, Eugene's IV Corps, over General Count Ostermann-Tolstoi's IV Corps of Barclay's 1st Army.

Napoleon, hearing that the Russians were at Witebsk, rushed on to catch them. The French had some 28,000 men and twelve guns against 20,000 Russians with twenty guns.

Seven kilometres from Witebsk Osterman's advanced guard (two squadrons of the Life Guard Hussars and a company of horse artillery) clashed with Bruyères's division. The Russians advanced rashly and were thrown back by Pire's brigade, which mauled them. In the following combat, many more units on both sides were involved. The Russians lost over 2,500 casualties and six guns. French losses, however, were a surprising 3,334.

The 7th Hussars (I Cavalry Corps) charge the Russian rearguard at Ostrowno on 25–27 July 1812. Albrecht Adam.

The clash at Jakubovo, 28 July. A village in the central sector, near the River Dwina, 10 km west of the town of Witebsk. A Franco-Polish victory. Marshal Murat with General Niemoiewski's 15th Light Cavalry Brigade, I Cavalry Corps, Castex's 5th Light Cavalry Brigade, 6th and 8th Infantry Divisions, II Corps. On the Russian side, Osterman-Tolstoi's IV Corps, as for Ostrowno. The 8th Polish Lancers broke a Russian square in this action; about 800 of the infantry were captured.

The first clash at Krasnoi, 14 August. A village in the central sector, 40 km south west of Smolensk. A French victory (Marshal Ney's III Corps) over General Neverovski's 27th Infantry Division, VIII Corps, 2nd Army of the West.

Barclay ordered General Neverovski to take his newly-formed 27th Division south, over the River Dnieper to watch the approaches to Smolensk on that bank of the river. Napoleon sent Ney's III Corps and Murat's cavalry to force their advance on the city. The French cavalry (Ney's corps did not come into action) had 15,000 men with thirty guns; the Russians 7,200 men and fourteen guns. After initial combat, Neverovski realised that he was hopelessly outnumbered; he formed his division into one huge square and withdrew, fighting as he went. Despite Ney's repeated pleas to Murat to draw his cavalry off so that his artillery could engage the square, Murat stupidly persisted in throwing his precious regiments in futile charges at the Russians, who skilfully withdrew until nightfall and safety. The French lost 500 men; the Russians 640 men and seven guns.

On 27 July, about fifty members of the Red Lancers were ambushed in the town of Babinowitz by the lancers of the Russian Imperial Guard under Grand Duke Constantine; only an NCO and three men managed to escape. Albert de Watteville, commanding a squadron of the 2nd Lancers of the Guard, wrote that night from Orscha:

> We have constantly been out in front of the whole army corps, sometimes 25 to 30 Meils. The campaign continues to be murderous. Except for the Prince of Eckmühl[2], who has defeated Bagration at Mohilev,[3] I do not believe that there has been any fighting other than by the vanguard, and then only occasionally. The Emperor has crossed the Duena at Orscha at a time when the Russians were leaving their camp to take refuge in Witebsk; they must have found themselves in even greater difficulties… We have been in Orcha for ten days now, using food from the Russian supplies. The enemy's manoeuvres at Witebsk compel us to bring together all our forces before moving forward. If, when we first reached this town, we had had half the cavalry that is now here, and a little artillery, we could have reached Moscow without firing a shot; and we could have spread terror to Witebsk. They are completely routed.

King Friedrich Wilhelm III of Prussia. His indecision, and terrible sense of timing, led to the crushing defeat of the Prussian army at Jena and Auerstaedt in 1806. General von Yorck's Convention of Tauroggen, with the Russians in December 1812, was key to bringing Prussia into the allied camp against Napoleon.

Not quite yet.

By this point, the chronic lack of food supply had seriously eroded the bonds of discipline in all units of the *Grande Armée*. Entire tactical formations left the march route to go foraging – or marauding – for food. Had they not done so, they would simply have died. It was only at Witebsk that the advance was halted and some of the stragglers could catch up. The Red Lancers of the Imperial Guard now had only 600 horses left; they had already lost 400 since the start of the campaign, and only fifty of these had been in combat, the rest by sickness and exhaustion. On 28 July, Segur tells us:

> Napoleon rode forward into the site of the camp just abandoned by Barclay's 1st Army. Everything he saw spoke of a mastery of the science of war; the favourable situation of the camp, the symmetrical layout of its parts, the exact and exclusive observance of the use for which each had been designed, and the resultant order and cleanliness. Moreover, nothing had been left behind, not a weapon or personal possession, no tracks – nothing to indicate the route the Russians had taken in their sudden nocturnal flight. There was more order in their retreat than in our victory! Defeated, they left us as they fled the sort of lessons by which the victorious never profit, either because success thinks it has nothing to learn, or because we put off improving ourselves till misfortune has struck.

Colonel Thomasset, commanding officer of the 3rd Swiss Infantry Regiment (9th Division, II Corps), described the terrible conditions of this initial advance to contact in a letter to Colonel von May in the regimental depot in Lille on 10 July:

You can have no concept of what we have suffered in this campaign. We have not had any bread for two months; only a little flour of which each soldier carries four pounds in a small sack. The entire country is devastated, the house are looted, the peasants have fled. We have lost an incredible number of men due to the forced marches that we have had to make. We had to march 12 Meilen in 24 hours which drove our agony to the limit and meant that two thirds of the men fell out and are now with the stragglers. They are trickling back day by day; I have met many, particularly from the 3rd Regiment – the waggons are always behind due to lack of horses; we replace them with whatever we can find, but the regiment loses about 20 per day despite this. The [regimental] artillery is without teams; the regiment now has no more than ten of the horses that we bought in Nimwegen. There have been two skirmishes with the enemy in the advance so far, one east of Wilna, one at Wilkomir; we only had to deploy two infantry regiments to put to flight a corps of 25,000 men. There are rumours of an early peace; I hope they are true and that we can leave this terrible land. The war in Spain was child's play [*une plaisanterie*] compared to this, where we are short of everything; I haven't drunk any wine for two months.

Another Swiss, Captain Rosselet, added his contribution to the record of this desperate period:

A detail of the clash between Russian and Saxon cavalry in the final struggle for possession of the Grand Battery at Borodino. Photographed from the great painting in the Rotunda museum in Moscow.

Fusiliers of the Portuguese Legion foraging on 4 August at Liozni; sketched by Faber du Four. The infantry of the Legion served in the 6th, 10th and 11th Divisions. Author's collection.

> By day great heat; terrible storms with thunder and hail; by night, floods and cold in our wet clothes. It's terrible to bivouac in these conditions. Many have dysentery.

After several days of terrible heat, a gigantic thunderstorm burst over the weary columns as they struggled forward, bringing five days of torrential rain and a sudden, sharp – and unpleasant – drop in the temperature. The 'roads' and fields were flooded; all movement of the lumbering waggons stopped as their teams of starved, exhausted draught animals collapsed and died in the mud. The already bad supply situation for the troops became catastrophic; the bivouacs in the fields of half-grown barley became swamps. The problem of stragglers was already serious and quickly became acute and chronic as thousands left their regiments to forage on their own account; many never to return to their colours, many to die at the hands of the enraged Russian peasants.

At the end of July Napoleon's patience – ever in short supply – was steaming rapidly out of both his ears at the absence of real success or of any response from the Czar. He looked at Witebsk and was unimpressed.

Segur furnishes some revealing imperial quotations, all dated on 28 July in Witebsk:

> Do you think I have come all this way just to conquer these huts?
> How many reasons have I for going to Moscow at once? How can I bear the boredom of seven months of winter in this place?
> Am I to be reduced to defending myself – I who have always attacked? Such a role is unworthy of me... I am not used to playing it... It is not in keeping with my genius.

And in answer to a request that they stay in Witebsk, Napoleon responded: 'Of

General Nikolai Nikolajevich Rajewski, Russian commander of the Grenadier Corps and defender of the Grand Battery at Borodino. He went on to fight in 1813 and entered Paris with the allied troops in 1814.

course I see that the Russians only want to lure me on. Nevertheless, I must extend my line as far as Smolensk, where I shall establish headquarters …' But then, according to the same source, he said: 'How far must we pursue these Russians before they decide to give battle?… shouldn't all this make us decide to stop here on the border of old Russia?'

Also from the Witebsk quotations is this:

We must take possession of it [Smolensk] so that we may march on the two capitals simultaneously. In Moscow, we'll destroy everything; in St Petersburg we'll keep everything. Then I'll turn my arms against Prussia and make her pay the cost of the war.

When Napoleon asked his minister (Pierre-Anton Daru, Minister for War) his opinion of this war; the latter replied:

It is certainly not a national matter. The importation of some English goods into Russia, even the creation of the kingdom of Poland are not sufficient reasons for waging war with such a remote country. Neither your troops nor ourselves see the object or the necessity for such a conflict. Everything warns us to stop where we are.

And in yet another mood swing, Napoleon said: 'Peace awaits me at the gates of Moscow…' Daru said to the Emperor (to quote Segur) 'Your army has already diminished by one-third, either through desertion, famine or disease. If supplies are scarce in Witebsk, what will it be like further on?'

The Emperor spent fifteen days in Witebsk, so obviously his need for speed had suddenly abated and his indecision had increased dramatically. Every day, at six o'clock, he attended the guard mounting ceremony in front of his palace, at which the presence of everyone in his extensive entourage was also required. As he soon found that the available space was too small, he had some houses pulled down to provide more room for the spectacle.

But some, such as General Raymonde-Aimery de Fezensac, were still fascinated by Napoleon's spell. Napoleon famously once said: 'In war men are nothing, one man is everything.' And in this case, that one man was himself. General de Fezensac wrote of the state of the army at the end of July 1812:

Here I may mention that no general ever paid more attention to the subsistence of his troops and to the hospitals of his army than Napoleon. It is not sufficient, however, to issue orders: those to whom they are given should have it in their power to execute them. The orders themselves should be practicable; yet how could this palpable truth be realised in the present state of things? The rapidity of the movements, the concentration of so many, the bad state of the roads, the difficulty of obtaining forage, all interposed to prevent any methodical issue, or any complete organization of the hospitals.

The soldiers, who never troubled themselves with these difficulties, contented themselves with inveighing at the want of zeal, and sometimes the want of honesty, of the commissaries and contractors. They were heard to say, when perishing on the road, or dying in the ambulances, 'It was sad thus to die when the Emperor interested himself so much about them.'

And if you'll believe that...

As of 14 August, the 1st and 2nd Lancers of the Guard formed a brigade under General Baron Colbert. The combat reputation of the Red Lancers among the Cossacks was not high; the Dutchmen seemed to have been less than expert with the use of the lance.

Notes

1 Actually about 90 km west of Smolensk.
2 Marshal Davout.
3 AKA Saltanovka.

Chapter 8

The northern flank – Polotzk

In mid-July, Barclay de Tolly detached Wittgenstein's I Corps to cover the road to St Petersburg at Polotzk, on the north bank of the River Duena. Napoleon sent Oudinot's II Corps after him. There followed a series of sharp defeats for Oudinot from 28 July to 2 August. Wittgenstein had achieved local superiority.

Oudinot sent a call for help; the Emperor, still chasing after Barclay, but concerned that his lines of communication might be cut, ordered Saint-Cyr's Bavarians to reinforce the hard-pressed Oudinot.

The VI Corps, the Bavarians, lost two cavalry regiments on 12 April, at Napoleon's command. These cavalry regiments were sent to join the 17th Light Cavalry Brigade of General Jean-Baptiste Dommanget, in Grouchy's III Cavalry Corps. On 14 July the Bavarians were reviewed by the Emperor at Wilna. He was so pleased with the remaining four regiments (3rd, 4th, 5th and 6th Chevaulegers under General Graf von Preysing-Moos) that he took them and Captain Widemann's horse artillery battery and sent them off to the Reserve Cavalry as well. Thus the Bavarians were without any cavalry for the whole campaign; a great tactical disadvantage. As Preysing-Moos wrote in his diary:

> When we reached Pokoinje on 1st July, there was an absolute lack of every sort of supplies. We crossed the Niemen next day at Gogi. As it had been raining heavily for several days, the roads (inadequate at the best of times) were transformed into extended swamps, through which we moved the guns and vehicles only with the greatest effort and trouble. Even the slightest hillock became a major obstacle, on which many horses collapsed. From now on until we reached Wilna, we lost hundreds of horses every day.
>
> At midday on the 8th [July] Pino's 15th Italian Division passed us; they were in such a bad state, that they left some hundreds of men dead on the sides of the road from starvation and exhaustion.
>
> On 14th [July] we, and several other corps, were reviewed by Emperor Napoleon, who was on a hill just this side of Wilna. The army was perhaps the finest, mightiest and best-organized army that had been gathered together at one spot. He was most impressed with our cavalry regiments; but this was to have drastic consequences. The next day I was ordered to leave VI Corps and to join up with the Imperial Guard.
>
> I left my whole herd of cattle and all unnecessary baggage with the corps and set off for my new duty station, without a war commissar, without any money and without any supplies of clothing, as I thought that I would shortly return to my corps.

Detail of the cavalry action at Borodino. A unit commander of the Russian Cuirassier Guards, with his attendant trumpeter close behind him. Photographed from the great painting in the Rotunda museum in Moscow.

On 25 July Preysing's division was attached to Montbrun's II Cavalry Corps and thus was destined for Borodino and all the horrors of the retreat.

Another Bavarian eyewitness was Captain Maillinger[1] who, while admiring Saint-Cyr's undoubted military talents, sheds less flattering light on the marshal's personality. On 1 April 1812 Saint-Cyr took command of the VI Corps; following the wounding of Marshal Oudinot in the first battle of Polotzk on 18 August, Saint-Cyr assumed command of both corps. Relationships with the Bavarian commanders were extremely strained from the beginning and were to get much worse.

Maillinger described Saint-Cyr as avaricious, greedy and vindictive. When supplies of food and wine were found in the Jesuit monastery in Polotzk, he confiscated them for his own use instead of allowing them to be used for the starving sick and wounded in the field hospital. When Maillinger discovered some supplies in the Polotzk area one day, he passed some of them to the field hospital; Saint-Cyr learned of this and was most enraged.

Saint-Cyr's chief of staff was Colonel Count Philippe François d'Albignac, a French officer thrown out of the service of the Kingdom of Westphalia in 1810 for misappropriation of funds and foisted off onto Saint-Cyr by the Emperor early in 1812. Saint-Cyr cordially hated d'Albignac and suspected him of theft and almost any other crime which occurred in or near his headquarters, including the theft of some of his cash.

From Wilna, the VI Corps marched through Danielowice on 20 July to Globukoje two days later. Here a hospital was set up for the 600 sick and soldiers who had no shoes.

At this point, Napoleon's main body was south of the Duena, in the area between Witebsk (on that river), Minsk and Orscha, half way between Minsk and Smolensk. Exhaustion had caused so much straggling that a pause in the advance was needed. Some interpret this as being a cunning move on Napoleon's part to 'allow' Barclay and Bagration to concentrate their two armies, something he had almost wrecked his own force trying to prevent since mid-June. The superiority of the Cossacks in maintaining a protective cavalry screen around their rearguard, and their proven ability to inflict repeated defeats on the allied cavalry undoubtedly added to the new-found caution shown by the *Grande Armée*.

Wittgenstein had taken up a position behind the River Duena between Duenaburg and the abandoned camp at Drissa on 24 July. His task was to block any thrust on St Petersburg and to act as a link with the Russian forces in Riga. He then moved eastwards on his own initiative for about 40 km to intercept Oudinot's II Corps as it probed north from Polotzk, towards the Russian summer capital. They met at Kliastitzy.

The first clash at Kliastitzy, 28 July. A village in the central sector. 35 km north of Polotzk, on the River Swolna. A Russian victory of General Kulniev's Advanced Guard (one squadron of the Life Guard Hussars, the Grodno Hussars and the Cossack Pulk of Platow IV) and the 5th Division, over Legrand's 6th Division and Corbineau's 6th Cavalry Brigade. This was the opening action on the Polotzk front. The light cavalry of Oudinot's II Corps groped towards Wittgenstein's Russians – and met with a bloody repulse. The 7th and 20th Chasseurs à Cheval lost 167 prisoners.

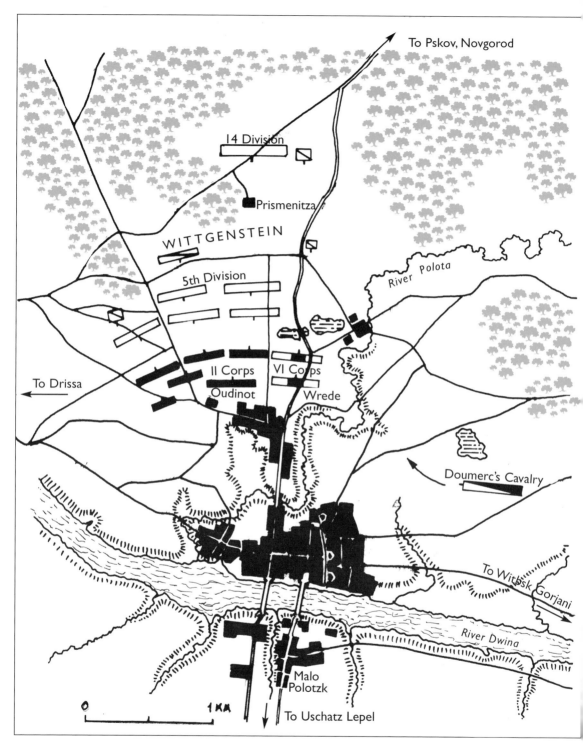

To Pskov, Novgorod

14 Division

Prismenitza

WITTGENSTEIN

River Polota

5th Division

II Corps
Oudinot

VI Corps
Wrede

To Drissa

Doumerc's Cavalry

To Witebsk Gorjani

River Dwina

Malo
Polotzk

0   1 KM

To Uschatz Lepel

1st Polotzk 16–18 August. *After seven minor defeats at Russian hands, Oudinot's II Corps was joined by the Bavarian VI Corps under General Gouvion Saint-Cyr, to confront Wittgenstein's I Corps. After a hard fight, Wittgenstein withdrew to the north, still blocking any thrust at St Petersburg. The Franco-Bavarians lost some 6,000; Marshal Oudinot was wounded; Bavarian generals Deroy and Siebein were killed. The Russians lost 5,500 casualties, including generals Berg, Hamen and Kazatchkowski, who were wounded. There followed relative quiet until the 2nd Battle of Polotzk on 18 October. In this period the Franco-Bavarians dwindled rapidly away due to starvation and sickness. This map is after Bogdanovich.*

The second clash at Kliastitzy, 30/31 July–1 August. Also called Oboarszina. A town in the central sector. Another Russian victory; the 5th Cavalry Brigade, 5th and 14th Infantry Divisions of Wittgenstein's Corps over Legrand's 6th Division and the 5th Light Cavalry Brigade of Oudinot's II Corps. This action in close country lasted over three days, as the opposing sides sought to gain the upper hand. Effective Russian artillery fire held the French in check. Kulniev was killed leading one of the last Russian charges. Following this check, Oudinot withdrew south to Polotzk on the River Duena.

The clash at Golovchtitzy, 2 August. A village north of Polotzk, near the River Drissa. A successful Russian ambush by General Berg's 5th Division, over General Legrand's 6th, Verdier's 8th and Merle's 9th Divisions. Another French probe north from Polotzk had been ambushed and repulsed. The French had 9,000 men in the action and lost some 5,000; the Russians had some 13,000 and lost about 4,000 casualties.

On 31 July the Bavarians were at Beschenkowitschi, on the left bank of the Duena; here they stayed until 4 August, when they received orders to undertake a forced march to Polotzk to support Oudinot's II Corps. 'Dysentery had caused great damage to the army and there was still no food to be found', as the Bavarian Maillinger recorded. A Bavarian sergeant wrote that:

> For thirty-three days we have had no bread; on the 34th we received a little so that each loaf had to be shared among twelve men. The only water we had was that which we scooped out of the river; brackish and alive with insects.

Gouvion-Saint-Cyr and the Bavarians arrived in Polotzk on 7 August. Maillinger gave this description of the place:

> Polotzk is the oldest town in White Russia, with some 400 houses and 2,000 inhabitants. There are also five abbeys including that of the Jesuits, which was the largest and finest. It was here that Marshals Oudinot and Saint-Cyr set up their headquarters. Most of the inhabitants were Jews who carried on a not inconsiderable trade with Riga. From the remaining walls and deep ditches behind the Jesuit abbey and on the far side of the Malo Polotzk suburb, it is clear that the town had once been very well defended.

General Deroy, senior Bavarian officer of VI Corps, wrote the following letter to King Maximilian in Munich from his headquarters in Balaubanszyzna, describing the parlous state of his command.

> Food supply is very bad; there is no bread and we have no time to bake any. There is much sickness due to the bad weather and the dreadful diet of meat, which must be eaten without bread or salt. These factors depopulate our columns. The lack of money puts officers and men into a desperate state. Shoes, shirts, tousers, gaiters are in tatters and hang in rags from the men; many men march barefoot. It is no wonder that military discipline has suffered under these conditions and that morale is very low.

The clash at Swolna, 11 August. A town in the northern sector. Russian victory of General d'Auvray (standing in as commander of Wittgenstein's I Corps) with Berg's 5th, Sasanov's 14th Divisions, over Verdier's 8th Infantry and Doumerc's 3rd Cuirassier Divisions. Again Oudinot's II Corps, with 9,000 men, were bested by the Russians who managed to bring 20,000 onto the battlefield. Oudinot lost 1,200 killed and wounded and 300 captured; he withdrew again into Polotzk. The Russians lost 800 casualties.

When the Bavarians arrived at Polotsk on 15 August, they went into bivouac to the east of the town, on the left bank of the Polota stream, which bisects the battlefield. It was 1.5 metres deep, narrow, fast-flowing and set in a deep and winding cleft.

Maillinger was now living in the partially destroyed post office in Gamselewo, a village near Polotzk, on the road to Sebesch and Duenaburg. He records that on the evening of 12 August:

Napoleon's ADC, Hautpoul arrived with despatches for General Saint-Cyr. He came to me and asked me to have a meal prepared for him and to find him a spot to sleep for a few hours as he had had neither rest nor food for some days. I gave him what I had; a good soup, some mutton and a glass of good Schnaps and showed him to a corner where there was a heap of half rotten straw on which a couple of dozen men had already died. He fell upon it at once and asked me to wake him at 3 o'clock in the morning.

When I woke him next morning, with a cup of coffee cooked in Schnaps – which we often did, because the water was so bad – he couldn't thank me enough. He then set off to return to Smolensk.

Next day headquarters was moved to a fine castle in the village of Bjelaja; I had some flour with me and the nobleman who owned the place gave me some more. One of my company, Enderlein, was a good baker, so I had bread baked for the company. Every man received half a loaf; as there was plenty of meat and Schnaps, we were very comfortable on the 13th and 14th.

Next day, at 10 o'clock in the morning, we were attacked by Russian light cavalry and Cossacks; after exchanging some shots with us, they withdrew into the forest. At 4 o'clock that afternoon a more serious assault was launched on the castle; probably the owner had told Wittgenstein's men that the enemy commander was in his house.

Saint-Cyr made a withdrawal back into Polotzk with minor loss – apart from the next ration of bread that had to be abandoned in the ovens.

There followed the first battle of Polotzk. The II Corps had entered Russia with 30,000 infantry and 2,000 cavalry; on the eve of this battle there were only 11,000 infantry and 1,000 cavalry left. Of the Bavarians, only 10,000 were now fit for duty.

The first battle of Polotzk, 16–18 August. A town in northern Russia on the River Dwina, 95 km north west of Witebsk. A drawn battle between Oudinot's II and Gouvion Saint-Cyr's VI (Bavarian) Corps and Wittgenstein's I Corps, 1st Russian Army of the West. The combined allied corps totalled 18,000 men with 120 guns; Wittgenstein now had 22,000 men and 135 guns; the scales were beginning to tip in the Russians' favour.

The first battle of Polotzk on 16 August. This plate shows the western half of the conflict, with Bavarian troops of the VI Corps in the foreground right, Bavarian artillery and Swiss grenadiers to the left. The River Duena crosses the plate. Author's collection.

Wittgenstein advanced south down the road from Newel and at 8 o'clock on the morning of 17 August he launched an attack on the allied right flank, which was Wrede's division. The combat centred on possession of the village of Spas, in which were a stone church and a Jesuit monastery, both of which formed good defensive positions. Oudinot's conduct of the battle was unimaginative; the Russians made little headway and fell back into the woods in the evening. Deroy's 19th Division was in the second line, behind the 20th, and was not used, suffering only slight losses this day.

Deroy, eager for action, asked to be allowed to replace Wrede's battered command. St-Cyr agreed and the change over took place at dawn on 18 August. St-Cyr now convinced Oudinot to mount a counter-attack at four in the afternoon.

Nicolas-Charles Oudinot, Duc de Reggio, Commander II Corps

Oudinot enjoyed the dubious distinctions of being one of the most decorated, and the most often wounded, of Napoleon's marshals. Born on 25 April 1767 in Bar-le-Duc (Meuse) as the son of a brewer, he entered military service in June 1784 as a private. During his long career he was promoted and wounded many times: at Hagenau in 1793, at Trier in 1794 and again at Neckarau (Mannheim) in 1795. In action at Ingolstadt on 11 September 1796 he was wounded five times.

Oudinot was promoted to *General de Division* in 1799, and was appointed Inspector General of Cavalry at Bruges in late 1801; an odd appointment for an infantryman. In March 1805 he was awarded the *Grande Aigle of the Legion d'Honneur.* He was appointed to command the

Marshal Charles Oudinot, commander of the II Corps, wounded in the first battle of Polotzk.

1ère Division (of combined grenadier battalions) in Lannes's V Corps of the *Grande Armée* in August 1805, and was the victor at the clash at Wertingen before being wounded again at Hollabrunn. Due to the effects of this wound, Napoleon decided to split the command of his division at Austerlitz. Oudinot nevertheless continued to fight with his troops, breaking a leg in a fall from a horse in 1807 and going on to receive numerous annuities and honours for his trouble. In July 1808 he was created a count of the Empire, and in April 1810 he was created the Duc de Reggio.

For the 1812 campaign Oudinot became commander of the II Corps of the *Grande Armée* in Russia. He fought at Oboarszina (Kliastitzy), was wounded at the first battle of Polotzk and handed over command to Gouvion St-Cyr until October. He also fought at Borisov, was wounded at the Beresina on 28 November; wounded again on 30 November and was replaced by Victor on 8 December.

After action in the campaigns of 1813 and 1814, he became Minister of State in May 1814. A week later he was appointed commander of the *Corps Royal des Grenadiers et Chasseurs à Pied de France*. In June he received a knighthood in the Order of St Louis; two days later he was created a Peer of France.

In the Hundred Days, on 24 March 1815, he opposed the proclamation of the Empire at Metz, but was forced to leave the city due to the mutiny of the garrison against him. Napoleon called him to Paris on 26 March but he refused to join the Emperor and went into exile.

Following the second restoration Oudinot was showered with honours. On 3

May 1816 he received the Grand Cross of the Order of St Louis; in 1820 he became a knight in the Order of St Espirit. On 12 February 1832 he was appointed to command the I Corps of the army in the war with Spain, and on 29 July he became Governor of Madrid and commander in chief of Extremadura, Leon, New Castile, Salamanca and Segovia. For his services he received the Grand Cross of the Order of Charles III of Spain. Oudinot was made responsible for the disbandment of the Royal Guard on 11 August 1830, during the revolution. On 21 October 1842 he was appointed Governor of Les Invalides. He was wounded in action no less than 22 times in his life, but died on 13 September 1847 in Les Invalides.

The 19th Division, on the right wing, was to advance through Spas village. Legrand's 6th Division (II Corps) was in the centre and would move forward to Prismenitza and Verdier's 8th Division was on the left wing, resting on the Duena. His task was to advance along the road towards Sebesch. Up to midday all was quiet and Oudinot transferred his train to the south bank of the river to get it out of harm's way, should the day go against him.

At 4 o'clock the 19th Division crossed the Polota stream at spots concealed from Russian view, east of Spas, and formed up beside the village. Wrede's men moved out of the place and Deroy's 19th Division took their place. Wrede now opened the action by advancing to push the enemy outposts back; this attack was supported by thirty-four guns. The Russians then rapidly brought up their own artillery in much greater strength.

To join the combat line, Deroy's men had to file out of the gates of Spas then march to the right to form line of battle, and this under effective enemy artillery fire. Bavarian casualties were heavy and the appearance of a Russian force on their right flank caused them to falter. At this point, General von Raglovich (commanding the 2nd Brigade, 19th Division) was wounded; the Bavarians fell back. Deroy soon rallied them, however, and drove off the Russians.

By now, Legrand's 6th Division had been driven out of Prismenitza; his men streamed back onto the Bavarians and the whole mass rolled back to Spas. Russian artillery fire swept through the allied crowds and soon sergeants were commanding companies, as all the officers had been killed or wounded. The allies rallied; Legrand and Wrede advanced again, but the former's division was once more driven back, leaving the Bavarians alone. Despite this, they re-took Prismenitza. Wittgenstein decided that he would have to withdraw; to cover this movement, he threw his entire cavalry at Verdier's 8th Division on the allied left wing. Concealed by the great clouds of gunsmoke, the Russians burst onto the surprised II Corps, spreading panic. The Riga Dragoons and the Grodno Hussars took fifteen guns and advanced right up to the walls of the town. Corbineau's 6th Light Cavalry Brigade was also swept away.

A counter-attack by the Bavarian General Siebein restored the position and retook all but two of the artillery pieces. The Russians withdrew unmolested; the exhausted allies were too tired to pursue them. This had been one of the bloodiest battles ever fought by the Bavarians.

Marshal Oudinot (Duke of Reggio and commander of II Corps) was badly wounded by a canister ball in the shoulder in this action and General Gouvion Saint-

Shako of an officer, Voltigeur company, 2nd Swiss Infantry Regiment. All fittings gilt, French cockade. Author's collection.

Cyr took command of both allied corps. It was due to his energetic conduct that Wittgenstein was held in check until late September. The allies maintained their hold on Polotzk. General von Deroy, commander, 19th Division, was mortally wounded, dying on the night of 23 August.

After the battle, Maillinger did what he could to help the numerous wounded, including feeding them with food from Saint-Cyr's store. The general's ADC reported this to Saint-Cyr and the enraged general vented his spleen on the lowly captain, because he had 'wasted his rations'. Maillinger gives a further picture of the conditions under which the Bavarians now lived:

> There was scarcely ever any bread, but we did have some meat. As there was no salt, we used gunpowder to season the soup. The water was bad and undrinkable, as all the wells and streams were tainted with the corpses of men and horses.

Sergeant Schrafel[2] recorded that he and others drank water 'from a large puddle, which looked like brown paint and was full of countless tiny worms.' The shortage of food around Polotzk was now so acute, that foraging parties sometimes fought each other when anything edible was found. Even the Russians withdrew their garrison out of Polotzk in the summer, due to the fevers, which were caused by the mosquitoes in the numerous swamps in the area. All the houses of the town were filled with the sick and dying.

Following this battle, Wittgenstein remained quiet, rebuilding his forces in preparation for the second battle and watching his enemies dwindle away.

Notes

1 Maillinger was from the 1st Infantry Regiment König.
2 Schrafel was from the 5th Infantry Regiment, Bavarian Army.

A group of Cossacks with their ponies and the typical lances.

Chapter 9

The southern sector – Podubna/Gorodeczna

The allies had 18,000 men and 48 guns; the Russians brought up 26,000 men and 42 guns. On 11 August Schwarzenberg advanced south from Kobryn, through the Kossenbrod defile and closed up to Gorodeczna. Reynier's Saxons were close behind him. Tormassow had taken up a strong position on a low ridge, which commanded the few crossings of the very swampy river to his front; his left and right flanks were also covered by swampy areas. The paths across the morass at Podubna and Gorodeczna would only allow the passage of columns, six men abreast. One path was covered by the fire of twelve Russian guns, the other by thirty. The situation looked like a stalemate.

When the Saxons came up, they formed to the west of the Austrians, at Podubna. Reynier sent out patrols, who discovered an area of dead ground along the Russian left flank, in which was a forest. Even more surprising, there was a track, muddy but drivable, south from the village of Szedowa, along which cannon could pass. There were no Russian troops covering this flank at all.

Armed with this information, Reynier and Schwarzenberg rapidly formed a plan to exploit this chance. While the Austrians held the Russians in front, the Saxons were to cross the swamp and turn Tormassow's left flank. The move began that night.

Next day, Tormassow was shocked to discover the threat to his army and at once set a complete redeployment in force. A fierce combat developed between the Russians and the Saxons, which went on all day, while Schwarzenberg bombarded the enemy from the north. The Russian artillery fire was poorly aimed and overshot the Saxons, causing relatively few casualties.

The Saxons were nevertheless hard pressed, and part of Bianchi's division arrived at three o'clock to reinforce them. By now, Schwarzenberg could try to break through and the Regiment Colloredo Nr 33 pushed forward over the river. Finally, as night fell, Tormassow withdrew his right wing and abandoned his position; falling back south to Lutzk. His negligence had cost him dear; Russian losses were some 3,000 killed, wounded and missing. The Austrians lost 1,300 casualties, the Saxons 930. Had the Austrian commander used his initiative and supported the Saxons earlier, it is likely that Tormassow would have been very badly beaten.

Saxon Ulan Captain von Boehm reported as follows on this phase of the operations:

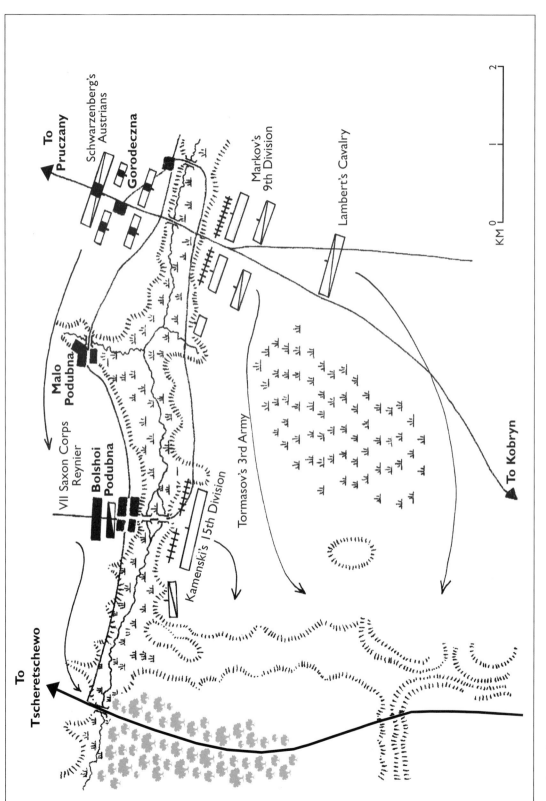

Battle of Gorodeczna (Podubna), 11 August 1812.

We fulfilled this task well. At Koszibrod on 10 August, and at Podubnie [Gorodeczna] two days later, we hit Tormassow hard. Our losses were 2,000 dead and wounded; the Russians lost 3,000. Later we held the field for three months in face of the far superior forces of Tormassow and Tschitchagow at the clashes of Luboml (29 September) and Rudnia (18 November).

In fact, the allies had begun their advance from Slonim on 3 August, south west with 30,000 men, looking to attack Tormassow. The 13,000 Saxons marched on their right, through Pruzany. Reynier was 50 km to the north, on a parallel course – surely too far distant for security.

For his part, Tormassow remained static at Kobryn and Antopoli (to the east), with outposts at Pinsk (in the centre of the Pripet marshes), Chomsk (General Tschaplitz, north east of Antopoli) and Malecz. Tschaplitz and the detachment in Pinsk (13,000 men in all) were to take no part in the forthcoming battle.

General Lambert, with 8,000 men, was at Pruzany, north of the swamps and on the Brest-Litowsk–Slonim road. He was surprised at Rudnia on 8 August by the Austrian advanced guard and thrown back south west on Tormassow with the loss.

The clash at Rudnia, near Kobryn, 8 August. A small village in the southern sector, east of Kobryn. A minor Austrian victory of parts of General Bianchi's 2nd, General Trautenberg's 1st and Frimont's Reserve Divisions over General Lambert's corps (5th Division) of General Tormassow's 3rd Army of the West. The Austrians had 4,200 men; the Russians somewhat fewer. Losses were minor on both sides. This was an insignificant action, but raised allied spirits.

The clash at Gorodeczna (Podubna), 12 August. A village in the southern sector, in Grodno province, 53 km north east of Brest-Litowsk. An Austro-Saxon victory (Prince Schwarzenberg with the 1st, 2nd and 3rd Austrian Divisions and the Saxons under General Reynier) over General Tormassow's 3rd Russian Army of the West.

The Austrians remained at Gorodeczna. Lieutenant von Wolffersdorff, of the Saxon Prinz Clemens infantry regiment, continues with his account of events:

> The Russians had used up all the resources in this sandy region; the heatwave of July had now given way to very cold weather. Without good clothing and rations, the number of sick began to rise. The Austrian advance was so slow, that we had to wait for them to catch up on 8 and 9 August.
>
> Next day, we attacked General Lambert's advanced guard of about 8,000 men at Pruczany and pushed them back. The Austrians came up too late to help us destroy them in front of the defile of Kossebrod.
>
> On 12 August my battalion came into action for the first time in this campaign.
>
> On 11 August we came up to the village of Podubna and found the Russians in a very strong position on the Kobryn road, to our left, at Gorodeczna. There were only two very narrow tracks and bridges over the swamps there. Our patrols found out that the swamps on the enemy left flank were not guarded. A battalion of our light infantry took post where the road from Tscheretschowo comes south to cross the marshes. General Reynier

decided to exploit this Russian omission. That night, most of the horses of the Austrian Hussar Regiment Kaiser broke their picket ropes and stampeded through our lines, causing great alarm. It seems that wolves had scared them.

At dawn on 12 August General Reynier climbed onto the straw roof of the inn in Zabin to spy out the land with his telescope. At 7 o'clock we advanced across the bridge, Reynier at the head of the cavalry of the advanced guard. Lecoq's division followed him. This move surprised Tormassow, who soon moved troops and artillery to oppose us. Lieutenant von Kauffberg, of the Regiment Prinz Friedrich, was killed. Grenadier Battalion von Spiegel, acting as guard to our artillery, lost a lot of men.

General Freiherr von Langenau, VII Corps' chief of staff in 1812.

Enemy cavalry charged our Light Infantry, but were driven off by them in short order.

On the Russian side, the divisions of Kamenski Markow and Tscherbatow and Lambert's cavalry were engaged; this was about 26,000 men against 16,000 Saxons and the Austrian cavalry of Zechmeister's brigade. It was not until 3 o'clock in the afternoon that Bianchi's Austrian division came into action to support us.

Now Schwarzenberg broke through on the other flank and as dusk fell, Tormassow withdrew south behind a screen of Cossacks. Reynier rode along the front of the Saxon troops and was cheered along the whole length.

My battalion had lost some killed; one officer and 20 men had been wounded, most by cannonballs.

Wolffersdorff continues:

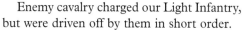

> That night was awful; all around were the groans of the wounded and dying. Next to me was a Russian with a stomach wound; his entrails were spilling out. We had him bandaged up. There was no water for anyone to drink. Next day we buried the dead. One man of my company had a ball in his thigh; it was simply cut out by the surgeon, as the man calmly smoked his pipe and drank the brandy that was given to him. At last we marched off.

Following this action, Tormassow seems to have lost his nerve; instead of utilising the good positions, which lay along the road, his rearguard abandoned them one after the other. The Saxons picked up about 400 prisoners along the route; with more cavalry, much more could have been done.

Tormassow withdrew all the way to Lutzk, some 240 km to the south, on the River Styr, destroying all the bridges behind him. Here he called in General Osten-Sacken's corps of 8,000 men and awaited the arrival of Admiral Tschitschagoff's Army of Moldavia, some 36,000 men, which was now able to leave the southern front against the Turks to join him in mid-September.

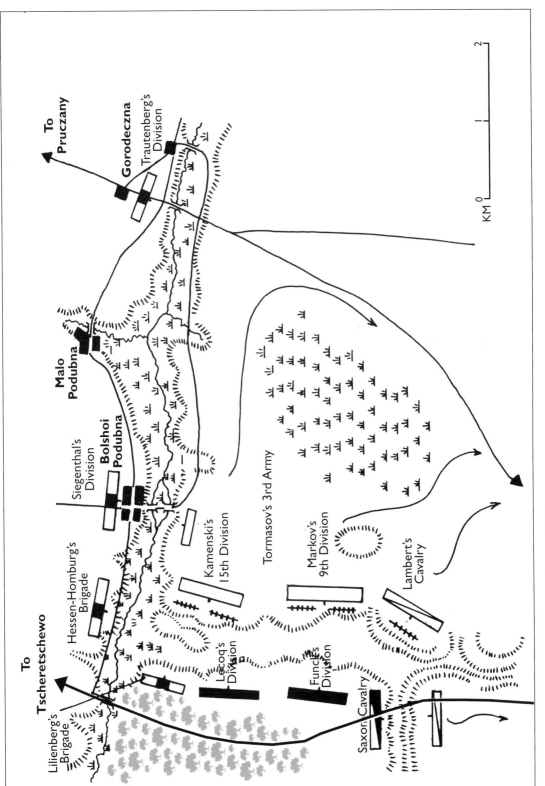

Battle of Gorodeczna (Podubna), 12 August 1812.

Schwarzenberg did not follow the Russians into the swamps and his two corps remained for several weeks in hutted camps in the area east of Brest-Litowsk, along the northern edge of the Pripet marshes. Here they were joined by the Polish Bug Division of 5,500 men under General Antoine Amilcar Kosinski. This formation operated on Schwarzenberg's western flank until January 1813. It consisted of the 1st and 2nd Provisional Cavalry Regiments, the Bug Jaegers[1], the 13th Infantry Regiment and some units of the Plotzk National Guard. It was dissolved in February 1813. According to the Austrian officer, Wilhelm Edler von Gabler: 'Kosinski's troops were without uniforms, weapons, equipment and saddlery; only the 13th Infantry Regiment was any good.'

The Austrian division of General Mohr was sent south east to Pinsk on the Pripet River, to observe the II Russian Reserve Corps of General F.F. Ertell at Moszyr, which gradually increased to a strength of 12,000 men and 22 guns.

Wolffersdorff left us some observations on his opinions of the Russian army:

> The Russian army was not yet that which it became in 1813. Their line infantry fought with great bravery and did not withdraw, even from bad positions, until they were surely forced to. They held their dressing well, but once they had lost it, they had great difficulty in restoring order. Their tactics were too mechanical. Their dispositions indicated that their senior commanders and general staff were functioning well, but their middle commanders lacked practice and decision; they often failed to exploit opportunities.
>
> They did not understand how to skirmish in open order, unlike our Sharpshooters, who could rapidly deploy from close to open order and back again. In close combat they lost more men than we Saxons even though they had better muskets and ammunition. In general, all their equipment was better than ours. Their artillery shot at very long range but with little accuracy; they had excellent gunpowder, but tended to use too large a charge, so that the balls mostly went over our heads. 'The closer to the enemy the safer it will be from artillery fire' was our motto.
>
> Their artillery was also too static on the battlefield and failed to move as the tactical situation demanded. Their infantry and cavalry moved far too slowly on the battlefield.
>
> All the military virtues which the line troops lacked, appeared among the Cossacks in profusion. Each one of them was led by the correct instincts and acted in the best interests of the entire corps. As scouts they are unequalled by any other nation and a position guarded by them can never be surprised. But they are far less courageous than other Russian soldiers. Their courage is fuelled only by hope of loot and is based on outwitting the enemy. If they meet a determined foe, even when they are in superior numbers, their bravery evaporates. If they are covering a withdrawal, they are masters of slowing the pursuit by repeated sallies.

The diary of Sergeant Vollborn, of the Infantry Regiment Prinz Clemens, contained a section on his experiences after the battle of Podubna:

> Marching through the swamps of Wolhynia meant that the men were wading through water and mud all day, half undressed. The battalion

pioneers went ahead under escort and cut trees to build bridges over the worst spots. Those who have not seen the spectacle of an army of half-naked soldiers, floundering through such mud will have no idea of what it looked like.

On the first day we all laughed to see how the regimental band got on; but the sutleresses were the funniest. But one gets used to all sorts of things.

It went on for days; wading along all day, bivouacking in the swamp at night, no bread since over a week, not even biscuit – only some captured Russian biscuit, which was the baked crusts of black loaves – it was awful.

Anyone who discovered one of the haystacks, which dotted the swamps, and could sleep in them was a happy man. It was a miracle that the whole army did not go down with fever, or that discipline did not collapse.

We then heard that the commander of the Regiment [Prinz] Anton had been arrested by General Lecoq, who had caught some of his regiment maurauding. If you put your hand on your heart, you know the cause of this maurauding; it was the failure of the ration supply system in this terrible piece of country.

Evidence that we had taken many prisoners was seen every day in the piles of destroyed weapons at the sides of the track. We sergeants each received fine Russian swords and discarded our sabres... In the Russian cartridge boxes we found finely made cartridges of the best vellum – made in England. What a massive difference to ours, which adopted the English pattern only in 1820, and even then without vellum paper.

At the end of August, Vollborn's regiment reached the River Styr and the pursuit of the Russians ended:

During our time on the Styr we saw the second, and final, public execution. Two soldiers, who had slept on guard duty, were made to run the gauntlet. Apart from this, discipline was rapidly restored once we were able to set up orderly, hutted camps again. The whole secret is: regular supply of rations. The supply organization was solely to blame for the lack of clothing resupply, which they ought to have arranged at least as far as Wlodawka on the Bug. We were now all in rags; everyone was cutting pieces from their greatcoats to patch elbows and knees. The men often had no breeches and gaiters any more; they wore shoes and boots taken from peasants and prisoners, and self-made trousers cut from peasant smocks. My own costume consisted of home-made green trousers, gaiters and a dark grey overcoat, reaching to mid-thigh.

Following the battle of Podubna, the Saxon corps took up quarters north of the Pripet marshes, between the Austrians to the east and the Polish Bug Division. Von Wolffersdorff's regiment was initially around the Kobryn area, but on 16 August they moved westwards to Brest-Litowsk on the River Bug.

In the midst of the horrors of war, there were occasional, almost incredible, islands of peace and tranquillity – at least in the southern sector – as this account illustrates:

One battalion of the Regiment Prinz Clemens was in the town itself, Lieutenant von Goeckel, myself and some men were quartered in the Ursuliner Nunnery, with the administrator's family. That fine evening we sat out in the garden under a large fruit tree and drank tea with a wonderful arak. The battalion choir was nearby and sang Saxon folksongs. The administrator's wife had a beautiful, clear voice and he accompanied her on the mandoline... On 26 August we were attached to the Austrian Colonel Soden for a reconnaissance south east to Rudnia.[2] Next day we pushed the Russian rearguard back to Macewo. The area was filled with lakes and streams; the roads were the usual log tracks. We advanced as far south as the village of Szazk,[3] where we stayed three days. The maps and the inhabitants told us that the entire surrounding area was impenetrable. We pushed on south to Luboml, where we clashed with the enemy. The corps then pushed on south to Turijsk, where we took up a position along the Turija River. It was here that our General Lecoq received the commander's cross of the Order of Heinrich. We also heard that the Army of the Moldau, of five divisions under generals Langeron, Bulatow, Woinow, Sabanjew and Essen was advancing northwards, up the left bank of the Dnjestr on us to support Tormassow. The Army of the Moldau could be on us by early September. Our further advances were thus cancelled and we restricted ourselves to frequent patrols to our front and flanks. The Saxon troops now went into hutted camps, the 1st Division at Kiselin,[4] the 2nd at Maskowicze,[4] an hour north of Turijsk. Kosinski's Polish division was at Pawlowicze[4] to the west of the Saxons.

Jean-Louis-Ebenezer Reynier, Commander VII Corps

Born on 14 January 1771 in Lausanne (Switzerland), in May 1790 Reynier was a pupil in the *Ecole des Ponts et Chaussées* in Paris, an engineering school. He entered military service in September 1792 as a volunteer gunner and was posted next day, but was soon recalled to Paris to work on the fortifications. His career in the staff soon began, and he served at the battle of Jemappes, the siege of Maastricht and at the battle of Neerwinden.

In June 1794 Reynier was nominated *General de Brigade*, but refused to accept on the grounds that he was too young. Nevertheless, he was promoted to acting general in November in Macdonald's division and this was confirmed in January 1795. He travelled widely, serving in the conquest of Holland, occupying Gozo off Malta and fighting in the battle of the Pyramids in Egypt, later becoming Governor of Charquieh province in Egypt. In January 1799 he went on the expedition to Syria and was at the capitulation of Fort El Arish on 20 February. At the battle of Alexandria on 21 March 1801 Reynier openly opposed General Menou and was arrested by General Destaing and sent back to France on a ship called *Le Lodi*. He landed at Nice on 28 June. He then published a book on the Egyptian campaign which was critical of Menou; this was siezed on the orders of the First Consul.

On 5 May 1802 Reynier fought a duel with Destaing in Paris, killed him and was exiled from the city. He entered the service of the Italian Republic and commanded troops successfully in many exploits, for which he became a *Grand Officer of the Legion d'Honneur.*

Further important commands ensued, including taking over the French army in Calabria in place of Massena in 1807, and taking command of the 2e Division of the *Armée d'Espagne* in 1809. In May 1811 Reynier was created a Count; in June he became second in command to Marmont of the *Armée de Portugal*. On 23 January 1812 he was called to the *Grand Armée* in Germany and given command of the VII (Saxon) Corps; he fought on the southern flank together with Schwarzenberg's Austrians at Gorodetchno, Wolkowysk and other clashes.

Reynier received the Grand Cross of the Order of the Two Sicilies and was created Commander of the Order of St Heinrich of Saxony. On 3 April he was also awarded the Grand Cross of the Order of the Reunion. His corps fought at Bautzen, Reichenbach, Gross-Beeren, Dennewitz and lifted the siege of Wittenberg on 12 October. His remaining Saxons went over to the enemy on 18 October at Leipzig; he was captured after the battle and returned to France on 12 February 1814. He died in Paris on 27 February.

Austrian headquarters was now at Kowelj,[4] later in Goloby,[4] in order to cover the left flank of the Saxon corps and to maintain contact with the main body of the *Grande Armée*. [now nearing Borodino].

The Russians had now withdrawn south to Luzk and had taken up fortified positions behind the River Styr; west of Lutzk was General Lambert's corps, which extended south west along the upper reaches of the river to include the town of Berestezko, on the border with Galicia.

Horses of the Italian Dragoons in bivouac. Faber du Four.

We built our huts on some high ground, taking materials for them from the surrounding villages; in this process some of the Russian houses were completely demolished. Each battalion built a large wooden barn to serve as an inn and social centre, in which our sutleresses did brisk business.

That which we needed, and could not draw from our stores, we took from the surrounding areas. Sometimes we were lucky enough to find dry straw or a smoked ham, which was then shared out in our 'inn'. There was always a good supply of excellent brandy and the Austrian sutleresses brought in Hungarian wines. Generally we closed our inn (which we christened 'Eilenburg' after our garrison town in Saxony) at 11 o'clock at night. The officers and men then went off to their huts and the sutleresses went to bed under their carts, draping sheets of canvas to form rooms there.

This type of warfare meant that we were supported at the cost of the country, and Wolhynia offered us goods in abundance. The country was rich in grain and fruit, the lush meadows supported plenty of cattle and the gardens, protected from the east winds, were full of all sorts of fruit and vegetables. The ponds were full of fish, the farms had plenty of poultry and the cellars were full of brandy, which, due to the ban on trade, had been building up for years.

Then comes a side-swipe at the French methods of treating the assets of the country in which they were operating:

Despite all these assets, the French commissars managed to plunder most of it bare and to ensure that almost none of it found its way to their own troops – or to any others.

It was noticeable that the local Jewish merchants always managed to undercut the army sutleresses in price.

Thus it was that we had to mount regular requisitioning expeditions. I was sent out on one on 15 September, with 60 men, to a village three hours distant, to requisition horses and rations.

We set off at dawn, making a wide detour through the meadows in order to escape being seen; we then passed through some woods to come out in a clearing containing several paddocks with horses grazing in them. This was the stud farm of a rich landowner.

The Jew, whom we had brought along as a guide suddenly vanished and we had to find our own way, but finally we found our village, by a lake in the middle of the forest. We found plenty of supplies of bread, wild honey and cattle, as well as traces that Cossacks had also been here.

I kept my men together, gathered up quickly what we needed and set out sentries to avoid being surprised. Half an hour later, one of my sentries came running back with the news that enemy cavalry was approaching from the next village and could be here in thirty minutes.

I sent my wagons off as fast as they could go; we hid ourselves behind the houses... Then I saw three Cossacks appear in the distance and we heard the rattle and clatter of a large body of cavalry behind them. We stayed under cover; I had to be prepared to fight off an attack by superior numbers. Finally

1. Russian infantry drawn from life by Georg Adam in Nuremburg, Germany, in 1814. This plate throws
up some teasing questions, possibly illustrating the differences between the purely theoretical uniform
regulations and what was actually worn in the field after a hard campaign and miles away from the
regimental depot. The central officer and the private to his right with the brass, double eagle cap plate
of the Pavlovski Grenadiers are apparently of the Imperial Guard, as is the private with the black
plume. None of them, however, wear guards' lace to collar and cuffs. The figure on the extreme right,
with a black fur busby and light blue facings, would appear to be from a militia unit.

2. Once again, Georg
Adam has given us
campaign dress. In
the foreground we see
a member of the
Starodub Kuerassiers.
To his right is a
member of the
Lifland Mounted
Rifles; to his right a
member of the Ulans,
but the Czapka and
lance pennant colours
make identification
impossible. The
dragoon seems to be
from the Kasan
Regiment.

3. A group of Austrian cavalry officers from various regiments. Note the imperial cipher 'F' on the helmet plates and the forage cap of the groom holding the horse on the left. plate by Theodor Weigl, Vienna.

4. Officers and men of various Austrian hussar regiments. From left to right they are: trooper, 8th Regiment (poplar green dolman and pelisse, light red breeches); officer, 3rd Regiment (ash grey shako, dark blue dolman, breeches and pelisse); officer, 5th Regiment (red shako, dark green dolman and pelisse, crimson breeches); officer, 4th Regiment (light blue shako, poplar green dolman and pelisse, light red breeches); trooper, 9th Regiment (black shako, dark green dolman and pelisse, crimson breeches); officer, 3rd Regiment (ash grey shako, dark blue uniform).

5. The *Aigle-Garde* of an infantry regiment. In the Army Museum in Vienna is an example of the brass helmet with red fur crest worn by some members of this guard when in action. By the brothers Suhr in Hamburg. Author's collection.

7. Below: Private, Garde-Jaegers, parade dress. Musician, Silesian Grenadier Battalion.

6. Below: Gunner, Silesian artillery brigade. Pioneer, marching order.

8. Troopers of different cavalry regiments. Left to right: Leib-Chevauxlegers-Regiment, Jaeger-Regiment zu Pferd Nr 4, Chevauxlegers-Regiment Nr 1 Prinz Adam, Jaeger-Regiment zu Pferd Nr 3, Herzog Louis. A Knoetel plate. Author's collection.

9. Left to right: three infantrymen, a trooper of the Chevauleger-Regiment. Wuerzburg retained traditional white uniforms for its infantry. The cavalryman's costume reflects Austrian fashion. A plate from the Augsburger Bilder. Author's collection.

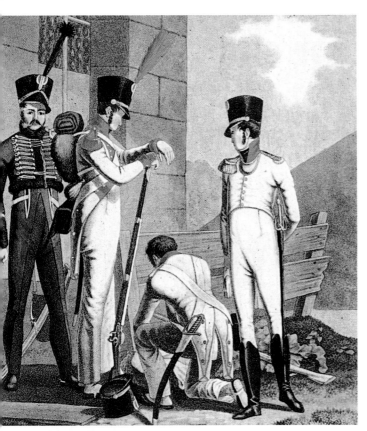

10. Again, Frankfurt retained the traditional white uniforms of the Catholic states of the Holy Roman Empire, whilst introducing French-style badges of rank and red and green plumes and epaulettes for the grenadier and voltigeur companies. Augsburger Bilder. Author's collection.

11. A *sappeur* of a line infantry regiment. As in the British regiments, the sappers went unshaven. The leather apron, the axe and a saw-toothed sword completed his toolkit. By the brothers Suhr in Hamburg. Author's collection.

12. Left to right: officer in undress uniform; fusilier; grenadier in service dress; grenadier in parade dress; voltigeur; pioneer; musician. Knoetel plate. Author's collection.

13. Left to right, grenadier, Schwerin (note Prussian style of the uniform); centre – officer, Schwerin artillery, with the usual black facings; officer, Strelitz infantry battalion. Mecklenburg-Schwerin's infantry regiment served in the 5th Division, I Corps, while Mecklenburg-Strelitz's infantry battalion was with the 3rd Division of the same corps. Knoetel plate. Author's collection.

14. Right: Left to right, infantry officer, private, Leib-Regiment (the regiment was the only one of the infantry of the grand duchy to wear the lace loops to collar and cuff flaps), private Jaegers, private Garde-Grenadiers. Knoetel plate. Author's collection.

15. Officer and troopers, Kuerassier Regiment von Zastrow. This cavalry regiment (and the Garde du Corps) were detached from VII Corps, brigaded together under General von Thielmann and transferred into General Lorge's 7th Heavy Cavalry Division, in Latour-Maubourg's IV Cavalry Corps. They fought at Borodino and were the regiments that finally took the grand battery. Author's collection.

16. This formation of infantry and cavalry was raised by the French from Portuguese prisoners of war from the campaign of 1808 in Portugal.

Left to right: chasseur (background), grenadier (rear view), two fusiliers, seated voltiguer (foreground), officer of Chasseurs (mounted), infantry officer, mounted chasseur. Augsburger Bilder. Author's collection.

17. These troops fought with the VIII Corps under General Jean-Andoche Junot (after King Jerome was sent home by Napoleon).

Left to right, officer of grenadiers of the line, officer of light infantry. Knoetel plate. Author's collection.

18. This regiment was with the 6th Regiment, Confederation of the Rhine, in the 34th Division, XI Corps of Marshal Augereau. Together with the 5th Regiment (see below) they entered Russia, relatively intact, in mid-November 1812. The XI Corps then had 14,000 men; it was reduced to 1,500 within four weeks. Augsburger Bilder. Author's collection.

19. This regiment was with the 5th Regiment, Confederation of the Rhine, in the 34th Division, in Marshal Augereau's XI Corps. Knoetel plate. Author's collection.

the first shots rang out, echoing ten times as loudly in the surrounding trees. We formed up to do our duty, and after about ten minutes of musketry, fifty Cossacks rode away; our casualties were very light, there was just one man hit in the thigh, but he could still march.

In Kiselin we received a long-awaited shipment of new clothing, but it didn't help much, as the cloth was damp and rotting from the long journey. Part of the shipment had been taken by the Cossacks.[5]

The regular attrition of operations, which steadily ground down the armies even in 'quiet' periods, is mentioned here.

The frequent patrols that we sent out to the Styr often caused us casualties. On 7 September Lieutenant of Engineers, Geise, was sent off with an escort of Lieutenant von Mangold and fifteen hussars to scout the river bank; they were captured. The same fate befell a patrol of the Austrian Hussar Regiment Kaiser at the same spot next day. They lost two officers and 37 horses. After these events, only strong patrols were sent out.

Russian General Ertell now attacked Austrian General Mohr with superior force and pushed him back to Cubieszow; Mohr lost some hundreds of men.

Napoleon's entry into Moscow was a watershed in our fortunes. From early September, the Russian pressure against us grew.

Obviously the entry into the Russian capital was not, of itself, a trigger in this event; it merely occurred at the same time as the Russian mobilisation efforts began to deliver more troops and guns to the front line formations.

The action of Schwarzenberg in deploying his forces deep into the Pripet marshes, with miles of fragile defiles behind them, is difficult to understand. It would have been more advisable to remain on the northern edge of this major obstacle, with regular patrolling activity forward into the swamps. The enemy would then have had to cope with the difficulties of advancing through the miles of deadly morasses. As we shall see, when the allies were forced to withdraw, the exercise was a nightmare.

Notes

1 The same unit that had excited Napoleon's ire in Wilna on 7 July.
2 Ratno.
3 Now Sack, about 90 km south of Brest.
4 I have been unable to locate these villages.
5 In December, when it was very cold, cloth was requisitioned in Rozana in order to have greatcoats and trousers made for the men, who were running around in rags. They had to buy the items at one Thaler each, because they were not official issue items.

Chapter 10

The central sector –
the battle of Smolensk

'Here I remain. Let us rally our forces. The campaign of 1812 is at an end.'

The chase of the 1st and 2nd Russian Armies of the West by the main body went on to Smolensk, where, on 16 August, the armies of Barclay de Tolly and Bagration finally united. Napoleon, expecting a battle, seemed to want to halt for the year. Murat advised advancing further; the Emperor responded: 'In 1813 I shall be at Moscow; in '14 at St Petersburg. This war will last three years.' But next day, just prior to the battle of Smolensk, he said:

> Russia cannot continue this sacrifice of her towns. Alexander can only begin negotiations after there has been a major battle. No blood has yet been spilled. Even if I have to march as far as the holy city of Moscow, I am determined to force a fight and win!

The battle of Smolensk, 17/18 August. A Russian city in the central sector, on the River Dniepr. A drawn battle between Ney's III and Prince Poniatowski's V (Polish) Corps and elements of the combined 1st and 2nd Russian Armies of the West.

The city of Smolensk lay astride the river. To the north was the small new town, or St Petersburg suburb. Across the bridge lay the old city, still surrounded by the massive, red-brick, medieval walls and towers, five kilometres long, and a moat. There were three gates, to the west, north and south. The fortifications had been allowed to fall into disrepair and extensive suburbs of wooden houses had sprung up on the glacis, obscuring the defenders' fields of fire. There was no time to clear them.

Napoleon concentrated 50,000 men and 84 guns on the day of the battle; Barclay opposed him with 30,000 men and 108 guns. At five o'clock on the afternoon of 15 August, Murat's cavalry and Ney's infantry closed up to the western side of the city. The main body of the army did not come up until late next day. Nonetheless, Napoleon ordered an assault on 16 August.

Ney's III Corps and Grouchy's III Cavalry Corps managed to push in the defenders of Kolubakin's 12th Russian division (2nd Army of the West), who were in front of the Krasnoi suburb, but were unable to penetrate the city. The Emperor called off his dogs.

Trooper of the Italian Dragoons in bivouac. Albrecht Adam.

That night, the rest of the 2nd Russian army, and all of the 1st, arrived to the east of Smolensk. But Barclay decided – once again – to avoid a pitched battle and to adhere to his policy of drawing the invaders further to the east. His 1st Army would lead the way; Bagration would provide the rearguard.

Next day, Napoleon had 183,000 men in the area. Still in the city were Dokturov's VII Corps, the 3rd Infantry Division of Konovnitzin's II Corps, Neverovski's solid 27th Division and the 6th Jaegers of the 12th Division. This made a total of 20,000 men and 180 guns.

On the right wing of the *Grande Armée* were Poniatowski's V Corps and Murat's cavalry on the eastern flank. Then came the I Corps (with the Guard behind them) and Ney's III Corps up against the river. A general assault began at three o'clock in the afternoon; the Russians were soon forced back inside the old city. The suburbs were soon ablaze and a French attempt to break into the centre of Smolensk was repulsed with heavy loss. Three other assaults were treated in the same manner. By seven o'clock the whole city was ablaze. That night (17/18 August) the Russians evacuated the ruins and withdrew eastwards.

Napoleon had lost 8,564 men, the Russians about 6,000. The Imperial Guard was not engaged.

Caulaincourt, a usually reliable source on Napoleon, recorded that the Emperor actually considered halting the campaign for 1812 at this point. Watching the retreating Russian columns, Napoleon mused:

> By abandoning Smolensk, which is one of their holy cities, the Russian generals are dishonouring their arms in the eyes of their own people. That will put me in a strong position. We will drive them back a little further for our own

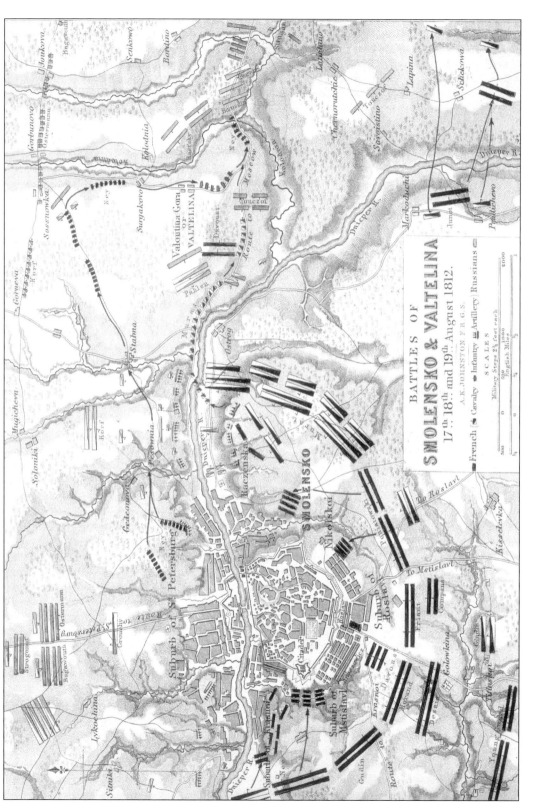

BATTLES OF
SMOLENSKO & VALTELINA
17ᵗʰ, 18ᵗʰ and 19ᵗʰ August 1812.
A. K. JOHNSTON F.R.G.S.

French (█ Cavalry ● Infantry ▬ Artillery) Russians ▭

SCALES

Military Steps 2½ feet each

English Miles

Smolensk 17/18 August and Valutina Gora (Lubino) 19 August. *This is a Blackwood map; the complex movements of this three-day conflict are shown on this composite map. It was largely due to General Junot's refusal to attack that the Russian army was allowed to slip away to the east. Napoleon lost some 18,000 casualties, Barclay de Tolly and Bagration lost 11,000. They withdrew towards Borodino.*

comfort. I will dig myself in. We will rest the troops and dominate the country from this pivotal position and we'll see how Alexander likes that. I shall turn my attention to the corps on the Dwina which are doing nothing [a reference to the II and VI Corps, facing off against Wittgenstein at Polotzk]; my army will be more formidable and my position more menacing to the Russians than if I had won two battles. I will establish my headquarters at Witebsk. I will raise Poland in arms and later on I will choose, if necessary, between Moscow and St Petersburg.

Indeed, a strategic pause at this juncture would allow Napoleon's tired and much diminished army to rest, refit, reorganize and integrate the drafts of young, scarcely-trained reinforcements that were trickling in from western Europe. The shockingly inadequate supply situation could also be addressed, although it must be said that without active – and massive – Russian cooperation, there was not the slightest hope of supporting even what was left of the *Grande Armée*; the vast majority were already doomed to die of starvation whatever Napoleon did; it was just a question of where their bones would lie. One thing was certain: on any further advance towards Moscow, the supply situation would only get worse; the Russian army would see to that.

According to Segur, Joachim Murat told him at Smolensk, on 18 August, of his attempts to make the Emperor see reason: 'I threw myself on my knees before my brother-in-law and implored him to stop. But he could see nothing but Moscow. Honour, glory, rest – everything was there for him. This Moscow was going to be our ruin!'

On 19 August, Bagration wrote to Araktchejev from Michaelowka, just west of Dorogobusch:

> Your Minister might be good in the ministry but he's no good as a general!... I'm losing my mind with rage! ...Organize the militia because the Minister is leading our guests right into the capital! The army is very much against ADC Wolzogen; they say that he is more for Napoleon than for us and he is advising the Minister!... It's not my fault that the Minister is indecisive, cowardly, stupid, slow to make decisions and has all the bad characteristics. The whole army insults him. Poor Pahlen I is dying of grief and all are being driven mad with rage and sorrow. We have never been so depressed as now... I would prefer to be a common soldier than a commanding general at this time, and that even under Barclay. I have written the whole truth.

These letter extracts give us some idea of the divisions that were ripping the very fabric of the Russian high command apart at this strategically critical juncture; the atmosphere is one of near-mutiny. That the Russian army could give such a good account of itself as it did at Smolensk, after weeks of demoralising withdrawals, abandoning their homeland to the ravages of the horde of the Antichrist (as Napoleon was held to be by most Russians) and with practically no faith in their commander, speaks volumes for the high quality of the army and all its members. It also demonstrates how ineffective Barclay was at communicating his strategic concept to his junior commanders, and even to the Czar, because all of Bagration's letters to Alexander's close adviser had had their effect.

Giesse, with the Westphalians, relates the incident which caused the unfortunate VIII Corps to miss this battle, and to earn Napoleon's enmity:

> Until Smolensk, we had rarely seen the Duke of Abrantes, only when he

galloped through marching columns of troops, lashing out left and right with a large riding whip at any unfortunate who failed to get out of his way quickly enough.

At that point we didn't know that he had formerly been a sort of a 'Leibmameluke,' or valet, to Napoleon and owed his rise through the ranks to this. On 15th August the corps was ordered to become the right flank guard of the army. This involved a march to the right, around V Corps, with the aim of being at Smolensk the next day. The march was to go via a village named Tscherkowiczi, which no-one seemed to be able to identify. The Duke of Abrantes appeared before the troops, early in the morning. After much secretive discussion with his staff, poring over a map and looking towards all points of the compass with obvious signs of impatience, he ordered an officer to go off and get a peasant.

General Andoche Junot, commander of the VIII (Westphalian) Corps after Vandamme's removal. He was judged to be mentally unstable, a proven and unrepentant squanderer of several fortunes. He committed suicide on 29 July 1813.

A peasant was duly produced; a lame geriatric who at once fell at the feet of our Duke. A great blow from the Duke's whip brought him very smartly to his feet again.

There was not one officer in Junot's retinue who could speak Russian or Polish; this did not worry the Duke for a second. He pulled Berthier's order from his pocket and proceeded to read the word 'Tscherkowiczi' gravely to the peasant, several times.

No response.

Another great blow from the Duke's whip.

The peasant fell back a step and shouted what sounded like: 'Ziverowiczi!' and waved his hand off to his left rear.

Even if this was the right direction, Junot – or one of his officers – should have become suspicious, because that was the direction that we had just come from.

The Duke, however had no such doubts; ordering one of his staff to take the peasant on his stirrup leather, he rode to the head of the column, shouting: *'Filons Messieurs!'* and set off in the direction indicated by the peasant.

We marched for some hours; no village appeared. This made the Duke annoyed, as he laid great value on a good breakfast and it was time for a long rest period.

He was about to ride off with his suite in order to spy out the *'château d'un bon baron,'* when General von Hammerstein[1] rode up and pointed out a distant castle with the words: *'Mais Monseigneur, voilà notre bivouac d'hier!'* (But Sire, that is our bivouac of yesterday).

The Duke stared silently in the direction of the castle; motionless. Then he galloped back to the unfortunate peasant, cursing and screaming, flogged him briefly with his beloved whip, then drew his sabre and cut and hacked at him. Not satisfied with that, he ordered him to be shot, and galloped off towards breakfast in the castle.

Thus the VIII Corps took no part in the battle of Smolensk.

In the battle of Smolensk on 17/18 August the *Grande Armée* lost over 8,560 men; the Russians lost some 6,000 and slipped away to the east. The city was destroyed by fire; no quarters here. Away to the north at the same time, Marshal Oudinot, with the II and VI Corps, had fought General Count Wittgenstein's Russians to a bloody draw; no resounding French victory here either.

On 19 August another opportunity for Napoleon to catch the Russians at the defile of Valutina Gora was missed, largely due to Junot's blatant – and expensive – mishandling of his VIII Westphalian corps. Again a captured Russian general was asked by Napoleon to carry a message of peace to the Czar; the plea was mixed with many threats of what destruction would be wreaked on Russia if no peace ensued.

The letter was written and delivered; it was never answered. Alexander had learned to play poker with the big boys very well.

After the Russian left, General Rapp asked the Emperor whether the army was to advance or retreat; the answer was: 'The wine is poured out; it must be drunk to the last drop. I am for Moscow… Too long have I played the emperor; it is time I became the general once more.'

At long last the fateful die had been cast.

But the months of uncharacteristic, querulous indecision on Napoleon's part betrayed the changes that were taking place in his thought processes – or was it just that Lady Luck's face was now turned against him? This indecision was to surface again in the 1813 campaign.

★★★★★

On 18 August General of Infantry Prince Michael Giliaronovich Goleichev Kutuzov was appointed supreme commander in Barclay's place. His task was to revitalise and reunite the army, restore morale and to offer battle to the invaders as soon as possible. Kutuzov was 67 years of age, heavily overweight, ponderous both physically and mentally, and blind in the right eye from a wound received in the wars with the Turks. He had served in the army for 52 years and had 'commanded' at the Austro-Russian defeat at Napoleon's hands at Austerlitz on 2 December 1805. 'Commanded' is probably not the correct formulation as Czar Alexander was present in his headquarters and was playing at soldiers.

This new, aggressive policy could not, of course, be adopted overnight; a suitable defensive position had first to be found to tilt the playing field in favour of the Russians in the face of the enemy's numerical superiority. But there was the proviso that it had to be found somewhere between the armies' present location and Moscow; to abandon the capital without a fight would be totally unacceptable to the army and to the populace.

A group of men of the Italian Royal Guard in bivouac. Albrecht Adam. Author's collection.

French cavalry search for rich pickings in a Russian town. Albrecht Adam. Author's collection.

The battle of Valutina-Gora (Lubino), 19 August. A village in the central sector, 8 km north east of Smolensk. Another drawn battle. On the French side were the I, III and VIII (Westphalian) Corps; on the Russian side, under General Tutschkov I, the II, III and IV Corps.

Following the action at Smolensk, the Russians pulled back eastwards, their extensive trains offering a tempting target to the allies as they struggled through the defile of Valutina-Gora. Murat's cavalry and Junot's VIII Corps crossed the River Dnieper at the ford of Pruditcheva to the south east of Smolensk and had a chance to cut off the Russian rearguard, but Junot refused to advance and the Russians were allowed to slip away to the east. French losses were some 9,000 of the 41,000 men involved; General Gudin was killed. The Russians had 22,000 men in the action and lost about 5,000.

The Westphalians, who had missed the Russians at the start of the campaign, and who had missed the battle of Smolensk, were – unwittingly – to consolidate their reputation for ineptitude this day. Giesse's tale is continued:

> On the morning of the 19th August, VIII Corps crossed the River Dniepr on two pontoon bridges. By midday they had reached the village of Tschebonkowo, when their advanced guard came up with the Russians, who were moving so slowly, that it was in Junot's hands to bring them to battle. The troops were eager for a fight; the sounds of heavy gunfire showed that action had already been joined. General von Ochs[2] records that if Junot continued his march, they would have taken the enemy rearguard in flank and destroyed 10,000 Russians.

Horse artillery advancing at the battle of Smolensk. Albrecht Adam. Author's collection.

A scene during the battle of Smolensk, 18 August 1812. Wuerttemberg infantry of the 25th Division, III Corps, skirmishing in the outskirts of the city. Faber du Four. Author's collection.

Junot now decided to call a halt and took a siesta.

After his rest, Junot continued his march, but by now, Russian cavalry had come up to cover the exposed flank. Despite being exhorted by his generals to attack, Junot just sat and watched the spectacle.

He eventually could be moved to send out the 2nd Light Infantry Battalion and the voltigeur company of the 1st Light Infantry Battalion. These troops were far too weak to affect anything.

The latter unit was attacked by a swarm of Cossacks and formed square; they then fired a volley too soon; the Cossacks charged in and cut them down to a man.

This took place in full view of the rest of the corps, but Junot did nothing. He was roundly cursed by many an officer and man.

Westphalian participation had been eagerly expected by the other allied corps commanders. After a time, the King of Naples galloped up, cursing and shouting: 'Where is General Junot?'

Murat's appearance on the scene evoked roaring cheers from the Westphalians, who thought that at last they would have a chance to prove their worth in battle.

Murat confronted Junot and hotly demanded to know why he was not attacking the enemy.

Junot replied that he had received no direct orders from Napoleon to attack, that he did not trust the Westphalians, they were untried troops, they might endanger his artillery, and the responsibility was too great.

At last, Murat rode back along the front of the VIII Corps shouting: '*Eh bien, Westphaliens! Si vous êtes aussi braves que vous êtes beaux! Chassez-moi cette canaille – là!*' (So, Westphalians! Are you as brave as you are handsome? Chase this mob off for me – go!) And rode back to the main army.

Stung into some sort of action at last, Junot ordered Hammerstein's light cavalry to advance through the defile into action.

Defiling took some time; when the brigade at last formed line, they were attacked by the Russians, who outnumbered them by three to one. Despite being repeatedly urged by General von Ochs to send them some support, it was some time before he allowed a battery of artillery to be sent up.

Meanwhile, General von Hammerstein, on his great Turkish grey, had challenged any Russian daredevil to come out and face him in single combat. At last a Russian hussar with a lance came forward. He circled around von Hammerstein and fired his pistol at him. The general sat quietly while this went on, then suddenly spurred his horse forward and cut the Russian through the shako and head to his shoulders.

The Russian slumped to the ground like a sack. The general caught his horse and gave it to a hussar to take to the rear. 'Just a little determination and you can get all those fellows like that' he said to his men.

Apart from these minor skirmishes, that was all that VIII Corps was permitted to contribute to the day's events. We stood and watched as the Russians moved off into the forests.

Von Lossberg's feelings are of interest:

> I share the feelings of all those who say that it is a disaster for our corps that we have lost Vandamme and gained Junot. If the former were still here, some of us would not be alive now, but the living would at least have earned honour and fame, which it seems we shall lose under Junot, and that is worse than death.

A scene during the battle of Smolensk. Albrecht Adam. Author's collection.

View of part of the battle of Valutina Gora, 19 August, by Paul Hess. Author's collection.

According to Segur, Napoleon, on the field of the drawn battle of Valutina Gora, on 19 August, said:

> This battle has been the most brilliant exploit in all our military history. You soldiers who are listening to me are men with whom one could conquer the world. The dead here have earned immortal names for themselves.

He was less than pleased with his old friend, Junot, and removed him from his command for a brief period, replacing him with General Rapp. Junot's friends interceded for him, however, and much to the chagrin of the Westphalians, the Duke of Abrantes was soon flogging his way through his marching columns again.

The Imperial Guard was not engaged in the battle of Smolensk, or in that of Valutina-Gora. The Russians withdrew before the *Grande Armée* in a most professional manner, leaving behind nothing of value. Their view of events was radically different from that of the invaders – doubtless moulded by the needs of public relations as much as any bulletin.

On hearing that *Te Deums* were being sung in St Petersburg to celebrate alleged Russian victories at Witebsk and Smolensk, Napoleon burst out indignantly: 'What! Te Deums? Then they dare to lie to God as they lie to men!' The Emperor was obviously annoyed that anyone else had dared to infringe his copyright.

Notes

1 Commander of the Light Cavalry Brigade.
2 Commander, 24th Division.

Chapter 11

The central sector – from Smolensk to Borodino

*'The staff is useless; not one of the officers does his duty properly,
not the provost-general, nor the quarter-master.'*

The negative effects on the army of Napoleon's continued rush to catch the Russians were commented on by von Lossberg:

> If I could not see the great road to Moscow, I could follow it with my nose because of the stench! At least every hundred paces is a dead horse or cow, which has been slaughtered and whose innards are strewn all over the road. In every village or isolated house are unburied human dead, both the enemy's and ours, which no-one has bothered to bury. Truly, today has convinced me that Napoleon is so obsessed with the idea of catching and destroying the Russian army, that he pays no heed to the shattering effect that this pursuit has on his own army.

So the army trudged on eastwards, getting weaker, smaller and further from its bases with every weary step. The drain of manpower became obvious to the Emperor. On 2 September he ordered Alexander Berthier to write to the corps commanders on the topic:

> My Cousin: Order the King of Naples, the Prince of Eckmühl, the Viceroy, Prince Poniatowski, the Duke of Elchingen, to take a day's rest, to get in their stragglers, to have a rollcall at three in the afternoon, and to let me know precisely the number of men they can place in line.
>
> The staff is useless; not one of the officers does his duty properly, not the provost-general, nor the quartermaster. You have my order for the baggage. See to it that the first baggage wagons I order burnt are not those of the general staff.

A most revealing sentence considering that he had just condemned the lot of them as being 'useless'. And as he had selected all the senior staff officers personally, what did that say about his acumen for getting the right men in the right jobs?

Next day, again to Berthier, Napoleon ordered:

> Write to the officers commanding the army corps that we lose so many men daily because there is no system in the supply service; it is urgently

necessary that they should take measures in concert with their colonels to put an end to the state of things that threatens the army with destruction. Every day the enemy pick up several hundred prisoners. During the twenty years in which I have commanded French armies, I have never seen the commissariat service so hopelessly bad; there is no one; the people sent out here have no ability and no experience.

So, in just two days the scales had suddenly fallen from his eyes as to the efficiency of his general staff and his commissariat and to the extreme strategic attrition that his army was suffering, deep in hostile Russia. But why only now? Was he so insulated from what had been happening to his army even since before he crossed the Niemen on 23 June? Did he not see the thousands of corpses of *his* men and *his* horses lining the route of his advancing columns? Did he receive no daily and weekly parade states? Did he not read them and notice the dwindling numbers of men and horses day after day, week after week? Or did Berthier fudge all the figures? It seems hardly likely. The truth is that the welfare of his army only became a matter of concern to him when it was painfully obvious that it was falling apart, melting away. A state of affairs that might endanger his own personal aims.

> **Schewardino, 5 September.** A hamlet in the central sector, 3 km south west of Borodino. A French victory (Davout's I and Ney's III Corps) over Borosdin's VIII Infantry and General Count Siever I's IV Cavalry Corps.

This was the foreplay to the battle of Borodino. The redoubt here was a tiny earthwork, flanked by artillery batteries but isolated from the main Russian army to its rear. Napoleon ordered Davout's I Corps to attack it from the west and north and for Poniatowski to assault it from the south.

Defence of the work had been delegated to Neverovsky's 27th Infantry Division, which had performed so well in its baptism of fire at Krasnoi on 14 August. The Russians had deployed the 5th, 49th and 50th Jaegers in skirmishing order on the south bank of the Kalotscha (here merely a rivulet) north of Fomkino and then south in the scrub along the eastern bank of the Doronino stream. Other troops were in support.

In the late afternoon, Compans's 5th Division Jaegers out of Fomkino advanced in battalion columns to assault the redoubt itself. At the same time, Morand's 1st Division and Friant's 2nd pushed south through Aleksinki, Friant attacking the Russian artillery and dragoons north of Schewardino, Morand heading through Schewardino itself. Behind the infantry was the cavalry of General Bruyères' 1st Light Cavalry Division of Nansouty's I.

Holzhausen, a German eyewitness in VIII Corps, recorded:

> It was wonderful to see the keenness of our soldiers. The beauty of the scene was enhanced by the magnificent sky and by the setting sun which was reflected from the muskets and sabres. The troops marched on, proud to have been chosen to be the first to come to grips with enemy.

This pointless struggle for an insignificant and indefensible pimple of a hill had held up Napoleon for a few hours, had demonstrated what tough opponents the Russians were and how bravely the French and their allies could die, but all in all, it was a waste,

Staff officers of the IV Corps at Borodino. Albrecht Adam.

particularly when every man would be needed by both sides for the impending main battle. Barclay was disgusted with the affair, as was Yermolov. Rumour had it – and there was a fair ring of truth to it – that Bennigsen had chosen to fortify and hold the site and would not allow the troops to abandon it without a fight in order not to lose face.

The day cost Napoleon about 4,000 killed, wounded and missing and five guns. The Russian losses are less clear; Buturlin states: 'over 1,000 men' which is surely too few; Thiers shows '7–8,000' and Barclay de Tolly gives '6,000 and three guns'. To Napoleon's astonishment, not one prisoner had been taken.

Segur quotes Colonel Jacques Ricard of the 61e Ligne responding to Napoleon's question after the action: 'Where is your Third Battalion?' by saying 'It is in the redoubt, sire.'

Having seen the reconstruction of this feature, the quote must be taken with a large pinch of salt.

★★★★★

On 6 September 1812, at Borodino, Napoleon said 'At last we have them! Forward march! We are going to open the gates of Moscow!'

There are certain similarities between the strategic situation prior to the battle of Austerlitz and to that just before Borodino. In both cases, Napoleon had brought his army to the end of an extremely long and fragile line of communication; in both cases, campaign attrition had greatly reduced the strength of his army; in both cases, the enemy's army was still largely intact; in both cases, Napoleon desperately needed to

A sentry on the battlefield of Borodino. Albrecht Adam. Author's collection.

land his legendary knock-out blow so that he could end the campaign, dictate peace on his terms and get back to Paris to concentrate on the management – and expansion – of his empire.

Captain Franz Morgenstern[1] recalled how, on the afternoon of 6 September, he had the opportunity to see Napoleon at close quarters for the first time:

> He was dressed in an open, light grey overcoat, under this a green tunic on which a star was visible; white breeches, riding boots. On his head was his world-famous tricorn. He sat on his grey Arab with the reins hanging over the neck and used both hands to hold his telescope with which he studied various points of the terrain in the direction of the Russian lines. His peaceful, faintly yellow, marble countenance, the high, wide forehead – within which he was undoubtedly formulating tomorrow's battle plans – and the respectful silence of the high-ranking officers surrounding him (I recognized Berthier, Murat, Ney, and Junot) all made such a powerful impression on me that I could hear my heart pounding loudly. Yes, truly, the close proximity of this extraordinary man wove a spell and made it clear to me how his French soldiers, bleeding to death on the battlefield, would summon their last strength to cry out a last *'Vive l'Empereur!'*

Borodino, 7 September. Centre. A village on the upper River Moskwa, 105 km west of Moscow. A victory of Napoleon's main body of the *Grande Armée* over Kutusov's combined 1st and 2nd Armies of the West.

Borodino, 7 September: *This epic battle was preceded by the clash at the Schewardino redoubt two days previously. Borodino was nothing more than a bloody slogging match, with no dash of genius to leaven it. Napoleon lost about 28,000 casualties, the Russians, now under Kutusov, lost about 43,000 (largely due to their dense formations, which offered the French gunners such wonderful targets) and twenty guns. The Russian army was still intact. This is a Blackwood map.*

General Count Matvei Ivanovich Platow, Hetman of the Don Cossack Host. He defeated the French cavalry at Korelitchi, Mir and Romanowo early in the advance, and at Borodino his raid (together with Uwarow) on the French northern flank, won the Russians much valuable time on 7 September. Among his Russian decorations is the Austrian Order of Maria Theresa.

On 7 September a blood-bath, one of Napoleon's worst battles, was fought at Borodino, seventy miles west of Moscow. By this time, the cunning old General of Infantry Prince Micheal Illarionovich Golenischev Kutusov had taken command of the Russian army in place of Barclay de Tolly and the honour of the nation demanded that a battle be fought to save Moscow.

Prior to this battle, Napoleon received a dispatch from Spain reporting Marshal Marmont's defeat at Wellington's hands at Salamanca on 22 July. Perhaps the news caused him to be a little careful at Borodino.

On the eve of the action, Davout suggested a right-flanking manoeuvre; the Emperor dismissed this as being too risky; he was all for a head-to-head slogging match.

Emmanuel, Comte de Grouchy, General, Commander, III Cavalry Corps. Author's collection.

Kutusov expected the main enemy thrust to be along the new road to Moscow, north of the chosen battlefield. He thus devoted most of his available labour to digging fortifications in the woods against the River Moskwa in that area; a totally wasted effort as events proved. Other fortifications were built on the hill just south of the Kalotscha stream (the Grand Battery) and further to the south (the Bagration Flêches). Napoleon's massed artillery batteries were sited out of range of the Russian lines and had to be moved forward when this error was discovered.

At the start of the fighting, Eugene's IV Corps seized Borodino village. The Russians retook it and later mounted a cavalry raid north of the place, deep into the rear of Eugene's IV Corps. Although this raid was only partially successful – it had no infantry support – it caused Eugene to panic and to withdraw his corps from the area of the Grand Battery for some hours.

The emperor did not sleep well the previous night, partly due to his illness. Very many others also had difficulty in getting to sleep, mainly because of the tension of the coming action. Captain Morgenstern was a happy exception.

Later that evening I met a Cuirassier who was looking for his brother in our regiment and learned from him that our 2nd Kuerassier Regiment was bivouacked nearby. I went over to their camp to visit Lieutenant Colonel von Cramm, a boyhood friend with whom I had served in the army of Brunswick. We had not seen one another for years and our joy at meeting was great. With a bottle of wine and a hearty snack – the Kuerassiers were far better off than we poor devils – the time passed so quickly that it was late at night when we parted, each wishing the other the best for the bloody work of the morrow and that we might meet again, in good health, tomorrow evening. [Von Cramm survived Russia, only to be killed at Quatrebras in 1815.]

Morgenstern continues:

My sergeant wakened me from a deep sleep before reveille; it was 4am; a profound silence reigned. A signal gun was fired; all along the line, reveilles rang out to wake any still asleep. My company's roll-call revealed three officers, all the NCOs, 81 soldiers and 3 drummers as being present. I had the corporals inspect the men's muskets and ammunition. Our regiment was already drawn up on parade when the order reached us to put on full dress as quickly as possible. [this was often done for set-piece battles and usually involved putting on plumes, shako cords, epaulettes, medals and decorations]

Officers were allowed to remain in their blue, undress uniforms. After this had been done, the emperor's proclamation was read out before each battalion.

This stirring address was greeted by the French regiments with the usual '*Vive l'Empereur!*'; the Württembergers responded with : '*Es lebe der Koenig!*' [Long live the King!] The emperor's words had touched the spot in all our hearts!

Morgenstern's Westphalian corps was made up mainly of young conscripts (as were most other formations except, of course, the Imperial Guard) and he related the following interesting phenomenon, which took place as they stood for about an hour, inactive under the artillery fire.

> Already we had suffered casualties when my senior sergeant, who had seen much action in his past service in the armies of Hessen-Kassel, Prussia and Austria, delighted me with his sense of humour when he came up to me and suggested that I order the three flankers next to me to stick out their tongues. This I did and was surprised to see that all their tongues were as white as their uniforms! I at once ordered others to do the same; theirs too were white. The sergeant assured me that this was the case with all men who were going into action for the first time. Of course, I had to put this to the proof and demanded that he show me his tongue; he obliged immediately – it was lobster-red! 'And yours, captain?' he grinned. 'We'll just let that remain my secret.' I replied. The tongue test spread quickly to neighbouring companies and caused considerable hilarity as they were all white.

At about 6.30am, Napoleon, hearing that the battle for Borodino village was in full swing and calculating that Poniatowski's V Corps must be making good progress through the woods on the southern flank towards Utitza on the old Moscow road, ordered the first assault on the *flêches* to begin. Davout's I Corps was to lead the way with Compans's 5th Division aimed at the right-hand work. For this day's assault, the Emperor had arranged the command of the forces in the central sector so that Marshal Ney controlled all the infantry involved and Murat managed the cavalry. One effect of this arrangement was that General Junot, commander of the VIII Corps, was left without a job. Junot's obstinate and erratic behaviour at the battles of Smolensk and Valutina-Gora had deprived the Westphalians of any chance of earning Napoleon's praise on these days and they had no regrets that he would not be with them today.

The garrison of the *flêches* was Neverowski's 27th Division of Borosdin I's VIII Corps; in each work was a battery of twelve guns. General Prince Karl of Mecklenburg's 2nd Grenadier Division was in close support.

Compans had two objectives: the *flêche* itself and the woods directly to the south, which were infested with the 49th and 50th Jaegers. In good order Compans's regiments marched forwards into a storm of Russian artillery fire. It has been calculated that almost 300 guns of both armies exchanged fire in the intense struggle which took place in a sector of the field about two kilometres square. The din was incessant, deafening; through it all the regimental drums beat the *pas de charge*, shells exploded, the wounded and dying screamed and groaned, officers and NCOs yelled commands, wounded horses thrashed about on the ground or careered riderless through the ranks.

Many eyewitnesses have recorded how limited their vision was at this point as the air filled with the smoke of discharging guns, exploding shells and clouds of dust thrown up by the projectiles and by passing cavalry regiments. The chaos that reigned is difficult for anyone that has not experienced its like to comprehend; the shock to the nervous systems of those going into action for the first time was immense, numbing.

It was just before 7am when Compans's 5th Division approached the southernmost *flêche*. The artillery barrage had lasted about one hour. The French

Members of the Italian Guard in bivouac. Albrecht Adam.

Platow's Cossacks in the raid on the French northern flank on 7 September at Borodino. Had this raid been backed up with infantry and adequate artillery, this battle – and the entire campaign – might have had quite a different outcome.

Italian ration wagon of the IV Corps, returning from Moscow. Faber du Four.

infantry threw the Russian Jaegers out of the wood and advanced at the *pas de charge*, storming over and around the ruined work and evicting the Russian garrison. A rapid and spirited counter-attack threw them out again. Not to be robbed of their prey, the French regrouped, assaulted again and took the *flêche* for the second time. The fighting was fierce; the casualties mounted, particularly among the French commanders who were often too close to the front line for their own good. Compans was wounded by a musket ball in the right shoulder (his twenty-second wound), probably from General Schakhowski's Jaegers in the woods to the south. Then, in rapid succession, Generals Duplain, Rapp and Dessaix (commanding the 4th Division), who in turn took over from him, were wounded in their turn. Marshal Davout was also hit.

The *flêches* had been built with no ditch or rampart on the eastern sides; any enemy forcing their way into the fortification would be fully exposed to fire from the Russians standing in reserve. It was not long before the French were thrown out again by the 2nd Grenadier Division of Major General Prince Karl von Mecklenburg and the 12th Infantry Division of Major General Wasiltschikof. At last, some Russian reinforcements arrived on the scene from the north in the shape of General Sievers I's IV Cavalry Corps (Kiev and New Russia Dragoons, Akhtyrsk Hussars and Lithuanian Lancers), and with this 2,000-strong force, Sievers temporarily broke the French grip on the *flêches* and drove Davout's I Corps back to the edge of the woods.

General Yermolow attributed the fact that the Russians held on for so long in this sector against such crushing pressure to their superior use of the bayonet.

At one point, two regiments of Württemberg cavalry and the King of Naples were forced to fly for their lives back to the southernmost *flêche*. Here, Murat soon found himself in a critical situation; penned up by some cuirassiers against a part of the ramparts which was still intact and which his horse had no chance of climbing. He was saved by a troop of Württemberg infantry which, seeing his predicament, swarmed out over the ramparts, drove off the cuirassiers and thus bought him time to dismount and climb into the redan, upon which they followed him. This event was immortalised by the Württemberg artist Faber du Four who was present at the battle.

It was not until about 11.30am that the struggle for the *flêches* was finally decided in favour of the allies. By this time, General Prince Bagration had been mortally wounded and taken to the rear. The surviving Russians in this sector pulled slowly and sullenly back eastwards over the Semenowskaya stream.

Roth von Schreckenstein[2] gave us some idea of the desperate situation in which some of the cavalry regiments of the IV Cavalry Corps found themselves at about midday: 'As men and horses were being shot all the time, the men were fully occupied closing to the centre and telling off in their new files of three; this constant telling off never stopped.'

Latour-Maubourg, commander of the corps, saw that if he could move his corps somewhat to the left, they would benefit from the cover afforded by a gentle dip in the ground. He was loath to have his command carry out a full flank march to the new site in case the Russians should sieze the opportunity to attack them as they did so. He thus sent repeated orders to his subordinates, by means of his ADCs, to carry out several minor 'shuffles' in order to achieve the same objective. Not having his commander's aims explained to him, General Thielmann became increasingly frustrated by the repeated visitations of his minions with apparently pointless instructions, and eventually he boiled over.

It was the bad luck of one of Latour-Maubourg's ADCs, a young Pole, to come to General Thielmann's brigade to deliver the next order for it to move to the left just as this happened. He arrived just as Thielmann was between the Garde du Corps and the Zastrow Kuerassiers exchanging his wounded horse for a new mount. Not seeing the general, the ADC delivered the order directly to the regimental commanders. Much to Thielmann's surprise, his brigade began to move off, apparently of its own accord. Spotting the ADC, Thielmann rode up and demanded to know why the order had not been delivered to him. The hapless ADC replied that Thielmann 'had not been at his post'. This was the last straw for the general. Flying into a rage, he drew his sabre and charged straight at the Pole, chasing him all the way back to Latour-Maubourg. Here he explained to his astounded commander that he was not one of those who would allow himself to be ordered about by adjutants, much less be insulted by them. Furthermore, if the said ADC showed his face anywhere near him again, he would run him through!

It says much for Latour-Maubourg's regard for Thielmann's proven reputation as a brave and competent commander that he did not at once arrest him but calmed him down and took the trouble to explain his aims to him in detail.

Montbrun's II Cavalry Corps was subject to a similar ordeal when they advanced into line north of Lorge's division, just west of the Semenowskaja stream. The general himself was mortally wounded by a shell splinter as he rode at a walk along the front of his regiments. 'Good shot!' a Prussian trooper heard him murmur as he slid from his horse. Montbrun died at five o'clock that evening from the effects of his stomach wound; he was regarded among the Germans in the *Grande Armée* as being one of the most honourable men in the French army.

The next tactical feature to fall to the French was the fortified village of Semenowskaya, about a kilometre to the south of the Grand Battery; this exposed the

Allied cavalry before Borodino. Faber du Four.

southern flank of the battery. When Prince Eugene's troops returned to their position in front of the Battery, they prepared to make the third assault. This time, the infantry were to aim for the north flank of the structure; Montbrun's II Cavalry Corps was also to assault the northern side of it, but to strike before the infantry arrived, and the IV Cavalry Corps was to swing around into it from the south.

As Roth von Schreckenstein wrote, General Auguste de Caulaincourt[3] was by now attached to the II Cavalry Corps, but only in the capacity of a brigade commander, not at divisional or even corps level as some writers have suggested in the past. This error has been compounded by the King of Naples, who wrote in his report (as he related the capture of the heights of Semenowskaya by Latour-Maubourg between 10.30 and 11.30):

> *Je fis alors passer le General Caulaincourt à la tête du 2. Corps de reserve; à peine fut-il de l'autre côté du ravin, que je lui donne l'ordre, de charger sur la gauche tout ce qui se trouve d'ennemis et de tacher d'aborder la grande redoubte (Rajewsky Battery) qui, nous prenant en flanc, nous faisait beaucoup de mal, s'il trouvait l'occasion favourable. Cet ordre fut executé avec autant de célerité que de bravour.*
> [I got General Caulaincourt to lead the second corps of the reserve; scarcely was he on the other side of the ravine than I gave him the order to charge any enemies on the left and to try to take the big redoubt if he got a good opportunity, which, on our flank, was giving us a deal of trouble. This order he carried out with as much celerity as bravery.]

This *'occasion favourable'* did not occur until much later, after two o'clock, when Prince Eugene made his final assault on the Battery, probably at the same time as Thielmann received his orders for the same attack. At that point however, the King of Naples was close to the village of Semenowskaya and a long way away from the II Cavalry Corps.

By saying that Caulaincourt was 'at the head' of the II Cavalry Corps, Murat gives the distinct impression that he was actually in command of it. Chambray, on the other hand, has Caulaincourt at the head of Watier's division after this general had been wounded. Meanwhile, Lorge's 7th Cuirassier Division was suffering the continued effects of the Russian artillery bombardment with great stoicism. In fact, now that they had moved a little further to the left, into a slight dip in the ground, their casualty rate had decreased somewhat. This relief was amplified by the fact that many of the shells which landed among them now had their fuses set too long; instead of bursting in the air just above their target in order to create maximum havoc, most buried themselves in the ground, the fuses were snuffed out and the shells did not detonate. The situation became so relaxed that General Thielmann ordered the men to break out their weeks-old rations of hard tack biscuits and take a frugal snack.

Just before three o'clock, Eugene's infantry moved off to the assault. Shortly afterwards, one of Napoleon's ADCs galloped up to the impatient Thielmann and delivered to him the long-awaited message: 'On behalf of the Emperor, I bring you the order to attack!'

This same order had also been delivered to the II Cavalry Corps. Caulaincourt led Watier's 2nd Cuirassier Division forward against the north flank of the Battery, Sebastiani's 2nd Light Cavalry and Defrance's 4th Cuirassier Divisions advanced directly on the front of the work, while Lorge's 7th Cuirassier Division advanced on its southern flank. What actually happened in this massive allied cavalry assault has

Napoleon, giving orders as Bavarian cavalry move forward at Borodino. Prince Eugene is on the left. Faber du Four. Author's collection.

been obscured by dubious, partisan French reports, generated at Napoleon's instigation and scarcely questioned since then. Which regiment was it that was first into the Battery? Which regiment actually took – and held – it?

As we shall see, Napoleon's official rumour mill worked at top speed and with its customary efficiency to ensure that posterity would be forced to accept *his* version of events. In the years following the battle, however, small voices could be heard – by those willing to listen – which must lead us to treat this Napoleonic bulletin with the circumspection now accorded to so much else that he wrote, or commanded to be written.

Meerheim described the final assault on the Rajewsky Battery as follows:

> The redoubt lay at the top of a steep slope rather like the one which we had had to climb to get into Semenowskaya.[4] It was covered by a fairly wide ditch but built, happily, only of loose earth, without pallisades and obviously constructed in a hurry. On the side facing us there was a deep, narrow valley[5] like a second ditch which we also had to cross before we could storm the actual crest of the ridge. In the Battery itself were maybe 12 or more guns; the remaining space was filled with infantry. The ditch and the 'ravine' were also filled with infantry. Behind the Battery were several, fairly strong squares of infantry relatively close together and ranged along the far side of the valley east of the ridge on which the Battery stood. We saw (or rather felt) the presence of a strong force of artillery also on that ridge.
>
> Apart from this, we could see several lines of infantry and cavalry in reserve further back. In the dip towards Borodino[6] were more masses of infantry and cavalry which had previously been concealed from our view.
>
> We charged at the 'ravine' and ditch, the horses clearing the bristling fences of bayonets as they would have Chevaux de fris. The combat was frightful! Men and horses hit by gunshots collapsed into the ditches and thrashed around among the dead and dying, each trying to kill the enemy with their weapons, their bare hands or even their teeth. To add to this horror, the succeeding ranks of assaulting cavalry trampled over the writhing mass as they drove on to their next targets – the infantry squares – who greeted them with well-aimed volleys. [von Meerheim now speaks of Russian infantry in huts in the valley east of the Battery firing out of the windows at them but I can find no trace of a similar account of such constructions and the nearest village east of the Battery is Kniaskowo, over 1,600 metres away – DGS]
>
> Despite all the perils and obstacles we were unstoppable and burst over and into the Battery, inspired by the examples of our commanders, Generals Latour, Thielmann and our brigade adjutant von Minkwitz. The interior of the Battery was an indescribable mess of infantry and cavalry all intent on killing one another. The garrison of the place fought to the last.

Napoleon (and many historians since) attributed the final capture of Rajewsky's Battery to French cuirassiers under the leadership of Caulaincourt. This on-the-spot, eyewitness account, together with the carefully conducted investigation of Roth von Scheckenstein contained in his book *Die Kavallerie in der Schlacht an der Moskwa*, should finally lay this ghost.

On page 105 of his work, von Schreckenstein wrote:

> If I return again to the Report of the King of Naples of 9 September,

concerning the participation of the Reserve Cavalry in the battle, it is because this report contains a number of inaccuracies that have been repeated in subsequent documents including the Bulletin by the Marquis de Chambray of 10th September. In my footnote 30 to section 10 I have already shown how completely wrongly Chambray describes Latour-Maubourg's attack on Semenowskaya village. Chambray is equally unclear on page 180 concerning the capture of the Rajewsky Battery where he has Caulaincourt enter the work by wheeling to the left, having previously charged a line of the enemy. This is what he wrote: 'Eugene ordered the divisions of Broussier, Morand and Gerard to cease firing and to storm. At the same time, Caulaincourt, at the head of Watier's division, overthrew the line of the enemy that was opposite to him, then, wheeling left, charged through the troops close behind the redoubt then, turning back towards the work, entered it from the rear. Eugene stormed over the parapet from the front at this same instant; all who defended themselves were cut down. Twenty-one guns fell into French hands. Watier resumed his position on Eugene's right flank. Caulaincourt had been fatally wounded in the redoubt itself. It was now three o'clock'.

According to this, it seems that the Marquis de Chambray was ignorant of the fact that it was only Defrance's division which assaulted on the right of the redoubt and that Watier's division attacked it from the direction of Borodino, whilst the Saxon cavalry penetrated into it from the direction of Semenowskaya. This writer [Chambray] relates nothing of the active participation of Latour-Maubourg's [IV] corps here because there was nothing about it in the Bulletin and nothing in the Report. I feel that it is quite possible that Caulaincourt was wounded near the Battery, but I feel that it is quite unacceptable for the King of Naples to bury the victor's laurels with HIM.

Segur tells us that General Count Auguste-Danielle Belliard, Murat's chief of staff, was sent back to Imperial headquarters to urge Napoleon to throw in his reserve and decide the battle. He returned in consternation.

It is impossible to get the Emperor to send his reserve! I found him sitting on the same spot, looking sick and depressed, his face sagging, his eyes dull, giving orders languidly in the midst of the horrible din of war, which he doesn't even seem to hear. When Ney was informed of this, he flared up and shouted: 'Have we come all this distance to be satisfied with one battlefield? What's the Emperor doing behind his army? He doesn't see any of our successes there – only our reverses. Since he isn't fighting the war himself any longer and isn't a general any more, but wants to play the Emperor everywhere, why doesn't he go back to the Tuileries and let us be generals for him?'

The day wore on and still the grand battery held out.

Murat's heavy cavalry moved forward to make what was to be the decisive charge. Segur tells us that General Baron Auguste-Jean Caulaincourt rode past him at the head of the 5th Cuirassiers: 'You'll see me up there very soon – dead or alive!' he said. With that he dashed off and mowed down everything that stood in his way. Then, having led his cuirassiers around to the left of the grand battery, he was the first to enter this gory redoubt, but a bullet struck and killed him. His conquest became his grave.

Artillery coming up during the battle of Borodino. Albrecht Adam. Author's collection.

Segur wrote: 'We are too far away from our reinforcements. All Europe lies between Napoleon and France, and we must preserve at least this handful of men to be answerable for his safe return.' According to Segur, Napoleon, on hearing of the losses of his generals at Borodino, said: 'One week in Moscow, and this will not matter any more!' Years later, however, in exile on St Helena, Napoleon wrote of Borodino:

> Of all the battles which I have fought, that before Moscow was the most significant. The French showed themselves in it to have been worthy of the victory and the Russians earned the right to call themselves The Unbeaten.

He was also supposed to have said: 'Of all my fifty battles, Borodino cost me the most and brought me the least.'

Segur then wrote:

> Henceforth his victory at the Moskwa, incomplete as it was, would become his finest feat of arms. Thus all that might have contributed to his ruin would contribute to his glory. The next few days would decide whether he was the greatest man in the world or the most foolhardy; in short, whether he had raised himself an altar, or dug himself a grave.

History proved very conclusively which it was to be.

Allied losses were 28,000 including many of Napoleon's veteran generals. The Russians lost about 44,000 – the exact figures will never be known – but their army withdrew towards Moscow, still intact.

Following this bloody battle, the unfortunate VIII Corps was ordered to stay behind and clear up the site, rescue the wounded, bury the dead and secure usable guns and weapons. On 12 September they entered Moshaisk, where a battalion of the 6th Infantry Regiment was detached to the town of Wereja, some 15 km off to the south; more of those unfortunates later.

Other Westphalian units were left in Dorogobuzh, Gschatsk and Wiasma. The only Westphalian troops to enter Moscow were part of the 3rd Line Infantry Regiment, the 2nd and 3rd Light Battalions and 60 hussars commanded by Colonel Bernard.

Notes

1 Of the 2nd Westfalian Line Infantry Regiment, VIII Corps.
2 A junior officer in the Saxon Zastrow Kuerassiers in the battle.
3 One of Napoleon's ADCs and brother to the French ex-ambassador to the Czar.
4 This I cannot understand; the slope from the west up to the site of the Redoubt is level and gentle – DGS.
5 Not today! There is only a wide and shallow depression to the east of the Grand Battery – DGS.
6 Along the Goruzka stream – DGS.

Chapter 12

The central sector – on to Moscow

'I have been forced to abandon Moscow. But the city has been emptied of the people who are its life. In all the world the people are the soul of an empire. Wherever the Russian people are, there is Moscow, there is the Russian empire!'
Marshal Kutusov to the Czar

On 14 September Napoleon saw Moscow from Poklonny Hill. The city lay spread out before him, the many gilt onion domes of the numerous churches and monasteries glittering in the early autumn sun. 'Ah, the Russians do not yet know the effect that the fall of their capital will have on them!' said Napoleon, gloating over his fabled prize. After some minutes, the cavalcade rode down the slope, preceded by strong patrols. No life was evident; this enormous, semi-oriental capital city had been abandoned by all except a fraction of its inhabitants.

The Emperor felt cheated; where was the humble deputation of trembling city fathers, anxious to proffer him – the conqueror – the ceremonial keys to the place? He was incredulous; 'Moscow deserted? An unlikely story! We shall get to the bottom of this. Go, bring the Boyars to me!' But no Boyars came, neither could any be found. This is scarcely surprising; they had been abolished by Czar Peter the Great in the seventeenth century.

Bavarian cavalry general, Preysing-Moos, recorded his impressions of the Russian capital that day:

> Before we marched off at seven o'clock on the morning of 15 September, an Order of the Day was given out whereby no one was to enter the city until further notice.[1]

> With Guyon's Light Cavalry Brigade in the lead, we marched to the left around Moscow, making a halt of some hours at the village of Dworez in order to gather news of the progress of the other columns. During the recent marches, even in this well-urbanised area and so close to such a great city, there had been no sight of living human beings and the destruction of all food and forage supplies – and even the buildings – was much greater than heretofore. The newly-ripened grain had been deliberately trodden down, all the stacks of straw and hay were in flames and huge clouds of smoke poured up out of Moscow itself.

> Our march continued directly past one of the city gates without our seeing a living soul and we took up a miserable bivouac in a village called Maria Rostoka. One squadron took post on the road to Moscow. General Ornano

sent out two piquets each of 30 men; one of these soon came haring back, hotly pursued, right into our lines, by 60–70 cossacks. The 5th Regiment had 7 men wounded in this mêlée and lost 5 men and 8 horses captured. I reinforced this piquet with 30 men, deployed them in a more defensible manner and from then on, the situation remained quiet. The Viceroy[2] took up residence in the fine St Petersburg suburb.

The clash at Moshaisk, 10 September. A town in the central sector. 95 km west of Moscow and 13 km east of Borodino. A victory for Marshal Murat, with parts of I, II and IV Corps and II and III Cavalry Corps, over General Miloradovitch's II Corps. This was a rearguard action on the part of the battered Russian army. Miloradovitch's corps numbered 8,600 men with 24 guns. Murat had about 10,000 men and 30 guns. The action cost the Russians 2,000 casualties and a further 10,000 of their wounded from the battle of Borodino were also taken in the town. Murat lost about 2,000 men. The advance to Moscow went on.

The entire French retinue was dumbfounded as they walked through the silent, echoing streets to the Kremlin, that massive, red-brick citadel on the north bank of the River Moskwa, in the centre of the capital. The gates stood open; the Emperor entered, unopposed. The imperial suite took up residence within the fortress; the city was scoured for life, only a few beggars were discovered. But next day, fires broke out in several different spots around the Kremlin. Almost the entire city being built of wood, the fires spread wherever the wind took the sparks. It was then that the French found that all the fire engines of the city had been removed; they were powerless to fight the flames and to save the immense stocks of food and other supplies from destruction.

It is generally accepted that General Count Feodor Vasilievich Rostopchin, Governor of Moscow, had removed the fire engines, freed many convicts, then paid them to become arsonists to destroy the city to deny the invaders shelter and supplies.

Rostopchin's hatred of the invaders was implacable. He even set fire to his own mansion in the city and placed this placard on the ruins for the stunned French to read and contemplate:

> For eight years I have been improving this property, and have lived here happily with my family. The seventeen hundred tenants of my domain left their homes as you drew near, and I have set fire to to my own house to save it from being defiled by your presence. Frenchmen, I abandoned to you my two homes in Moscow, with furnishings worth half a million rubles. Here you will find nothing but ashes!

For the first time, Napoleon was confronted with the fact that *he* was no longer the centre of the universe, was no longer the arbiter of events on the world's stage. The strings with which he usually manipulated the puppet-like pygmies who dwelt in his world had suddenly and deftly been cut and he had not even heard the snip of the scissors. By sacrificing his capital city, Alexander had wrested the strategic and moral initiative from the invader. Not in his wildest dreams had Napoleon factored in the possible abandonment by the Russians of Moscow. As he himself had said: 'A good general may be defeated, but he should never be surprised.' With or without knowing

Moscow burning in daylight, seen from within the Kremlin. Author's collection.

Allied troops loot a Russian mansion near Moscow. Albrecht Adam.

it, the young Czar had become the first – and possibly the only one – of the omnipotent Napoleon's enemies to have outwitted him so utterly. To say that Napoleon was left this day, in Moscow, figuratively open-jawed and with egg all over his face, would be no overstatement.

'This forbodes great misfortune for us!' said Napoleon on the walls of the Kremlin on 17 September, contemplating the fires eating up so much of the city. Soon, the outbreaks had become so widespread, that it was decided to abandon the Kremlin and to move some miles north, up the road to St Petersburg, to the small palace of Petrovskoi there.

Their progress out of the burning city was most dramatic; the roaring of the flames made it almost impossible for them to hear their own voices, smoke obscured the sun and blinded them, their journey was punctuated with the crash of falling buildings. Several times thay had to change their route as the road ahead was found to be blocked by burning debris. There was not the slightest hope of combating the multiple fires; they were forced to stand aside and let them run their courses. After a few days, the fires died down of their own accord; about 75 per cent of the city had been destroyed, and random islands of intact buildings stood in the vast, smoking sea of ashes. But the Kremlin still stood, undamaged. Napoleon decided to reoccupy it.

Segur noted their progress through the ruins:

> The section of the city that he had to cross to return to the Kremlin presented a strange appearance. Enormous fires had been lit in the middle of the fields, in thick, cold mud and were being fed with mahogany furniture and gilded windows and doors. Around these fires, on litters of damp straw, ill protected by a few boards, soldiers and their officers, mud-stained and smoke

blackened, were seated in splendid armchairs or lying on silk sofas. At their feet were heaped or spread out cashmere shawls, the rarest of Siberian furs, cloth of gold from Persia, and silver dishes in which they were eating coarse black bread, baked in the ashes, and half-cooked, bloody horseflesh – a strange combination of abundance and famine, wealth and filth, luxury and poverty!

On 17 September, Major von Lossberg, of the 3rd Westphalian Infantry Regiment, set down his impressions of life in the ruins of the Russian capital:

> It is not individuals who are looting, but whole detachments of all nations, commanded by subalterns, or even field officers. These groups... go from house-to-house, or from cellar-to-cellar if the house has been burned down. In this way they uncover many stores of all types. Our regiment and the two light battalions have occupied the church and neighbouring houses in the Smolensk suburb. I live very comfortably in one of the houses and want for nothing. In particular, I am enjoying 'Kolonialwaren'[3] and several types of fish. As we also have meat, bread and wine, we have everything that we could wish for.
>
> Something which is not less vital, is the fact that our foraging soldiers in the capital have brought back supplies of cloth to be made up into trousers and overcoats, and also a lot of leather including suede, and, most importantly, sole leathers for the soldiers' shoes. I have had workshops set up.

So, there was some forward thinking going on in Moscow, but it was at grass-roots level.

Notes

1 In fact several regiments did enter the city this day.
2 Prince Eugene.
3 Imported British goods from the colonies.

Chapter 13

The southern sector – the final phase

The clash at Neschwitz, 20 September. A village in the southern sector, on the upper River Styr, near the town of Lutzk in the Pripet marshes. A minor Russian victory for General Count Lambert's composite cavalry force, over General von Zechmeister's Austro-Saxon-Polish cavalry brigade.

This ambush heralded a new Russian offensive; they achieved surprise by dressing fifteen German-speaking Tartars in Austrian dragoon uniforms and placing them at the head of their column, shouting out that they were allies. They lost only five men in the entire action.

The Austrians were completely surprised; the O'Reilly Chevauxlegers and a detachment of hussars and dragoons suffered heavy losses and the O'Reilly regiment lost three standards. Czar Alexander sent them back to Kaiser Franz of Austria – a telling political gesture.

Admiral Tschitschagoff's Army of the Moldau closed up to the River Styr on 21 September. He now commanded 66,000 men with 233 guns. He was opposed by 43,000 allies with 107 guns. His aim was to cut Schwarzenberg off from the River Bug in the west and to throw him into the Pripet marshes. With this in mind, he crossed the Styr at Berestezcko on 22 September and pushed Kosinski's Polish divison back, while Tormassow held his position at Lutzk.

Lieutenant von Wolffersdorff's diary contains the following extract of interest at this time; it demonstrates the perils to which the allied troops were exposed by being in this forward deployment, deep into the swamps.

> On 25 September, the enemy seemed to want to take the offensive. A strong column, with artillery support, pushed against our right wing and drove in the outposts of General Kosinski's division. This move threatened our links to the Austrian Army of Observation in Galicia. We then heard that the Russians had already crossed the Styr in strength, and General Reynier could no longer hold that line.
>
> It was clear that the enemy wanted to throw us into the swamps. Despite this, we held on for a whole day to give our heavy baggage train time to get clear on the roads, which had been washed out by days of heavy rain. Following a night march, during which many of the men had to go barefoot despite the cold, we reached the hamlet of Turijskat midday next day, closely followed by Cossacks. We resumed living in our old huts.

On 26 September the 1st Division fell back to Dolsk. General von Sahr's brigade and Grenadier Battalion von Spiegel occupied Turijsk castle and the Turija crossing.

Shortly after the 1st Division had left, still before midday, several groups of enemy cavalry appeared along the far bank of the river. At midday, heavy masses of infantry came up the road; they then brought up guns and bombarded our old hutted camp and the island on which the castle stood. A couple of attempts to cross by the charred remnants of the bridge were beaten back. Night fell.

On 27 September, von Sahr's brigade also left Turijsk and rejoined the other troops that evening.

By means of fire and movement, the enemy were constantly confronted with new defensive positions; not knowing our real strength, the Russians were cautious, even though they sent some artillery shots over our cavalry bivouac. We joined up with the Austrian corps at Luboml on 29 September.

Sergeant Vollborn's account of the same sequence of events adds some more colour:

We marched out of our camp at 2 o'clock in the morning of 24 September; each of us said a sad farewell to the treasures which we had accumulated there. I left at least three bushels of strawberries and apples, a large pot of pork dripping and an axe that I had found. Strict orders were given that nothing was to be damaged. I wonder what the Russians thought of these wonderful presents?

Nothing dampens the spirits of a soldier more than continual rearward marches after every engagement with the enemy. It is even worse when the rigours of punishing night marches are added. The soldier only judges things by his exhaustion and the increasing numbers of those dropping out of the column. Despite the irregular, often very meagre rations, I never heard any moaning during this difficult period.

At the crossing of the Bug I lost my faithful dog Cornet, who had stuck with me during these last difficult marches. He had always been my hot water bottle in the bivouac. I hoped to find him again in the village on the other side of the Bug, but it was not to be. Apparently he fell off the bridge or was knocked into the water. Even now I mourn the loss of that faithful little animal, which I was given by a minor nobleman in Radom on whom I was billeted.

After crossing the Bug, we joined up with Durutte's division, a mixture of French, Portuguese, Spanish and Germans (Würzburgers). Despite the welcome numbers of the reinforcements, we were all worried by their extreme youth.

Sergeant Vollborn's diary entries paint the wider picture for us:

Several Russian attempts to throw us out of the place [Turijsk] failed. As darkness fell, we withdrew in the usual order. It was pitch dark and raining steadily; you couldn't see even the man in front of you. Reynier had let the path be marked by frequent small bonfires, each tended by a soldier, with orders to stay on duty until the last unit came past. This was an excellent idea. Some of the 'firemen' thought that the last unit had already passed and joined its tail, leaving the fires to burn out. At some places we found the fires out and the sentries asleep from weariness. But there were still enough burning to show us the way. Without them, the march along the narrow track, with the many junctions, would have been very difficult. Most of the march was made off the roads, through the mud and across fields and swampy meadows, where it was only possible to walk along the beaten trail.

The many wagons and guns had so cut up the ground, that the 2nd Division, which was the rearguard, had the greatest difficulty to get on and the men were often in danger of sinking into the mud. But the danger in leaving the narrow track, getting lost and not finding the column again, meant that there was no alternative but to press on, as best we could, along the track. The train caused the worst chaos; in order not to get stuck in the deep mud, the drivers whipped up their teams, with the result that they crashed into the wagon in front. We were all aware of the seriousness of our situation; deep silence was maintained, but no enemy attack disturbed our retreat.

The bad turn in the weather added to our misery; at the end of September it became very cold and we had many more men sick, especially with dysentery. My uncle, General von Steindel, fell ill with this, but he stayed with his men, using his wagon only when utterly exhausted.

The constant wet weather of the last few days had brought me down a lot. Due to the closeness of the enemy, we had to stand to under arms, every morning at first light and wait until dawn. This rigid duty sapped the last of my strength; the retreat to Luboml was a real torture for me. I was so weak that I could not hold myself on my faithful little Polish pony, a wonderful animal, which never put a foot wrong. I thus sought out my uncle's wagon, which followed the brigade...

The chaos of this night march was increased by some of the train drivers, who fell asleep and increased the confusion immeasurably. It would not have needed many enemy cavalry on this night to cause the complete destruction of our column.

Such episodes are the hardest tests on the often thorny path of a soldier's career. Not the enemy's bullet, not the raging of the elements are to be feared as much as the danger of losing one's honour, and thus the most precious thing that one has...

The march went on all night and the next day without pause; towards evening we reached the area, about 3 km above Wlodawka, where the great lake of Szazk reaches a point of three hours at most from the Bug. The intervening area was one of rows of low, sandy hills, running almost perpendicular to the river, in swampy woodland. Lecoq's division formed up along the first ridge, with its right wing on the river; the 2nd Division was on their left and formed a refused flank. The cavalry, which had joined the corps as rearguard in Opalin that morning, was in front of the refused wing. The Cossacks followed them, but there was only some light skirmishing.

From the hills we could see over into the area of Wlodawka [on the western bank], where the Austrian corps was in the act of crossing by pontoon bridge... The rest of the ground was deep marshes, in which we could see several mills and even some villages.

Here Reynier was having two pontoon bridges built; all approach routes to them were occupied and our troops, as well as the enemy, thought that we would cross the river at Wlodawka and follow the Austrians.'

There follows an account of how the VII Corps was allowed to extricate itself from the trap into which Schwarzenberg had placed it.

On 1 October, at 9 o'clock in the morning, the 1st Division withdrew to the next range of hills and formed line again. The 2nd Division moved off at 10 o'clock, but marched through a trough to the river and crossed the bridges, to cover the other troops from the Polish bank. The cavalry followed them and formed up beside them. Finally, Lecoq's division moved off; simultaneously, a regiment of Austrian cavalry appeared on a hill to the rear and scared off the Cossacks and still had time to march off to Wlodawka. Reynier was the last one to ride over the Saxon bridges, which were now pivoted across the river and taken out of the water.

Not a man, not a wagon, not a pontoon was lost, even though the enemy was so close, that we saw them forming up on the ridge before the last pontoon was loaded. The guns of the 2nd Division prevented them setting up a battery to disturb us. We had escaped just at the moment that they thought they had us, separated from the Austrians and trying to cross a river. When Reynier rode up to the 2nd Division, the men received him with a great cheer, as if we had just won a battle; they realised just what sort of peril he had led them out of.

The Austrians had crossed the river at Wlodawka, all except one division, that was to cross at Brest-Litowsk. The rest of the two allied corps marched there in three days. [The distance is about 70 km.]

Here, both allied corps recrossed to the right bank of the Bug and took up a position behind the Muchawiec, with the right wing on the Bug.

By means of prompt withdrawals to the western bank, Schwarzenberg and Reynier evaded this outflanking movement and managed to unite at Luboml on 28 September.

The clash at Luboml, 29 September. In the southern sector. A village just east of the River Bug, 60 km south of Brest. A minor victory for Russian General Count Langeron's corps of Admiral Tchitchagoff's Army of the Danube, over Austrian General Bianchi's 1st and part of General Frimont's Reserve Division. The 3,600 Austrians were outnumbered and pushed back after a brief struggle. Losses were light on both sides. The 32nd and 33rd Austrian Infantry Regiments distinguished themselves.

However, far from staying behind the Bug, Schwarzenberg moved north west to that river and crossed it at Wlodawka to the eastern bank again, in the presence of Tschitchagoff's forces, which did not attack them. These allied withdrawals, through very difficult terrain, were some of the most skilfully executed operations of the entire campaign. Not a gun was lost; no mean achievement.

Karl Fuerst zu Schwarzenberg, Commander of the Austrian Corps

Born on 15 April 1771 into an old and distinguished Franconian family which had been elevated to princely rank in 1670 and had provided several senior generals and statesmen to the Austrian state in the past, Schwarzenberg's father was Fuerst Johann Nepomuk, who died on 5 November 1789. Schwarzenberg entered military service in 1786 as a captain in an Austrian imperial contingent regiment. In 1788 he fought in the wars against the Turks and served together with Prince Poniatowski, a friend. In 1790 he was promoted to major and accepted into the '*Arcieren Leibgarde*'– a Viennese palace ceremonial unit – as a sergeant.

During his military career Schwarzenberg was repeatedly distinguished and promoted, being awarded the knight's Cross of the Order of Maria Theresia in 1794. In September 1800 he was again promoted to *Feldmarschallleutnant*.

At Hohenlinden in December 1800 he saved the Austrian right wing from defeat. His division was the only allied formation not to lose a gun in this action but he did lose 30 officers and 1,200 men fighting off the divisions of Bastoul, Grenier and Legrand. In 1803 he wrote: 'The glue which holds the machine [the army] together, is just subordination and again subordination; one should indulge oneself utterly in it.'

In 1805 he was appointed Vice President of the Aulic Council and commanded a division in the Ulm campaign. On hearing of Mack's plans he said: 'Oh, how incredibly irresponsible! This frivolous fool led the Austrian army – totally unprepared in every respect – across the Inn on 8 October to invade Bavaria!'. He advised Kaiser Franz against fighting at Austerlitz but was overruled. In July 1806 he was awarded the commander's Cross of the Order of Maria Theresia.

Schwarzenberg was sent to Paris in 1809 to negotiate the marriage of Princess Marie-Louise to Napoleon. The Emperor thought very well of him. At this time Schwarzenberg wrote: 'Napoleon is the greatest prince of his time, but does this mean that he cannot be beaten? And if this can be done, why should it not be me that does it? I am not worried by the prospect of standing against him.'

In 1812 Schwarzenberg commanded the Austrian corps in Russia; won the battle of Gorodeczna (Podubna) against Tormassow and extracted his corps skilfully from the general debacle. On hearing that Napoleon had proposed that he be promoted to field marshal, he wrote to his wife: 'This is fatal for me. I am not worth it. My deep inner satisfaction is my reward; the trust and respect of my comrades – that is my pride.' In March 1813, now a field marshal, he was sent to Paris to conduct negotiations with Napoleon aimed at securing peace (as envisaged by Metternich, the Austrian Chancellor). He was received by Napoleon with great friendliness: '*Mon cher ami!*' said the Emperor in greeting, '*Vous avez fait une belle campagne!*'. [My dear friend! You have fought a fine campaign!] Nevertheless, the negotiations failed.

Schwarzenberg left Paris for Vienna on 30 April. On 8 May he was appointed to command the Army of Bohemia - an utterly thankless task with the three allied monarchs stealing his time and dabbling in his strategic planning. He fought at Dresden (where his failure to assault Saint-Cyr's weak garrison on 25 August ensured the stinging allied defeat in the battle the following day), Kulm and Leipzig. He was greatly honoured after Leipzig, receiving numerous awards. He also pleaded with the Kaiser for the unlucky Mack to be released from arrest in the Spielberg fortress and rehabilitated; his request was granted.

Schwarzenberg retired on 5 May 1815. Later he was appointed President of the Aulic Council. In 1817 he suffered a stroke, which left him partially paralysed, and he eventually died of a further stroke on 15 October 1820 in the Thomas house on the main square in Leipzig.

Tschitschagoff followed on the eastern bank, forcing Siegenthal's Austrian division to evacuate Ratno and Mohr's brigade to leave Pinsk; both withdrew to the north. Siegenthal's division rejoined the allied main body, but Mohr's brigade was forced off 150 km north to Mosty on the Niemen by General Ertell. From Mosty, Mohr took up communications with the Duke of Bassano in Wilna.

Tschitschagoff's aim was now to turn the allied eastern wing and crush them against the River Bug, but his advance was slow and poorly coordinated. Schwarzenberg was able to withdraw some 10 km north to a new position, behind the swamps, at Ljesna, still on the eastern bank of the Bug. The Russians did not press him. Lieutenant von Wolffersdorff's diary contains the following account:

> On 8 October the enemy attacked the Austrians along the road from Kobryn [from the east], but their attack failed due to our good position. Prince Liechtenstein was wounded.
>
> We all had the impression that our army had been placed in a very dangerous situation by the enemy movements to our front and left flank, which could lead to our destruction. We were caught in a box, with the Muchawiec in front, the Ljesna, a river almost parallel to the former, not wider, but deeper, the Bug to our right and a very superior enemy in our left flank. We could not dare to cross the Bug to Terespol, because it could only be approached by one narrow track, where only six men could march abreast and the bridge was weak. One accident, or the failure of the bridge, would mean disaster.
>
> The only thing to do was to withdraw again, straight to the rear, over the Ljesna. This could be done with several columns, in order to reach the left bank of the Bug below Brest via this diversion.
>
> But even this withdrawal was one of the most daring and dangerous. Everything depended upon it being kept secret from the enemy, for the column on the left wing – which would be the right as we marched off – would have to move in close proximity to their outpost line. If the Russians detected this movement, the only outcome would be a desperate battle, probably one that we would lose, and which would result in a rout. We also had to cross the Ljesna as quickly as possible, as we had firm intelligence that the enemy intended to attack us early on 11 October and he might also think to move on our rear beforehand to cut us off.

This Saxon officer had every right to be extremely worried; by crossing back to the eastern bank of the Bug, Schwarzenberg had stuck out his chin to a bigger opponent and was asking to get it severely dented. His army was caught up against a major obstacle, with only one hazardous way out.

The clash at the Muchavietz River (Trycziner Hof), 11 October. In the southern sector, a river crossing between Brest-Litowsk and Kobryn. A victory for Schwarzenberg with his three divisions and part of the VII (Saxon) Corps, over part of the Russian Army of the Danube under General Osten-Sacken. The Austrians had 11,300 men and twelve guns, the Saxons 9,000 men and twelve guns. The Russians brought up some 24,000 men and twenty-four guns. Losses in this action are not known.

Von Wolffersdorff's diary continues:

With the greatest control and in utter silence, the army left the position at Brest on the night of 10 October. Deep darkness hid the dense columns and by dawn we were over the Ljesna. The bridges were broken and we occupied the village of Klinicky and an isolated manor farm. The 1st Light Infantry Regiment and a battery of foot artillery covered the crossings. My brigade was deployed in the bushes along the bank of the Ljesna. At 10 o'clock the enemy attacked Klinicky and the partially destroyed bridges. My battalion at once advanced to support the six companies of light infantry. After suffering heavy losses, the enemy managed to capture and repair the small bridge, which led to the manor of Klinicky. Some companies of Russian grenadiers ran over; there was a bitter mêlée. It was man against man, the butt and the bayonet came into play. Before my 5th Company reached the fight, Major von Metsch, commander of the Schützen, had been killed. This enraged his men so much, that there was a massacre such as I have not seen. After the fight, about 25 Russian bodies lay on the ground. My company, deployed in a line for skirmishing, maintained a steady fire. Our artillery set Klinicky on fire; the Regiment Prinz Anton occupied the village of Pecky close by. The enemy continued to mount attacks on us until dark, but without success. Our skirmishers were so close to the enemy, that we could clearly see their faces. My Premierleutnant von Neitschitz was a good shot; he duelled for some time with a Russian Jaeger. Four bullets slammed into the tree behind which he was sheltering, before his shot hit the Russian, who fell over backwards. A loud cheer rang out from our ranks. The four days rest at Brest had allowed me to recover completely and I threw myself into the combat with all the energy of my twenty years.

As with the rest of the 5th Company, we had not had a bit of bread since 4 o'clock that morning. Von Neitschitz and I complained of this to our men; shortly after this, Sergeant Müller, who, with some men had entered an isolated building to the right of the bridge at the risk of their lives, brought us some flour and bacon. My servant worked these into a sort of porridge; in the cover of some thick trees, this odd dish was much enjoyed under a hail of bullets. The smoke of the small fire on which it was cooked attracted the attention of the enemy at dusk.

We lost four wounded in the 5th Company; the rest of those that had been in the fight lost up to 100 killed and wounded. At dusk we left the position on the Ljesna, without being able to do anything at all to feed the men, and marched off for Wolczin. It was an awful night, pitch black and cold and the fact that we kept crossing with Austrian vehicle columns meant that there were repeated stoppages. Many stragglers lost contact with the column and fell into the hands of the prowling Russian light cavalry. My Captain von Bünau lost his servant and a fine horse this way... but the thing which he missed most was his coffee mill, which also went missing. Thus the loss of a thing makes one aware of its true value.

Some time prior to this action, Schwarzenberg had sent his ADC, Major Graf Paar, to Moscow to obtain orders as to the action the southern army should take; on 12 October Major Paar returned – empty handed.

The clash at Biala Podlaska, 13 October. A village in the southern sector, 39 km west of Brest-Litowsk. A successful Austrian rearguard action by General Bianchi's 1st Division over the Russians under General Count Lambert. The Austrians had 7,300 men and twelve guns. Russian totals are not known, but the following regiments were involved: 7th, 14th and 38th Jaegers, Tartar Ulans, Tartar Regiment of Evpatoria, Alexandria Hussars, Arsamass, Schitomir and Starodub Dragoons, Cossack Pulks of Grekov VIII, Grekov XI, Melnikov V and Babarantschikov IX and two batteries of horse artillery. Losses are not known.

The Russian advance was stopped – but only for a moment.

Our situation was still extremely dangerous. Our aim had to be to reach the left bank of the Bug, further below Brest, via a diversion. The problem was that our left flank column was always in close proximity to the enemy. They could always threaten to cut off our line of retreat. The Russians could also throw their whole force at Warsaw, for there was nothing in their way.

Finally, after four marches, we crossed the Bug into Poland. Reynier had a bridge thrown over the river at the village of Klimczice. The Austrians crossed at Drohyczin, seven kilometres further downstream.

We now had a free hand and marched back up the Bug on 15, 16 and 17 October to behind a swampy stretch of the Biala stream, up against Brest and were – once again – facing the Russian army.

Much to our surprise, we carried out this movement in peace, for the Russian main body was still at Brest. They had only sent Colonel Tschernitschew with 4,000 cavalry against Warsaw. He got only as far as Wegrow, when our movement caused him great concern and he withdrew again in a wide arc.

We had no idea what the Russians were doing; thus a squadron of Ulans, under Major von Seydlitz, was sent to Brest. They met General Essen's corps advancing on Biala, and were pushed back onto our outposts. Essen now attacked us. My regiment had to cross the swamps at Kosulamühle to threaten their right flank, while the Light Infantry crossed at Bialkamühle. After exchanging heavy skirmishing fire, the enemy withdrew. It seemed as if it was just a reconnaissance in force. Lieutenant von Zychlinsky and his platoon of sharpshooters managed to take a 12-pounder cannon, that had been set up in a copse. The Russians were so surprised, that they just ran off.

Saxon losses in this action were nine officers and 186 men. General Reynier expressed his satisfaction in a special order of the day. According to our prisoners, it was one of General Essen's divisions and part of the 9th Division, with forty-eight guns, which made the attack.

The Russians were so confused with our various manoeuvres that they sent detachments off in all directions. [It seems that the real reason for the lack of serious pursuit was the call for the Russian forces to close in on the Beresina crossing to the north east.]

I spent the following night in the shop of a Jew; a wounded Russian officer was brought in, he spoke German well and was named Bajardinsky. He had a bad head wound. In order to give the troops some rest and to establish contact with Warsaw, we withdrew to Siedlicze and Drohyczin, on the left bank of the Bug. The Austrians also fell back and stayed there until 27 October.

But the rough, cold weather was another enemy and we found little comfort in our hutted camp. Here we were joined by Durutte's [32nd French] Division of 9,000 men.

In these last combats in the withdrawal we had come to know the Russian Jaegers well, especially those which had joined Sacken's corps. They were good shots, equipped with long-range muskets and they caused us some damage. Our corps now numbered not quite 12,000 men. The weather was wet and cold, our clothing in rags and the ration supply in this exhausted province was barely sufficient. But, even with all these difficulties, no-one thought that things would very soon get so much worse. But we all hoped for support from the *Grande Armée* as it fell back; it had to be strong enough to defend the borders of Warsaw for the winter and be ready to resume the offensive in the spring.

It is clear from these passages that Schwarzenberg had risked both his army and the city of Warsaw by his decision to cross back to the eastern bank of the Bug. A more energetic Russian commander would have made him pay dearly for these errors. His decision to return south, upstream to the Biala Podlask – Brest position could also be criticised; the position at Siedlice – Drohycin would have been less exposed and closer to Warsaw.

Schwarzenberg continued north west and crossed the Bug some 90 km downstream at Drohyczin. He then returned south to take up a new line from Biala to the Bug. The Saxons were at Biala, the Austrians against the Bug. The allies were not clear as to the enemy's intentions; they knew only that Tschitschagoff's main body was at Brest-Litowsk, east of the Bug, with forces at Mosty and Slonim to the east.

The only Russian forces west of the Bug were the *Streifkorps* of Colonel Tschernitschew.[1] He had pushed some 90 km westwards from Brest to Wegrow and had caused panic in Warsaw. General Frehlich's Austrian cavalry brigade was sent after him, and the Russian took refuge with General Essen's corps.

There was no news from the Emperor in Moscow, and the Russian aims were still unclear; Schwarzenberg now fell back north to a new line from Siedlice to Drohyczin, in order to better protect Warsaw. He had no idea that the *Grande Armée* was to shrink from over 500,000 men in June to a mere 108,000 on 19 October, when the retreat from Moscow began.

The new Austro-Saxon allied position allowed the easy reinforcement of 8,000

Austrians, Durutte's 15,000-strong 32nd Division to the VII Corps and some squadrons to Kosinski's Bug Division.

On 29 September, Tschitschagoff received the order to advance north east on Minsk to strike at Napoleon's rear and to make contact with Wittgenstein's I Corps at Borisov on the Beresina. By this time, Tschitschagoff had given up hope of defeating Schwarzenberg after he succeeded in withdrawing over the Bug. The Emperor was still wasting his time in Moscow at this point.

Schwarzenberg was to be merely watched by the Reserve Army, now under Osten-Sacken, as Tormassow had been called away to the main army. On 29 October Tschitschagoff set off from Brest on the River Bug to march north east through Pruzany and Slonim to attack the French depots in Minsk, some 375 km away.

At this same date the Austrians had 30,000 men, having been reinforced by 5,800 men on 26 October, the Saxons about 12,000 and Durutte 9,000. The total was about 51,000 men. On the Russian side there were 35,000 with Tschitschagoff, including Tschaplitz, Ertel and Lüders, Sacken's Corps of 27,000, and Ertel's Reserve Corps of 15,000 in Mozyrj, 236 km south of Minsk. On both sides, many men were sick at the end of October. Sacken was left at Brest to watch Schwarzenberg.

Tschitschagoff reached Slonim on 6 November, Minsk on 16 November and Lambert's advanced guard took the town next day. On 21 November Lambert threw General Dombrowsky's 17th Polish Division out of the town of Borisov on the Beresina River and destroyed the bridge there that was so vital to Napoleon's escape. The Russians had marched 460 km, in bad weather, in 23 days; no mean feat. By the time of the battle of the Beresina crossing, Tschitschagoff had 38,000 men and these were joined by 3,400 of Ertel's corps in Minsk.

On 30 October Schwarzenberg crossed to the eastern bank of the Bug at Drohyczin, learned that Tschitschagoff had left for Minsk with his main body, guessed why and at once set off to follow, and try to stop him. He marched with the Austrians via Bielsk, Swisloczi and Wolkowysk. The train made a wide detour to the north, through Liw, Zambrow, Suraz and Zabludow to Swisloczi, and the Saxons – to cover this movement from Sacken – marched south of them via Orlja, Narewka, Rudnia, Porosowo and Podorosk, through the supposedly impassable swamps of the upper River Narew. These towns may be found on the map between Bielsk Podlaski in the west and Slonim in the east.

Reynier was to wait in the area south of Wolkowysk (Porosowo – Podorosk) from 6 to 13 November, until the trains had cleared that town and were on their way to Slonim. The Russians had to cover 180 km from their start-point to Slonim; Schwarzenberg had to march 220 km to reach the same town. His supply train had almost 300 km of appalling roads, in winter, to work their way through. This was strange, overcomplicated planning, involving the fragmentation of his army in enemy territory, lack of supplies and the choice of the worst terrain for much of his force to cope with.

Reynier had advised Schwarzenberg to first defeat Sacken with his whole force, then to follow Tschitschagoff on the best roads in the region, with all his army concentrated. Why this eminently sensible suggestion was ignored is a mystery.

Lieutenant von Wolffersdorff's diary is eloquent on this trek:

> On 27 October the enemy outposts to our front pulled back. This could only be explained by their withdrawal to the main army. We sent out many patrols; it seemed that the enemy had withdrawn in the direction of Slonim and had left a corps of about 15,000 men behind. This caused our

commander in chief to throw two bridges at Drohyczin on 29 October, to cross the Bug and to take the road to Slonim.

As soon as it was established that Admiral Tschitschagoff had taken his main army off to operate in the rear of the French *Grande Armée*, it was decided to disrupt this operation.

It was decided that the allied Austro-Saxon corps would undertake a flank march in the area of Bielsk and across the Narew.

On 1 November the Saxons were back in the area that they held on 13 October. At Telatice the Austro-Saxon cavalry clashed with the enemy; in the skirmish Major von Seydlitz of the Ulans was killed by a pistol shot in the throat. Ulan Reiss managed to recover his body from the enemy. Seydlitz was one of the best cavalry officers.

Marching hard, we crossed the Narew on 5 November. The muddy tracks demanded all our efforts and made these marches the worst of the whole campaign. We bivouacked in the middle of the forest.

As our 2nd Battalion straggled into camp not sufficiently closed up, General Lecoq ordered all company commanders to be arrested. Even in the most difficult circumstances, the general insisted on the best march discipline. This later saved our corps from disintegration.

November brought a mixture of storms, rain and snow. We always broke camp in the dark on these short days. A dry bivouac was a luxury. It was again necessary for the men to find their own food. An officer of the general staff allocated each brigade an area in the surrounding region from which to draw their needs. Each battalion sent out a foraging party. The officer in charge was often unable to ensure that there was good order and no violence in the darkness, especially as everything had to be taken by force. Food, forage, straw for our beds, wood for the fire, even pots and pans, for in the six months of the campaign, our field kettles were worn out by the daily use.

Uniforms and shoes were also missing. We took fur coats, skins, woollen blankets, which we tied around us with string, and peasant smocks.

But, even if the odd crime was committed under these circumstances, the inner discipline of the units was upheld. Very rarely did men go missing. We had to drive the Cossacks out of almost every village that we entered, and they became ever more bold.

They knew of every patrol that we sent out. Our cavalry – now down to 1,200 men – was no longer able to hold them back and we were literally confined to barracks. With every day we missed Thielmann's cavalry brigade, which had been detached to the *Grande Armée*, more and more.

Vollborn's diary has this to say:

> The march through the Narew swamps was utterly exhausting. In four days we lost six men from our company; where did those worn out men end up?
>
> The cold got worse and worse; our clothing ever more ragged. My servant brought me a sheeps wool peasant's smock in Rudnia; I had this turned into trousers by the company tailor, Hensel, in the bivouac, and they lasted me until we marched back into Saxony.
>
> We turned a blind eye to soldiers who supplemented their clothing; we were just pleased that they still had sufficient sense of survival to do it.

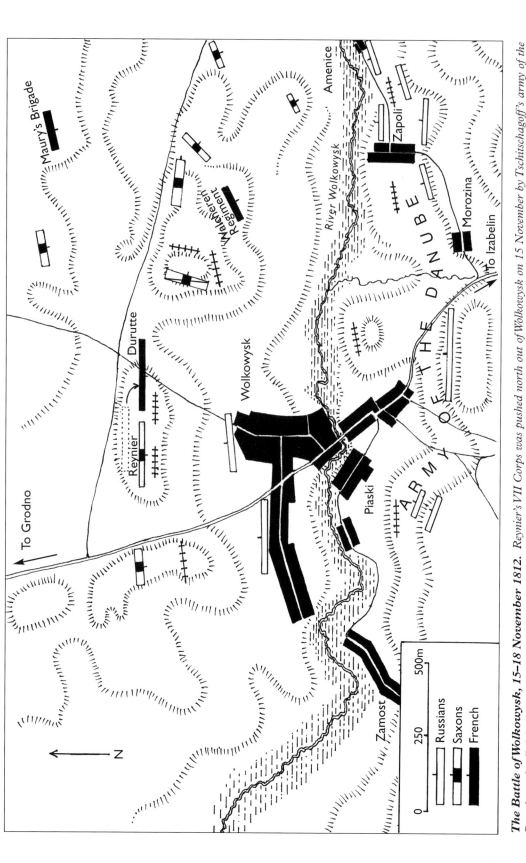

The Battle of Wolkowysk, 15–18 November 1812. *Reynier's VII Corps was pushed north out of Wolkozwysk on 15 November by Tschitschagoff's army of the Danube and called for help from Schwarzenberg's Austrians. Durutte's 32nd Division, XI Corps and the Wuerzburg Infantry Regiment came up in support of the Saxons and held the line of the hills. Schwarzenberg's corps arrived on 16 November in the Russian rear and caused them to flee the field. The allies lost 1,800 men, the Russians lost 4,000.*

In the following days there were repeated orders issued against looting, maurauding and so on. One quarter of the men had to stand guard around the camp. As the guard was changed only every six hours, this was a great strain on the men. The daily clashes of the next few days soon made us forget these troubles. The general dangers were stronger than mens' rules. The good spirit of our corps saved the individual as well as the corps itself.

Sacken learned on 8 November that the allies were on the move, and advanced on Wolkowysk from Brest-Litowsk by the most direct road through Rudnia, Nowy Dwor and Porosowo. On 7 November his patrols, emerging from the swamps at two widely separated points, bumped into the Saxons south of Swisloczi. Reynier wished to attack him together with the Austrians, but Schwarzenberg insisted that he adhere to the agreed plan, and continued on after Tschitschagoff.

Reynier was left at a disadvantage, but withdrew skilfully north to Wolkowysk, which he reached on 14 November. The previous day Schwarzenberg had arrived at Slonim, some 56 km to the east, and at last decided to turn back to help Reynier. Wolffersdorff takes up the tale again:

> On 7 November we reached Swisloczj; on the 8th Porosowo. The pressure of the enemy on our rearguard was so great, that our continued march to Slonim was not practical, even though the Austrians pressed on. In order to save our artillery and park, we had to turn back to Swisloczj on 11 November, and didn't turn back to Lapenica, south of Wolkowysk until the 12th. The 13th was supposed to be a rest day, but we were attacked at 9 o'clock by General Lambert, in such superior strength, that our outposts were forced back, even though they were supported by the five battalions of von Sahr's brigade. The battle was for the woods to our front and the fighting was bloody.
>
> We brought about 100 wounded back out of the combat area. Their condition aroused our deepest sympathy. We had nothing on which to move them in the sharp frost and the terribly cut-up tracks except the rickety local farm carts of the region. Only a few of these unfortunates reached the hospital; even many of those with only minor wounds died on the way.
>
> Reynier could not hold the poor position at Lapenica, due to the presence of Sacken's corps and the fact that the Austrian troops were 42km away. In the night of 13/14 November he pulled back[north] to the heights north of the little town of Wolkowysk, with the town to our front.'

The clash at Wolkowysk (Izabelin), 14–16 November. A town in south Russia, on the river of the same name, 70 km south east of Grodno. An Austro-Saxon victory over General Osten-Sacken's corps of the Army of the Danube. Sacken launched a night assault on Wolkowysk on 14/15 November. Renewed attacks were made on 15 and 16; they failed. On the afternoon of 16 November, the tables were turned, when Schwarzenberg took Sacken in rear. The Russians suffered a defeat; fled south to Kobryn and then back to Brest on the Bug. The allies concentrated 28,000 men and 76 guns for this battle; the Russians had 27,000 men and 92 guns. Allied losses were 1,800 men in all. Russian losses were 1,500 killed and wounded, 2,500 captured on the battlefield. Most of their baggage train was lost. The Saxons followed them up and captured 4,700 men along the way.

Wolffersdorff takes up the tale again:

> The 1st Saxon Division was on the right wing, covering the road to Mosty and Grodno. One battalion of [Prinz] Friedrich covered the crossings of the Rossa and Wolkowysk streams. Our left flank was covered by swamps. Thick woods ran around to the back of our position.
>
> Wolkowysk, a small town built mostly of wood and inhabited mainly by Jews, lay in the valley, scarcely a quarter of an hour before us. A battalion of Light Infantry occupied it. Reynier set up his headquarters in it.
>
> Durutte's division[2] came in from Grodno and joined us; it was composed mostly of prisoners of war, conscripts, deserters and criminals; a cross-section of the worst that Europe had to offer.
>
> It was rough on the troops who had to bivouac; there was a foot of snow, we were short of straw and dry wood and we had only ship's biscuit to eat. The night was bitterly cold.
>
> At 3 o'clock in the morning, the Russians assaulted the town. The signal horns blared, the salvoes roared, the wagons and horses clattered up the hill. It was a devil of a noise. Soon flames lit up the combat and two of our battalions were sent down into the town.
>
> The entire headquarters would have been lost had it not been for Leutnant von Petrikowsky's presence of mind. He had held his picket hidden at the priory until the Russians reached the bridge and then fired into their right flank to such good effect, that it slowed their advance right down. This gave everyone in the town time to get themselves together. Reynier rushed to the town square and almost fell into Russian hands together with his ADC, Major von Fabrice, whose horse was shot and wounded.
>
> In a night attack, the attacker must be very bold right at the start; that which is omitted in this phase can never be made up for later. If the Russian cavalry had attacked our camp at the same time and occupied the exits of the town, the results of the raid would have been much greater.

Von Wolffersdorff explains that the advantage of having experienced soldiers is that they are calmer in tough situations. The troops were never allowed to take off their clothes, and if they were close to the enemy they even slept with their bandoliers on and their packs under their heads. If the alarm was sounded, the men would run to fall in. On the night in question, the men were all in their ranks when the generals, some partially clothed, reached the camp. His tale continues:

> With soldiers like this you can do anything, but we also needed a man with Reynier's rapid decisiveness to get us out of the pickle in which he still was.
>
> General Essen, who commanded the Russians here, had not achieved his main aim, but most of the town and the bridges were in his hands. There was wild confusion in the town. Drivers were rushing about with their horses, wagons were overturned or broke and blocked the streets. The grenadiers and the Light Infantry Battalion still held the exits from the town and thus gave the train time to evacuate the place; only three or four wagons were lost. The rest, including the war chest and the intendance supplies managed to escape to Mosty.
>
> Eventually, the two battalions had to fall back, after having had a series of

bitter fights in the back streets. The enemy poured after them, but were in such confusion that they were quickly pushed back to the bridges. They went into the houses of the town to plunder and their officers had a hard job to get them back in the ranks. At 10 o'clock next day we could send details into the town to look for food and forage. That which we could not buy for any price yesterday, now lay in the streets. Sugarloaves, heaps of coffee beans, which the Cossacks had thrown away in order to make room for more precious items in the sacks, furs, woollen blankets, whole bales of cloth. Only brandy was missing; the enemy had left none of that behind.

Aware of the peril of our situation, General Reynier sent one of his ADCs to Prince Schwarzenberg in Slonim, 43 km away, to ask him to come and take the Russians in the right flank or rear.

On 15 November the enemy advanced in heavy assault columns against our left flank. A strong force of cavalry attacked our hussars and the Polenz Dragoons that were there. These were pushed back by the first charge, but stood their ground, supported by the horse artillery battery, for the second, then forced the Russian cavalry back. Colonel von Engel of the hussars was badly wounded here. He was already in the hands of the enemy, when he was rescued by his son.

The enemy repeated his assaults two or three more times that day, but without success. One of my friends, Lieutenant von Zeschau, was wounded in the lower stomach; we bandaged him up, but he died shortly afterwards. Later the Russians bombarded our camp with 12 pounders and caused us some loss.

Both sides remained under arms that night; the Russians in the town. It now became so cold, that the blood from the wounded froze. This bivouac was a severe test, as we were short of everything: food, straw, firewood, even drinking water and the snow was no substitute. I shall never forget the night of the 15/16 November.

Luckily, my servant had found some bacon and eggs in an abandoned house. Together with a soup made of ship's biscuit, we shared this with my uncle, General von Steindel. Then I stretched myself out on the snow, without a fire to warm my frozen limbs. My poor horse had to eat straw. So we lay there, dumbly wondering how many more such nights we would have to face.

On the morning of 16 November, the enemy renewed his attack on our position. Every time the fog cleared, all we could see were more and more enemy troops pouring down the hill into the town. They might come charging out of it at any time. At three o'clock a large mass formed up opposite our right wing. Just then, with indescribable joy, we heard the welcome sounds of cannon fire as the Austrians came up behind the enemy. At the same time, Durutte's division made an assault on the town, which took fire. The Russians were driven out under a hail of fire. Everybody shouted: 'The Austrians are here! Long live Prince Schwarzenberg!'

In order to break out once and for all, General von Sacken had packed troops into the town; as the burning bridge set the houses alight, the Russians rushed out at this side to escape, cannon and ammunition wagons blocked the bridges and all resistance ceased. Our troops could not miss the great targets that were presented.

The darkness was lit by the burning buildings of Wolkowysk and the flashes of occasional shots. The whole scene was fascinating; we forgot our fatigue. Then we realised that the danger was gone; we all went back to our huts, anyone who had anything to eat was busy, boiling and frying. Everyone was telling of what he had seen and done that day.

Our losses on these two days were heavy, but those of the enemy were much worse, especially in the last two hours. There were about 1,500 dead in Wolkowysk, and 1,700 wounded in the priory alone. Many of these were captured. In battle one's human feelings are suppressed, but they come to the fore in increased degree when the action is over. You just don't think of the man who is killed at your side; you have no time to think and to feel. But the impression that you feel, when looking at a battleground, covered with corpses is shattering... A light snowfall covered the bodies and made the scene even more weird. In the distance were the odd peasants, clutching items that they had taken from corpses. Ravens circled overhead.

The Austrians had captured the Russian headquarters, including their war chest. We saw Austrian soldiers with handfuls of gold coins; they offered horses, jewellery, gold crosses, furs for sale. Prince Schwarzenberg presented some dromedaries to General Reynier, but they died of the cold.

On their retreat the Russians had abandoned many guns that they could not move and had thrown the barrels into the swamp. We found just the wrecked limbers.

The fighting was mainly over for the Austro-Saxons, but the struggle to survive the vicious climate went on unabated. On 25 November Schwarzenberg, in Kobryn, received an order from the Duke of Bassano: 'March at once to take Tschitschagoff in rear and so relieve the *Grande Armée.*' The pursuit – and likely destruction – of Sacken's corps was thus abandoned.

Schwarzenberg was in Slonim on 5 December; here he received news from the Duke of Bassano, implying that something had happened to the *Grande Armée*. Two days later, Reynier, in Rozana, heard much more definite news from Berthier.

The Austrians withdrew north west to Grodno, then south west to Bialystock. The Saxons fell back west to the River Bug, to Wolczin,[3] just north of Brest-Litowsk. Kosinski's poles held Brest and Pruzany. This was the end of the significant fighting in the southern sector in 1812; at least here the campaign ended with a tactical victory.

In the southern sector, Schwarzenberg had held his position against superior Russian forces; but things were soon to change, as Ulan Captain von Boehm tells us:

All these deeds were buried by the gigantic catastrophe of the retreat from Moscow. Right towards the end, we were called upon to help at the Beresina; the Prince was ordered to: *'manoeuvrer dans le sens de la position actuelle.'* [manoeuvre in the sense of the current position] But absolutely no clue was given as to where this *'position actuelle'* was. This was at a time when the Saxons were being assaulted on 14–16 November, by General Osten-Sacken's corps.

On 19 December the VII Corps reached Wolczin, a village on the Bug, downstream from Brest-Litowsk. Here they were joined by a Saxon reinforcement battalion of 1,000 men and the Grenadier Battalion von Eichelberg, which had been in Bialystock. The corps now numbered 8,000 men. The river froze over and on 22 December

Reynier sent the train of the corps over the ice to the west. Finding food was difficult but possible. Wolffersdorff's servant even managed to buy the ingredients to make something almost like a traditional German *Stollen* or Christmas cake.

On 22 December, Russian General Wasiltschikow came to Schwarzenberg's headquarters to agree upon a ceasefire and the allied withdrawal to Warsaw. On condition that the Russians would not invade the Grand Duchy for a time, this was agreed upon. The Austrians withdrew to Ostrolenko, Pultusk and into Warsaw. In contravention of this agreement, the Russians advanced, step-by-step, westwards.

On Christmas day 1812 the Saxons crossed the Bug at Drohyczin and marched to Siedlce. Wolffersdorff survived the campaign with only a frost-bitten hand. The Austrian corps finally set off to return home from the city of Warsaw on 5 February 1813. The terrible campaign of 1812 was over; that of 1813 was about to begin.

Polish General Kosinsky's division had meanwhile been caught by Tschitschagoff's Army of the Danube at Kaidanov (30 km south west of Minsk) on 15 November and forced to surrender.

Novo Schwerschen, 13 November. North central section. A village 40 km south east of Smolensk. General Kossecki's Polish division (one battalion each of the 18th, 19th, 20th and 22nd Lithuanian Infantry Regiments and a combined cavalry regiment) were defeated by a Russian force from Admiral Tschitschagoff's Army of the Danube, including the 10th and 14th Jaegers. General Kossecki's 3,500 men were very badly mauled by General Count Lambert, losing 1,000 killed and wounded and their only gun. Russian losses were very light.

The clash at Kaidanowo, 15 November. A village in the central sector, 30 km south west of Minsk. A victory for the cavalry of the Army of the Danube under General Count Lambert, over General Kossecki's division which had been badly mauled at Novo Schwerschen two days before. It had now been joined by some Württemberg infantry and 300 French cavalry and totalled 1,300 men. They were all captured by General Count Lambert (except for one Württemberg sergeant who carried news of the disaster back to Minsk) for insignificant loss.

Notes

1 Seven squadrons, three regiments of Cossacks and four guns.
2 32nd Division, XI Corps.
3 Probably now Voucyn.

Chapter 14

Summer and autumn in Latvia

Up in Latvia, the conditions under which Marshal Macdonald's X Corps were operating bore absolutely no relation at all to the misery and deprivation being suffered by those in the central sector. At this point, Marshal Macdonald was closing up around Riga.

On 15th August the General Intendant of Courland, M. Chambaudoin, celebrated Napoleon's birthday with a splendid ball. In the morning a *Te Deum* was sung and in the evening the town was illuminated, as was the ballroom. There were plenty of fine refreshments; 300 bottles of champagne were drunk, as well as Madiera[1] and Hungarian wine; Medoc and other French wines were drunk from beer glasses.

We heard that Napoleon was at Witebsk on 22nd July; I bet he entered Moscow on his birthday!

Hartwich's naïve trust in the Emperor is slightly touching. He continued:

On 21st August I was sent to Shagory, to gather up local carts, horses and drivers, to form a convoy for some supplies that were expected. By 21st August I had about 116 wagons ready; the goods on the convoy from Okmiany were off-loaded onto these and sent on to Shagory. The only way to communicate with the Lithuanian peasants was with the Kantschu[2] and you can quickly become absolutely sick of such a business. We had to watch the drivers more so than their horses, as they were forced men and wanted to get back home. We had to keep 500 drivers and 200 horses locked up in two barns, guarded by an officer and 35 men. They had to live on what they had brought with them – I had nothing to give them. Their misery rose day by day. I very soon found myself forced to let two horses and half the drivers from each team go home. Each day we toured the local farms to requisition bread.

The clash at Dahlenkirchen, 22 August. A village on the left bank of the River Duena, 14 km south east of Riga, also known as Olai and Schlock. A Russian victory (Rear Admiral Moeller, the 25th Infantry Division and a flotilla of gunboats) over the Prussians (Colonel von Horn's 2nd Brigade). Colonel von Horn, with 1,450 men, bit off more than he could chew here and took on an enemy 3,000 strong. The Prussians lost 800 men to less than fifty Russian casualties. The Russians occupied Dahlenkirchen, but abandoned it again on 26 August.

On 13 August von Yorck's Prussian division was 16,800 men strong; as a percentage of the march-in strength, this was an amazingly high figure, when compared with the formations of Napoleon's central army group, where most of them were down to the 50 per cent level by this time. Prussian Captain von Schauroth had fought here; he was in Ruenthal on leave on 30 August and told Hartwich of his experiences that day:

> The Russians, led by a deserter from the 'Brown Hussars'[3], rushed upon the outposts giving the Prussian passwords, and cut them down. They raced on until they reached the lines of the unprepared Pommeranian, East Prussian and Silesian Fusiliers, cut them down and scattered them. Most of the officers were killed or wounded. The surviving fusiliers alarmed their main body, which drove the 800 Russians back to Riga.

The clash at Olai, 22 August. A village in Latvia, midway between Riga and Mitau. A Prussian victory (Colonel von Raumer's 3rd Brigade), over General Wiljeminov, with part of Riga garrison. A minor action in the continued low-key bickering, which characterised this front.

The second clash at Schlock, 22 August. A Baltic coastal village, on an island in the mouth of the River Aa, 18 km west of Riga. A minor Prussian victory (6th Infantry Regiment, 3rd Hussars, some 900 men), over an Anglo-Russian force of 3,300 under Rear-Admiral Moeller. This was another combined operation with the British gunboats transporting Russian infantry into the river. Losses were very light on both sides.

Meanwhile, up in Latvia with X Corps, things were rolling along at a comfortable clip, as Julius Hartwich recorded:

> On 30th August Captain Senes and Lieutenant Fourcade of the French artillery and Lieutenant Muck of the 13th Bavarian Line Infantry Regiment came through with 50 heavy guns and ammunition wagons... We left Labiau on the 8th August. . . and reached Mitau on the 18th.

Up in Latvia, Julius Hartwich visited Ruenthal castle on 6 September, apparently a gem of a building, built by the Duke of Courland and presented by Czarina Catherine to her lover, Prince Subow, when Russia annexed that province. It was a most impressive building, sited within formal gardens and containing an extensive, multi-lingual library –'as elegant as it was comprehensive'. All the artillery and engineer parks had been concentrated here:

> There were 42 officers, as well as generals Darencay and Taviel.[4] About 1,500 French gunners and engineers were lodged in the outbuildings of the castle and in huts. All the artillery parks [of the X Corps] are concentrated in Ruenthal... Among them is the Elba Sapper Battalion.

Hartwich recorded that it froze hard in Latvia on the night of 6/7 September. His tour of duty, requisitioning drivers and teams for convoy duty, ended on 15 September. He returned to Mitau, just in time to hear the gun-salutes and to attend the *Te Deum* in the German church there, which was being sung in thanks for news of Napoleon's 'victory' at Borodino.

Julius Hartwich had been sent to the island of Schlock, in the mouth of the River Aa, about 3¹/₂ Meilen from Duenamuende. He did duty here from 17– 26 September. In Duenamuende lay some twenty gunboats, which were often used to transport troops behind the allied coastal garrisons to mount spoiling raids. Garrison duty at Schlock – which was a post to be evacuated if seriously threatened – was considered a high-risk occupation. His duty here was cut short by a change in the local balance of forces.

> On the night of 26/27 September General von Yorck sent us an order to evacuate our post. Steinhiel's division[5] from Finland had arrived in Riga, and the Russians now intended to make a push for the corps' artillery parks in Ruenthal. The Prussian outpost at Dahlenkirchen had been pushed back and it was expected that the gunboats would be used against Mitau.
>
> We could thus not fall back up the River Aa, but would have to go through the woods via the hamlet of Tuckum. These woods were partially swampland and very hazardous to cross. The existing tracks were made up of logs and would often break under the weight of a horse.
>
> We left Schlock at 2 o'clock in the morning... As it grew dark, we set up a bivouac and drew rations from the manor farm of Hardersch in Bershof. We set off again at 4 o'clock on the morning of 28 September and reached Mitau at 11. Here we were given billets; I was sent to the Hotel St Petersburg, where I was well taken care of. There was a beautiful, heavy quilt in my room; I asked Herr Morell, the owner of the inn, if he would sell me it on credit; he at once agreed... To my delight, it folded down so that it would fit into my knapsack.

The 2nd Clash at Eckau, 27 September. A village 12 km east of Mitau (now Jelgava), 40 km south of Riga in Latvia. A Russian victory for General Count Steinheil's Finnish Corps (3,000 men and six guns) over Prussian General von Massenbach's cavalry brigade of 850 men and twelve guns. The Prussians lost 203 casualties; the Russian losses are not known.

The expected Russian offensive in Latvia began, but it was extremely cautious and the Prussians fell back south before it. Their main target was Macdonald's siege train at Ruenthal. Julius Hartwich takes up the tale:

> At two o'clock [on the afternoon of 28 September] we began our withdrawal to Ruenthal. We joined General von Kleist's corps... Marching in column is as boring as it is tiring, especially if it takes place in the rain and through heavy mud... We reached Ruenthal, after covering 5 Meilen, at 4 o'clock in the morning of 29 September. We all slumped up against the trees and were quickly asleep. I did not wake again until the sun was high in the sky.
>
> Mother Roerdanz, the queen of all sutleresses, a harpey for her country and a benefactress to most of the battalion, was my special protectoress since I had once saved her from a beating which the major had ordered. She had carefully watched for my 'resurrection'. I was scarcely awake, when she pressed a mug of steaming coffee into my hand, then spiked it with a generous dose of Cognac.
>
> We were on the left wing of Yorck's corps, which had been defeated the previous day and pushed back to here. We were about 2,000 paces north of Ruenthal. In front of us were the [artillery] parks, some arranged in a circle,

some of the guns, mostly 12-pounders, were deployed as batteries. We were to occupy the intervals between the batteries. We were set to work, rolling the larger cannonballs out in front of the guns, in random fashion, to disrupt any cavalry charges. We worked with a will; as the weather improved, so did our spirits... We ate our bread soup and the occasional jokes and songs were heard around the camp fires... At about two o'clock the order came to put on our equipment, then to take up arms.

General von Yorck, hearing that the Russians had stopped advancing, intended to mount an assault on their left flank and rear.

This was to be the clash at Mesoten.

The clash at Mesoten, 29 September. A village in Latvia, 30 km south east of Mitau, on the River Aa. A minor victory for Prussian General von Yorck's advanced guard over General Alexejew's 21st Division. The Prussians had 5,400 men and six guns; their losses were 'very light'. The Russians had 9,000 infantry, only 200 cavalry and twelve guns; their losses were also light. The superior Prussian cavalry was able to dominate the enemy in the open terrain.

As Hartwich previously told us, the Prussians in Latvia were to mount a flanking raid on the Russians from Ruenthal. The superior Prussian cavalry gave them the edge, but losses were very light on both sides. Hartwich's account of the action sets the scene:

If I am not mistaken, Mesoten castle belongs to the von Pahlen family. The first shot was fired at 4 o'clock, but the fighting was very low key. Our battalion was on the left wing up against the Aa. Action stopped at nightfall on our side of the river, but the 3rd and 5th Regiments, on the far bank, pushed the enemy back to Kiope and Graefenthal.

The clash at Graefenthal, 29 September. A village in Latvia, south west of Riga. A victory for Prussian General von Yorck, with the 2nd and 3rd Brigades, over Russian General Rachmanov's 6th Infantry Division of the Finland Corps. This was another low-key action; the Prussians had 7,000 men and ten guns; they lost some 260 men. The Russians had 1,800 men and six guns; their casualties are not fully known, but they lost 303 prisoners.

The clash at Lautschkruge, 30 September. A hamlet south of Riga in Latvia. A victory for General von Yorck's Prussian Corps over General Count Steinheil's Finland Corps. The Prussians had 12,000 men and sixteen guns and their losses were light. It is not clear what strength Steinheil had, or his total casualties, but 608 were captured when the Prussian cavalry caught two battalions of the 3rd Jaegers in the act of forming square and forced them to surrender.

Hartwich's account continues:

We broke camp and set off. We had gone scarcely a kilometre when we met the enemy. There were about five battalions, some in line, some in column, with their skirmishers deployed before them. 'They had four guns, as far as I can remember. Not long into our advance, a shot killed Major von Reuss' horse; then another knocked his shako off and a third hit the heel of his boot. Despite all this, he led us bravely onwards. We were three fusilier battalions, the Regiment Nr 2 (East Prussian), half a battery and three squadrons. The enemy had maybe 6,000 men... I was sent out with the 12th Company to skirmish; scarcely had we deployed, than Lieutenant von Hoepfner was hit in the foot. My flankman, Kulmey, one of the best one could wish for, was hit in the head at my side. The popular Fusilier Strutsch was badly wounded by a bullet and Fusilier Jenrich from Nitzahn was shot in the side. Muttering a silent 'Our Father' I asked God to keep me from harm, as it was pretty hot here. It was my task to push on to Lautschkruge, through a sort of sunken road, edged to both sides with willow hurdles. These were still occupied by the enemy, who retired when they saw that our advance was determined. We ran after them at full speed so as to enter the courtyard [of the farm] right after them... I was in the act of getting some twenty men together, when I saw, from the corner of my eye, a Russian Jaeger pop up over the hurdles to my left about ten paces from me and take aim at me. I had the idea to twist my pack around onto my chest, just as he fired. The ball penetrated the pack, but was stopped by all the thickly-folded blanket and clothing. It even dented the seal of my commission as I later discovered; I kept it as a souvenier.

Fusilier Burdewig of the 11th Company heard the impact, and shouted out: 'Herr Leutenant, that was you!' So I owe my life to that quilt from Mitau...The impact of the ball threw me to the ground, but I sprang up again and we took the farm, together with 30 prisoners, including my Jaeger. I had only grabbed him by the collar and the waistbelt, but he was in such shock, that he at once begged for mercy. We took some other farmsteads, each one involved a mêlée, then we turned on Kensinshof, where we were repelled. It was not until a platoon of the 5th Fusiliers took the place in rear, that it fell to us. Now the enemy, who had been retreating, turned on us and things really got lively. The Browns[6], and a detachment of the Green Hussars[7] took the enemy in flank and three battalions were captured. A squadron of Russian dragoons – I think the Smolensk Regiment due to their white collars[8] – and the Grodnow Hussars now rushed up, but were driven off by our Tirailleurs and those of the East Prussian regiment, which were hidden a in a copse. Lieutenant von Schack, of my detachment, won the Pour le Mérite for this action, and NCO Schildner captured Lieutenant von Firks of the Grodnow Hussars. This was end of the action for the day; the Russians opened up with heavy artillery fire from Annenburg, but it did us no damage, as most shots either went over our heads or dropped too short.

We bivouacked at Kensinshof and the men had their first hot meal for three days... Apart from the captain, I was the only officer not wounded that day. On the battlefield we had the chance to admire the excellent leather equipment of the 3rd and 5th Russian Jaeger Regiments.

The clash at the Garosse River, 1 October. A minor river, south of Riga. A minor Prusso-Polish victory over part of the Riga garrison under General Essen. Yorck's advanced guard and Kosinski's Polish contingent totalled 3,600 men and four guns. Details of the Russian strengths and losses are not known. They continued their withdrawal into Riga.

Close on the heels of their victory at Lautschkruge, the Prussians in Latvia closed up to the line of the Garosse River. It was a stream running through level countryside, with high, steep banks. At Garossenkruge, it joins the River Aa. There was a stone bridge over the former river, which became the target of both sides. The Prussian skirmishers were deployed in the bushes both up and downstream of the bridge and caused the Russians considerable casualties. The Prussians bridged the stream using willow hurdles and trusses of straw and took the enemy in flank. Julius Hartwich was shot across the face at point-blank range, but suffered nothing more serious than singed eyebrows. A Russian counter-attack drove them back over the Garosse, when the action again degenerated into a desultory artillery duel. The accuracy of the Russian artillery seems to have been extremely poor. The 5th Polish Infantry Regiment[9] and the Prussian Leibhusaren mounted a flank attack, which caused the Russians to withdraw. Julius Hartwich recalled:

King Friedrich of Württemberg, one of Napoleon's closest allies and absolutely unforgiving to his officers and men. Author's collection.

> After the enemy had withdrawn, I went into one of the barns and discovered a pig wandering about; we killed it with a musket shot and enjoyed an excellent supper. There was plenty of straw to use as bedding.

The Russians fell back to Riga. They had lost 3,400 prisoners alone. The Prussians lost forty-two officers, eighty-one NCOs, 1,094 men and 185 horses. Lieutenant von der Horst had defected to the enemy.

By his actions over the last few days, General von Yorck had foiled the superior Russian offensive and saved the artillery park of Macdonald's X Corps. On 4 October, the Prussians withdrew to Mitau and bivouacked around the state hospital there. Next day they took up a defensive position near to Garossenkrug. On 9 October, Hartwich's regiment marched to Eckau and built a hutted camp around the church there. Each hut consisted of a pit, three to four feet deep, roofed with sheaves of straw and held five men. Stone hearths were set to one side of the pit. Rations for the officers at this time consisted of a pound of meat, 100 grammes of grain cereal (which was sometimes replaced by 80 grammes of rice), one sixth of a pint of brandy and 20 grammes of salt. The men received only half an officer's ration of meat and brandy.[10]

This information is an astounding revelation. By this point, anyone outside the pampered circle of Napoleon's court or Imperial Guard in the central sector of the Russian invasion had been starving for months. It is almost incredible to read that Hartwich and his fellow officers became so bored with eating their daily soup and old beef, as 'the lads had their work cut out to keep us supplied with tooth-picks.' He also tells us that they had received no pay since 1 August, as the continual procession of 'allied' armies – as he put it – had exhausted all stocks of cash in Prussia.

> Occasionally we would save up our beef rations and steep it in vinegar, and instead of cooking the potatoes in butter, we boiled them in the marinade… We would like to buy a ham, but the whole area is bare, so we will just have to put up with the old bull's meat. I have discovered a source of butter, which I am keeping very secret, otherwise we would have to cook our potatoes in salt, like the other honest people.

The Prussians seem to have passed the time in Eckau very well, putting on concerts and organizing other games and entertainment for themselves. Once again, compare this with the wall-to-wall misery, death, destruction and deprivation which had trailed in Napoleon's wake for so many hundreds of thousands since June.

> On 14 October we moved off to the Misse, where we set up camp at Gallenkrug; the enemy had started skirmishing at Dahlenkirchen on 13 October and had pushed our outposts in. Marshal Macdonald thus ordered a general advance. For some days now, he has sited his HQ in Stalgen castle on the Aa, between Mitau and Bausk, right behind the centre of Yorck's corps. Previously it had been with Grandjean's [7th] division.
>
> We were with the advanced guard of Colonel von Horn's right wing of the Prussian corps, together with Colonel von Tresckow's Dragoner-Regiment Nr 1. At dawn on 15 October, I noticed that the Russians had withdrawn; we advanced to the customs post at Tomoschna,[11] where there was a large sugar refinery.

There followed a clash with the Russians, in which Captain Ledaskowsky's Polish half horse artillery battery[12] caught them wading across the shallow River Duena in a hail of canister and caused them heavy casualties.

> During this action, we could see the three fine, tall towers of Riga before us… Despite the cold wet weather, the bivouacs in the heavy timbers of the sugar beet stores were warm and there was plenty to eat.

On 17 October the Prussians were involved in another clash with the Russians – including the Grodnow Hussars and a regiment of regular Cossacks – around a brickworks, just outside Riga. The Prussians lost six men killed and 18 wounded, but took 70 prisoners. The quality of the Russian musketry again seems to have been as low as that of their artillery. Next day the Prussians fell back to Eckau, where they stayed, peacefully, until 23 October.

Hartwich tells us of a dramatic drop in temperature on the 21st of the month, with heavy snowfall. Next day:

> We were very pleased to be issued with fur coats. Those for the men were second hand items and were not very inviting; the dusty miller's old coat stood in the ranks next to the blackened item worn by the blacksmith and the tar-worker – but each one was a blessing. We officers each received a new, sheepskin coat, complete with a large hood, which fitted over the shako. The men wore their bandoliers over their coats; we officers wore our waist sashes over ours.

On 22 October, we took post about Eckau… There were two companies of French sappers at the castle, and on the other side of the sunken road to Mitau were two battalions of Polish troops and a Westphalian battalion.[13]

Next day – a Sunday – the Prussians had just finished church service in Eckau, when the alarm was beaten; but nothing transpired. Another skirmish took place on 29 October. It was at this point that the joyous news of Gouvion Saint-Cyr's victory over Wittgenstein in the 2nd Battle of Polotzk was received. The bulletin claimed 8,000 Russians captured; in fact, the contest was, at best, a draw and the allies were soon forced to evacuate Polotzk.

On 12 November we officers were called to Eckau castle to greet General Bachelu.[14] When I got there, Colonel von Horn asked me if I spoke French; I answered that I did… On 13 November Colonel von Hünerbein tested me in French, then took me to General Bachelu and introduced me to him as the Prussian ADC to Corps HQ. The general was most friendly and at once gave me some French orders to translate. Colonel von Horn gave me a horse – taken from a Cossack – and saddlery and I was allocated quarters in the attic of the castle.

Notes

1 More contraband.
2 The Russian horsewhip.
3 1st Silesian Hussars.
4 Albert-Louis Taviel was Chief of the Artillery, X Corps; Darencay was not a French general, according to Six.
5 Steinheil's Finland Corps would later move south east to join Wittgenstein in the second battle of Polotzk.
6 The 1st Silesian Hussars.
7 2nd Silesian Hussars.
8 The Smolensk regiment had yellow facings; it may have been the Finland or Mitau Regiments; the Irkutsk and Siberian regiments, which also had white facings, were with Barclay's 1st Army.
9 7th Division.
10 Exactly how this discrimination was justified would be of interest.
11 On the River Keckau.
12 1st Company, 1st Polish Horse Artillery Regiment, 7th Division.
13 7th Division.
14 Commanding 3rd Brigade, 7th Division.

Chapter 15

Moscow – waiting for Godot

'All that is left of Moscow must be burned...'

*'Oh, I know that from a purely military point of view Moscow
is worthless. But Moscow is not a military position, it is a political position.
You think I am a general, while I am really an Emperor.'*

Napoleon's stay in Moscow has something of the surreal about it. For the last three years he had been the undisputed master of mainland Europe, or so it appeared. He had invaded Russia to swat the last, annoying fly that disturbed his peace – and now, suddenly, he was waiting in Moscow. Waiting for his now-implacable enemy, the Czar, to save his failed gamble for him. He exhibited no initiative, made no plans for the coming winter, gave no orders for clothing, food or forage to be manufactured or collected. He was intellectually bankrupt; clutching at straws.

The rear zone of Napoleon's army became increasingly insecure as the partisans became ever bolder. The Red Lancers of the Guard were on the road from Moscow south to Kaluga on 25 September, when a patrol of twenty-five men of the regiment was ambushed and killed by the Cossacks near the village of Rakitki on the River Desna.

On 14 September (26 September) Denis Davidov's guerrilla group ambushed marauding soldiers in the countryside south of Wiasma.

> By 10 o'clock we had taken 70 men and two officers, one of whom had his pockets filled with looted seals, penknives and other stuff. It has to be said, however, that this officer was not French, but from Westphalia.
>
> On the morning of the 15th, around 8 o'clock, our sentries on duty spotted a large number of carriages with white covers on their way from a village of Tarbeyev. Some of us jumped on horseback and saw them as they moved along like a sailing fleet. In the blink of an eye, hussars and Cossacks galloped to cut them off. The first in line attacked those escorting the convoy, and after a few pistol shots they scattered in flight; then, when cornered by the Bug regiment, they laid down their arms. Two hundred and sixty men from different regiments with their horses, two officers and twenty carriages filled with bread and oats and harnesses fell into our hands.

General Preysing-Moos, near Moscow, throws some light on conditions for the troops on the front line, even in late September:

> On 28th the entire light cavalry of the IV Corps mounted a reconnaissance

to the village of Fedosino without making contact with the enemy. We bivouaced in misery in a small wood near Broussier's division. This night and the next were so cold, the weather so wet and windy and no food or forage available, that we were forced to seek better shelter in the devastated village of Judina. There we were at least able to find a church that could be heated in which to put the wounded and sick. On 30th we sent back to Moscow Major Gaddum, an ensign and 10 men who were seriously ill; 7 officers, 46 men, 59 sick horses, 88 unmounted men and 57 gunners were sent to the hospital in Rusa.

Back in Moscow, by 3 October, with his peace initiatives to Czar Alexander unanswered, Napoleon had another mood swing, as Segur recorded: 'We shall march on St Petersburg, where Macdonald will join us. Murat and Davout will be the rearguard!' declared the Emperor. Then, becoming aware of the stunned expressions of his staff, he said:

King Friedrich August of Saxony; hapless hostage to Napoleon in 1813 as his kingdom was extensively ruined by the fighting. Author's collection.

What! You are not inflamed by this idea! Has there ever been a greater military exploit? Henceforth, nothing short of that conquest will be worthy of us. We shall be overwhelmed with praise! What will the world say when it learns in three months' time that we have conquered the two greatest capitals in the north?

Not too much later, reality again asserted itself; the St Petersburg excursion was forgotten.

Just before this outburst, Russian partisans had become very active. Denis Davidov's raids had been very successful, for minimal loss:

On the morning of the 20th September we moved to Gorodistche where we could rest and also inspect the levies of the new militia formed at Znamensky. Besides, I was now laden with spoils. I found I had 908 men, 15 officers, 36 gun carriages, 40 supply wagons, 144 draught oxen, which I distributed, and about 200 horses, from which I chose the best to replace the poor mounts of the Cossacks. The rest I apportioned out among the peasants.

Davidov had also freed 400 Russian prisoners.

On 26th September we reached Andreyani, and I sent two peasants into Pokrovskoe to get information on the enemy detachment there. Within four hours two lads galloped over from Losmino with the news that the French were on their way from Wiasma, marching in the direction of Gzhatsk. My wishes were being granted.

Our party immediately headed for Monin. Towards evening we reached this village and captured 42 wagons loaded with food, 10 artillery carriages under the protection of 126 light infantrymen and one officer. This group was part of the detachment sent at the double to overtake us.

Just after this raid, Davidov's force was swelled by the 13th Cossack Pulk of the Don Host under Colonel Popov; together with the 1st Cossack Pulk of the Bug. Davidov now had some 700 men under his command.

On the evening of 10 October another group of Russian partisans under General Dorokhov attacked the small town of Vereja (16 km south of Mozhaisk) and overwhelmed the 450 men of the 1st Battalion, 6th Westphalian Infantry Regiment, capturing both the battalion commander, von Conrady, and the regimental commander, Colonel Ruella. The battalion's colour was taken, as was a large stock of bread and grain.

The next action of Davidov's group was to be north of the main road, near the River Wiasma.

> On 4th October... we halted in some woods, a few yards from a bridge over the River Wiasma. Hardly an hour had gone by when my scouts gave a whistled signal, having spotted an officer on foot with a musket and a dog. Ten men jumped on horseback to intercept him, surround him and brought him back. This was Regimental Commander Goethal, from the 4th Illyrian Regiment,[1] a keen hunter... Each time he noticed his dog, lying on a Cossack's coat, he assumed that stance of the famous actor Talma in the play *Oedipus*, and exclaimed aloud, 'Fatal Passion!'
>
> At this point we caught sight of his battalion. We got ready and when it came within range the whole party pounced on it – the first Cossacks in loose formation and the reserve in a column six horses abreast. Resistance did not last long. Most of the soldiers on foot threw down their weapons, but many, taking advantage of the nearby woods, scattered and saved themselves by fleeing. We captured two officers and 200 men.

Next day, a raiding party of the 1st Bug Cossacks captured a convoy of replacement uniforms and footwear for the 1st Westphalian Hussars[2] commanded by a Lieutenant Tiling, who was wounded and captured. The day's work had yielded 496 soldiers, four lieutenants and one staff officer captured, as well as the convoy of forty-one wagons. They were sent to Ukhnov. Lieutenant Tiling had been robbed of all valuables; he accepted this, but asked Davidov to return to him the ring his sweetheart had given him. Not only was the ring returned, but also a miniature portrait of the girl and a lock of her hair.

Davidov sent them on to Tiling (who lived in Orlov until 1814) together with a note in French:

> Receive, Sir, the effects which are so dear to you; may they help you remember your beloved and prove to you that courage and adversity are respected in Russia as everywhere else.

During his increasingly frustrating stay in Moscow (according to Segur) on 6 October, Napoleon revived the St Petersburg plan again. He wrote to the Marquis Louis de Caulaincourt, Duc de Vicenza, ex-ambassador to the Russian court, in October 1812.

> I'm going to march on St Petersburg. I know that the destruction of that city will distress you; but then Russia will rise up against Alexander, there will be a conspiracy, and he will be assassinated – which will be a great calamity. I esteem this sovereign highly, and will regret him, as much for my own sake as for France. His nature suits our interests, and no other prince could replace him advantageously for us. Therefore, in order to prevent this catastrophe, I have thought of sending you to him.

Caulaincourt refused to go. Napoleon then picked Marshal Jacques Lauriston for the task. According to Segur, the Emperor said to the latter: 'I want peace! I must have peace! I want it absolutely. Only preserve our honour.'

Lauriston dutifully went to the Russian headquarters, but was seen only by General Count Levin Bennigsen and Prince Wolkonski; they refused at first to allow him to speak to Marshal Kutusov. Later, when they relented, Kutuzov would not let Lauriston go to the Czar, but sent Napoleon's letter on with Prince Wolkonski and proposed a truce until the response come. Lauriston agreed and returned to the Kremlin.

Napoleon was very pleased to hear that the letter had been sent on, but ordered that the proposed truce was to be broken. In fact, it was observed. Shortly after this, the Emperor gave orders that all churches in Moscow were to be looted. 'It required all our efforts to remove the gigantic cross from the tower of Ivan the Great.' This tower was 320 feet high; the wooden cross was 32 feet long and covered with gilded silver plates.

To quote Segur, during October in Moscow, Napoleon, with astoundingly accurate foresight, said:

> Oh, I know that from a purely military point of view Moscow is worthless. But Moscow is not a military position, it is a political position. You think I am a general, while I am really an Emperor.

Those hearing this must have felt that his grasp of affairs was slipping. But then, as if to justify his inaction, he said:

> In affairs of state one must never retreat, never retrace one's steps, never admit an error – that brings disrepute When one makes a mistake, one must stick to it – that makes it right!

Those hearing this now knew that their suspicions were confirmed!

And still the ritual of imperial power was performed in the Kremlin, as Segur recorded:

> However, the rewards that the Emperor distributed so generously in his daily reviews were now received with a more restrained joy, even with a shade of sadness. The vacant posts he had to offer were still bloody; his were dangerous favours.

Just before leaving Moscow, it was discovered that there were not enough horses to pull all the artillery pieces; it was proposed that some should be left behind. 'Oh no,' responded Napoleon, 'the enemy would make a trophy out of it!'

Now Segur has an observation on Alexandre Berthier's effectiveness as Chief of the Imperial General Staff while in Moscow:

> The Chief of Staff was of little assistance to his superior in this critical situation. Though in a strange land, with an unfamiliar climate, he took no unusual precautions; and he expected the most insignificant details to be dictated to him by the Emperor, then they were forgotten. This negligence or lack of foresight had fatal consequences… Berthier of himself gave no orders, but was satisfied with faithfully repeating the letter of the Emperor's wishes. As for the spirit, he was constantly confusing the positive part of his instructions with the purely conjectural.

The French were becoming increasingly concerned at the frequency and severity of Russian retribution to the ravages of the 'foraging parties' sent out by the *Grande Armée*. On 19 October, Berthier wrote to Kutuzov:

> We urge you to regulate hostilities so that they will not force the Muscovite empire to bear more hardships than those which are indispensable in a state of war. The devastation of Russia is as harmful to the people as it is painful to Napoleon.

Kutuzov replied: 'It is impossible for me to suppress Russian patriotism.'

On 10 October, Murat wrote from Wiskowo to his chief of staff, General Auguste-Danielle Belliard, sick in Moscow:

> My dear Belliard, my situation is terrible; the whole enemy army is ranged against me. The troops of my advanced guard are reduced to nil. They suffer from hunger and it is no longer possible to to collect forage, without being sure that they will be captured. Not a day passes without I lose 200 men in this way. How will this end? I fear to tell the Emperor the truth, it will cause him concerns.
>
> Send us some flour or we will starve to death. Give me news, I know nothing.
>
> You will know that the Emperor has forbidden me to send out parliamentaries, and this is extremely unpleasant for me; as these were the only way that I could be sure that I was not going to be attacked; and in this manner foraging was easier.
>
> I am unhappy, farewell!
>
> When will the Emperor finally make a decision? What will happen to his army in the coming winter?
>
> The Russians are charming to me.

Russian charm had its aims...

The clash at Winkowo (Tarutino, Tschernischna), 18 October. A village in the central sector, 67km south west of Moscow. A Russian victory by Field Marshal Prince Kutuzov, with the II, III and IV Corps and the I and IV Cavalry Corps. They surprised and beat Marshal Murat with what was left of the I, II and III Cavalry Corps and the V (Polish) Corps.

The large-scale ambush at Winkowo on 18 October finally caused the penny to drop in Napoleon's mind. There would be no peace in 1812. No-one would be throwing him a life-line this time, as had been the case at Austerlitz. He had carefully manoeuvered himself out onto this limb and into this critical situation and must now fight his way out as best he could. He had embarked on the greatest game of poker in his career to date and his younger opponent (Alexander was 34 to Napoleon's 43 at this point) had outwitted him; had led him by the nose up the Russian garden path and into the fatal *cul-de-sac* of Moscow. Napoleon had made two major errors in this game: he had greatly underestimated his opponent and he had begun to believe his own propaganda of invincibility. The stakes in the game had been incredibly high; with his bluff called, he had to pay the price.

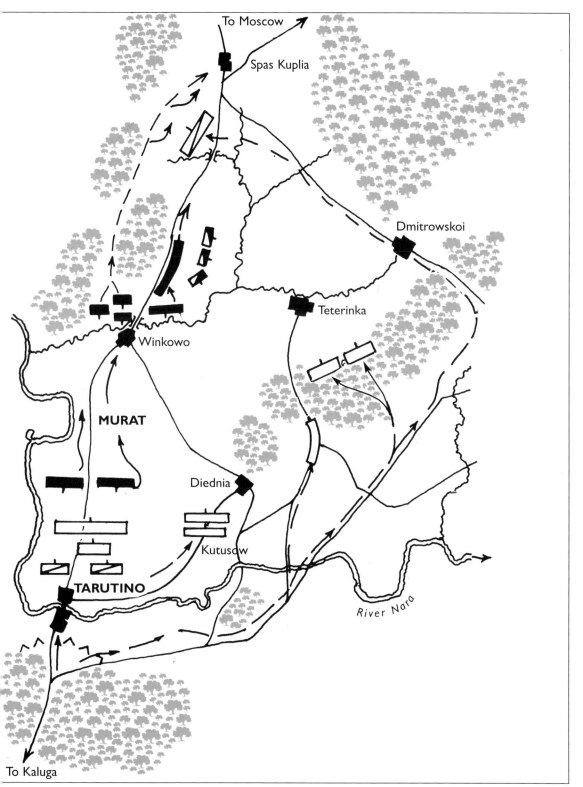

Winkowo. Battle of Tarutino, 18 October 1812. *Murat, in an isolated position, south-west of Moscow, had been lulled by the Russians into a false sense of security. When the Russians pounced here, they signalled the end of the phoney war. Murat lost some 3,500 precious cavalry and thirty-six guns. The Russians lost just 1,500 men; General Baggowut was killed. This map is after Bogdanovich.*

Preysing-Moos recorded how the retreat began for his cavalry brigade:

> Finally, on 19th October, we began our withdrawal. My 3rd and 6th
> Regiments were detached to General Ornano.³ With the rest, and the battery,
> I joined Broussier's division and we set off on the road to Kaluga to bivouac
> in the village of Scharapowo. After a march of four hours, we heard cannon
> and small arms fire from ahead. We sent out a patrol who reported that
> Ornano's baggage train had been ambushed by several hundred Cossacks due
> to the lax conduct of the escort. Many people had been cut down and killed
> or wounded and part of the convoy plundered. We hurried to reach the scene
> but could only capture a single Cossack. We marched on to Fominskija where
> the infantry halted. I took my cavalry and a battalion of Spaniards and took
> post half an hour ahead at the village of Malkowo.

This extract from General Preysing-Moos' account of the march from Moscow is
extremely revealing as to the state of the cavalry of Napoleon's army.

> On the information of a peasant that we had captured, that 10 Wersts⁴ [a
> Werst was about two-thirds of a mile] to our left hand side was an enemy force
> of 4 infantry and 2 cavalry regiments, I received the task on the 18th of taking
> two cavalry regiments, 300 infantry and one gun to reconnoitre in their
> direction. Just before we moved off however, the Chasseur outposts were
> attacked and driven back into the village. General alarm was sounded and we
> all rushed to our predetermined posts. Mine was on the left flank with the 5th
> and 6th Regiments. Several regiments of enemy cavalry were advancing against
> us and I was forced to form a hook by refusing my flank. This move was scarcely
> completed when we were attacked on three sides by a force of dragoons, lancers
> and Cossacks to the number of about 1,500 men, who charged at us whooping
> wildly. As my two regiments together numbered only about 400 men, and as it
> was impossible to goad our exhausted horses into a trot, I was forced to receive
> this charge standing. With admirable cold-bloodedness, my men took aim with
> their carbines and let the enemy charge up to within 15 paces of them. This
> steady conduct, and the shell and canister fire of two of our guns which had
> come up in our support, caused the enemy to break off the charge and retire
> into a nearby wood; taking some wounded with him and leaving some dead men
> and horses on the field. In the meantime, the 9e Chasseurs à Cheval had been
> overthrown and driven back with heavy loss. As this exposed my rear, I was
> forced to order the second rank of the 6th Regiment to turn about; this made
> my situation, in such close proximity to the enemy, even more perilous. Thus we
> remained until dark. The spare horses and the baggage were sent back to
> Fominskija where the wagons were formed into a circle.

The Emperor himself left Moscow before daybreak on 19 October. 'Forward to
Kaluga!' he cried, 'and woe to all who cross my path!'

But, as Segur noted, which confirmed Preysing-Moos' account:

> Still, that very first day on the road, he could not help noticing that both the
> artillery and the cavalry were crawling rather than marching... One could have
> taken it for a caravan, a nomadic horde, or one of those armies of antiquity, laden
> with spoils and slaves. How had it happened that in Moscow everything had been

forgotten? Why was there so much useless baggage; why did so many soldiers die so soon of hunger and cold under the weight of their knapsacks which were full of gold instead of with food and clothing? Above all, why, in the thirty-three days had not efforts been made to make snow-shoes for the men and the horses? If these things had been done, we would not have lost our best men at the Wop, the Dniepr and along the whole road. But why, in the absence of orders from Napoleon, had not these precautions been taken by by his commanders, all of them kings, princes and marshals? Had not the winter in Russia been foreseen?

And indeed, there was little resemblance of that loose mob to a conventional European army. It was a collection of motley individuals, many unarmed, including non-Russian male and female citizens of Moscow now too scared to stay and face the wrath of their ex-hosts when they came to view the ruins of their homes, lives and businesses. All were clad in a great variety of clothing, all were heavily laden down with all sorts of items precious to them, most of which would be discarded within hours or days as being not worth the effort of carrying. Carts and coaches, wagons of all kinds were mingled with the marchers. These too were piled high with treasured belongings, groaning under the weight, their teams staggering to move them.

But the fate of the sick and wounded moved Napoleon to action. He ordered each vehicle to be stopped and forced to accept a casualty as a passenger. As he wrote on 21 October to Marshal Mortier, still back in the Kremlin at this point:

> The Romans conferred civic crowns upon those who saved citizens' lives; you will be rewarded in a like manner, if you save soldiers. Have them carried on your horse and on those of your men. That is what I myself did at St Jean d'Acre.

Segur again confirmed the catastrophic state of the army:

> Men were already falling along the way. On 15th October, the first day of the retreat, we had burned wagon loads of provisions that the horses could no longer pull. Now the order to burn everything behind us was given and unharnessed powder wagons were blown up inside the houses.

In the early hours of 6 October, Davidov's partisans struck again at a French regiment in the village of Krutoy, near Wiasma. Again they were successful, taking an officer, a sergeant and 376 men prisoner. The Russians then went on to attack a French cavalry regiment in Losmino, about 20 km south of Wiasma. Again they were successful, taking 403 officers and men for the loss of only four Cossacks killed, fifteen wounded and fifty horses.

Notes

1 This is an error by Davidov; Goethal was in the Regiment d'Illyrie, which was in the 11th Division, III Corps. Martinien records him as being wounded this day.
2 With the 24th Infantry Division, VIII Corps.
3 Commander, 12th Light Cavalry Brigade, IV Corps.
4 1 Werst = 1.1 km.

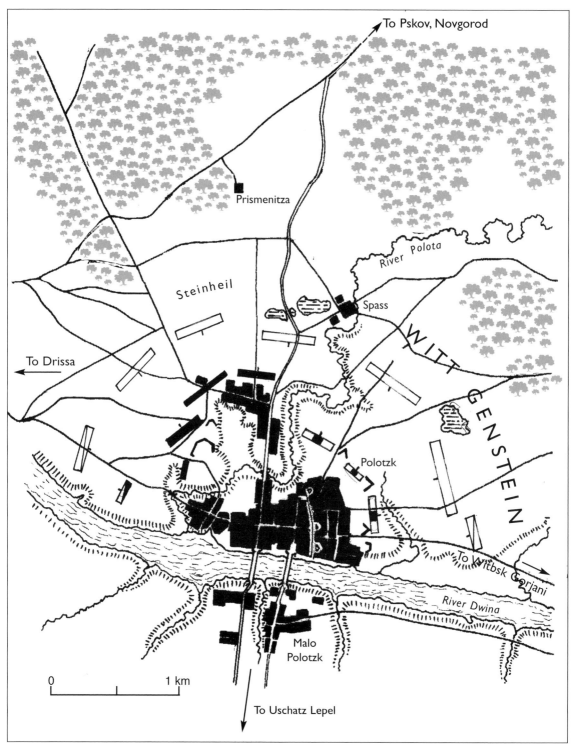

2nd Polotzk 18–20 October. *Wittgenstein had now been joined by Steinheil's Finland Corps and some newly-raised militia; he had 40,000 men and assaulted the 23,000 weakened Franco-Bavarians. Gouvion Saint-Cyr could hold on no longer and withdrew southwards, having lost 9,000 men. The Russians lost 8,000 casualties. This map is after Bogdanovich.*

Chapter 16

The northern flank, Polotzk – the finale

S ince the first battle at Polotzk on 18 August, action had been limited to patrolling and skirmishing. The town itself was mainly constructed of wood, which was used to build huts, feed the fires and to build defence works to the north of the town. By October, much of the place had simply disappeared. Abraham Rosselet,[1] recorded that:

General Prince Ludwig Adolph Peter von Wittgenstein, commander of the 1st Russian Independent Corps, which operated against the II and VI Corps of the Grande Armée around Polotzk. He was from a Westphalian family. In 1813 he commanded the allies at the battle of Bautzen on 20–21 May, where he was defeated; he then resigned and reverted to commanding a corps. At his throat is the Austrian Order of Maria Theresia.
Author's collection.

Le camp était assis dans la plaine en avant de cette place. Le camp était plutot un village; on s'y était établi dans de fortes et bonnes baraques, construi de manière a se garantir du froid, car on comptait y passer l'hiver. [The camp was on the plain in front of the place. The camp was a real town, made up of fine, strong huts, constructed as to be warm because we expected to overwinter there.]

The deadly fever and typhus continued to rage. In the four 'hospitals',[2] which the allies had built on the banks of the Dwina, there died about 100–150 men each day. As there were not enough men to bury the corpses, they were just thrown out of the windows into the river. As the river provided the drinking, cooking and washing water, the high mortality rate is scarcely to be wondered at.

Due to the absence of regular food supplies, the men were reduced to eating anything that they could find. Cowskins were cut into narrow strips and boiled, toads and frogs were fried, old fish, cats and dogs, herbs and mushrooms, animal entrails, offal and blood – it all went into the pot. Each corps was allocated an area from which to obtain its rations and fodder; that of the VI Corps lay between Uschatz and the village of Plissa. By this means, regular supplies of bread – even if only at half-ration level – were enjoyed for the next two months. By early September there was no more grain or bread to be found. The total absence of cavalry much reduced the effectiveness of these operations.

On 3 September a courier arrived from Imperial

headquarters bearing promotion for Gouvion Saint-Cyr to marshal. General von Deroy was created a count of the Empire, and eighty crosses of the Legion of Honour were distributed to officers and forty to NCOs and men.

The musicians of the 2nd, 3rd and 4th Swiss Regiments all fell ill and were sent back to the 'hospitals' in Kowno. As it was impossible to give them any money for this journey, few reached Kowno, and those who did, died there.

The VI Corps melted rapidly away. On 15 June 1812 it had 25,105 men; by 15 September this had shrunk to 7,814 and by 15 October it was down to 2,607. Indeed, Saint-Cyr gives the figure of 1,823 Bavarians present and fit for duty at the start of the second battle of Polotzk. The four Swiss regiments fared little better; in mid-September, the 1st Regiment had 864 men, the 2nd 983, the 3rd 314 and the 4th 664; a total of 3,025. These figures are without the foraging detachments.

There is a major question to be asked about Napoleon's management of his assets here. We are told repeatedly that he was able to reel off the parade states of his corps at will, with no reference to any documents. He knew how many men were available, where and when. If the men at Polotzk were dying at the steady rate of 100 each day, any fool could calculate that the 22,000 men of the II Corps and the 20,000 of the VI Corps, left after the first battle of Polotzk, would dwindle away to nothing within a finite time. So what went wrong in the fabled French high command? Was Saint-Cyr not rendering true parade states to the Emperor? Was Berthier falsifying the figures? If so, why? Why did Napoleon let two corps just sit in a poisonous trap and waste away? Why did Saint-Cyr just sit there and watch his command vanish? Why did he not pull back some miles and leave the miasma to the Russians?

Karl Philipp Wrede, Commander, 20th Division, then of the VI (Bavarian) Corps

Born on 29 April 1767 in Heidelberg, son of the *Regierungsrat* of Heidelberg, Ferdinand Joseph Reichsfreiherr von Wrede and his wife Katharina, Wrede studied law and in 1792 became the Commissar of the Palatinate with the Austrian Corps of FZM Fuerst Hohenlohe at Schwetzingen. In 1793 he was *Oberlandeskommissar* (Senior Commissar) with the Austrian army under Wurmser on the Upper Rhine.

On 18 June 1794 he was appointed titular colonel in the Bavarian General Staff; in this capacity he took part in all campaigns on the Rhine and was sent on special mission to the Duke of Brunswick with the Prussian army. He was then appointed Senior War Commissar in Rheinland Palatinate, before becoming colonel in the general staff with seniority from June 1794. He commanded a battalion in the campaign against France and was distinguished on several occasions. In December 1799 he was awarded the Military Medal.

Between 1800 and 1806 Wrede was involved in numerous actions, and he was awarded the Grand Cross of the Order of Maximilian Joseph for his services, along with the Grand Cross of the *Legion d'Honneur*. In 1809, after further distinguished military efforts, Napoleon created Wrede a count.

As *General der Kavallerie*, Wrede commanded the 2nd Bavarian Division in the VI (Bavarian) Corps in Russia in 1812. They fought at Polotzk; after Deroy's death, Wrede took command of his division as well. On 25 June 1813 Wrede was awarded the Grand Cross of the Military Medal. In July 1813 he commanded a 20,000 strong corps; after the signature of the Treaty of Ried Bavaria joined the allies against Napoleon. He fought Napoleon at Hanau and was wounded on the second day. He was defeated in this battle, largely due to the fact that his dispositions were tactically stupid and he had 'forgotten' his artillery park. Despite this, on 9 November he was showered with further honours.

In 1817, after further commands in the army, and following the fall of Graf Monteglas from the Bavarian government, Wrede took his place and did much work on the constitution of 1818. At the opening of the Chamber in that year, he was appointed to be its President. On 26 September 1822 he was appointed Minister for the Army. In 1826, while in St Petersburg on a diplomatic mission, he was presented with the Order of St Andrew in diamonds. On 29 April 1831 he was appointed colonel-in-chief of the 9th Line Infantry Regiment. He died on 12 December 1838 in Ellingen.

The final scene (without the enemy doing anything to hasten things along) would see Saint-Cyr and his ADCs, well provided with food and drink, sitting alone on the banks of the Dwina, surrounded by the 50,000 corpses that had once been their army.

But the enemy were not content to let nature take its course.

French communications from Moscow to Polotzk had broken down due to partisan activity; Saint-Cyr received his news from Maret in Wilna. The Russian General Count F.F. Steinheil now advanced south from Riga with his Finland Corps of 12,000 infantry, 1,250 cavalry and fifty-two guns to reinforce Wittgenstein. Together with local militia formations and this new corps, the latter could concentrate some 40,000 men. To oppose them, Saint-Cyr had only just over 20,000 weak, sickly, starving and demoralised men.

The stage was set for a showdown. Preliminary action opened on 14 October, when Wittgenstein attacked the II Corps right wing at Sirotino.

The 2nd Battle of Polotzk, 18–20 October. A drawn battle between Oudinot and Gouvion Saint-Cyr (II and VI Corps), and Wittgenstein's I Corps and Steinhiel's Finland Corps. The Franco-Bavarians could bring 23,000 men and 140 guns into line for this battle; Wittgenstein had 31,000 regulars, 9,000 militia and 136 guns.

This action coincided with the Russian surprise attack on Murat at Tarutino and was obviously well coordinated. Since the first battle in August, the wooden buildings in the town had been dismantled to provide materials for the bivouac huts of the troops and the various fortifications on the periphery of Polotzk.

There had been little action by either side in the intervening weeks. But now General Steinheil's Corps of Finland (6th, 21st and 25th Divisions and the 27th Cavalry Brigade) had come south to reinforce Wittgenstein and the combined force mounted an assault on the right wing of II Corps at Sirotino on 14 October. The advanced French and Bavarians withdrew on Polotzk with only slight loss.

Some of the VI Corps had been detached to occupy a bridgehead at Strunja, two hours march upstream from the town. On 18 October the assault began all along the line; the 2nd Swiss Regiment particularly distinguished themselves this day, losing their commander and twenty-three other officers in combat. General von Wrede, commanding in Redoubt Nr 2, had the guns moved out into the open ground so that they could rake an advancing Russian column with canister; the attack was beaten off.

The combat was broken off at six o'clock that evening.

Next day, the Russians commenced a great bombardment of the defences of the town and also attacked the Strunja bridgehead. Outflanking moves began to wrap around Polotzk. That night, Marshal St-Cyr evacuated that part of the town on the right bank of the river, broke the bridges and began his withdrawal to the south west to Arekowka.

Laurent Gouvion Saint-Cyr, Commander, VI Corps

Born in 1764 as the son of a butcher in Toul, Saint-Cyr adopted the surname Gouvion after his mother deserted her family while he was a baby. He studied art and tried to become an actor before entering French military service in 1792. He was defeated in the clash at La Grisuelle near Maubourg that year, but within two years he had risen to the rank of *General de Division*. In the 1796 campaign, he was initially commander of the two divisions of the left wing of Moreau's *Armée de Rhin et Moselle*. Later, he commanded the centre. Due to his cold, introverted, unsociable manner, he was quickly dubbed '*le hibou*' – the owl. He was an honest, principled man who despised his looting comrades, particularly the rapacious Massena, whom he had succeeded in 1798 as commander of the *Armée de Naples*. In 1799 he served initially in Italy in Joubert's army, which was defeated by the Austro-Russians at Novi on

Laurent Gouvion Saint-Cyr, commander of the VI (Bavarian) Corps in 1812. He was to receive his marshal's baton for the first battle of Polotzk. He was wounded in the second battle there on 18 October. In 1813 he commanded the XIV Corps and capitulated in Dresden.

15 August. He was then transferred to Holland, where he commanded the 1st Division of the French corps fighting the Anglo-Russian invasion. He then moved to southern Germany to serve under Moreau again in the *Armée du Danube*.

He then fell out with Moreau and was relieved of his command. From 1801–1803 Gouvion Saint-Cyr was ambassador to Madrid, and then to the court at Naples until 1805. He was apolitical and thus mistrusted by Napoleon, particularly as he refused to sign the proclamation supporting the latter's elevation to emperor. Not surprisingly, he was excluded from the first marshalate. In August 1808 he was appointed commander of the French troops in Catalonia. He was recalled for failing to capture Girona in August of that year. In 1812 he was given command of the VI (Bavarian) Corps in the invasion of Russia and rendered excellent service on Napoleon's northern flank.

Gouvion Saint-Cyr was wounded on 18 August in the 1st battle of Polotzk. For this, he at last received his marshal's baton, nine days later. He was badly wounded in the foot at the second battle of Polotzk on 18 October and had to give up command of his corps.

In 1813 he was appointed commander of XIV Corps, fought at Dresden on 26 and 27 August, and was commander in that city during the siege. He was captured when Dresden fell on 11 November 1813. After the Bourbon restoration, he continued to serve and refused to support Napoleon during the Hundred Days. In July 1815 he was appointed Minister for War, but was forced out of office by ultra-royalist intrigues the following September. His attempts to gain clemency for Ney were unsuccessful.

In June 1817 he was appointed Minister for the Marine, and two months later he was reinstated as Minister for War. By this point, he had been ennobled as a marquis. His reforms were very beneficial for the French army, but he resigned in 1819 to devote his time to his family, agriculture and writing. His military talents were recognised, even by his enemies, and his control of troops on the battlefield was thought to be exceptional.

The last allied troops to leave Polotzk were Swiss, and they had to cross the river in barges. The wounded and sick in the Jesuit Monastery were abandoned to the Russians. Losses in the three day battle were 9,000 for the allies (including 2,000 captured) and 12,000 for the Russians, whose infantry had suffered terribly from close range artillery as they repeatedly assaulted the town.

But while Russian losses could be replaced with increasing ease, the allies just dwindled away. On 23 October, Saint-Cyr (who had been wounded in the foot on 18 October) felt himself 'no longer able to exercise command of the army' and handed over to General Count Claude-Juste-Alexandre Legrand, previously commander of the 6th Division. His chief of staff, Colonel Laurencez, sent a message to inform General von Wrede:

> As Marshal Saint-Cyr can no longer exercise active command, he has delegated this to General Legrand. I already had the honour to inform Your Excellency of this, but it seems that the despatch did not arrive. The marshal requests you to consider yourself as reporting to General Legrand in all service respects, and to send the 7e Cuirassier-Regiment back to him tomorrow.

This must have been the last straw for Wrede. To be asked to place himself (and what little remained of the once-proud Bavarian army) under the command of a junior general was a calculated insult. He ignored the letter and took his own route out of Russia.

The subsequent retreat of VI Corps went through Kublitschi to Puichna, then westwards to Dogschitzi, which was reached on 27 October. Wittgenstein now abandoned the chase of the Bavarians to follow the remnants of Legrand's II Corps south east through Lepel and Tscheria, towards the Beresina.

There was to be one more misfortune to befall the hapless Bavarians. As the battalions were now so weak, all twenty-two regimental colours were packed into a treasury wagon and sent back to Uschatz with the artillery convoy. Unhappily, this convoy fell into Russian hands on 25 October.

So the conflicts on the northern flank ended.

Wrede led the VI Corps to join up with Marshal Ney on the River Niemen in mid-December.

Notes

1 Swiss Lieutenant-Colonel in 9th Division, II Corps.
2 There were no medical staff, no medicines, no bandages.

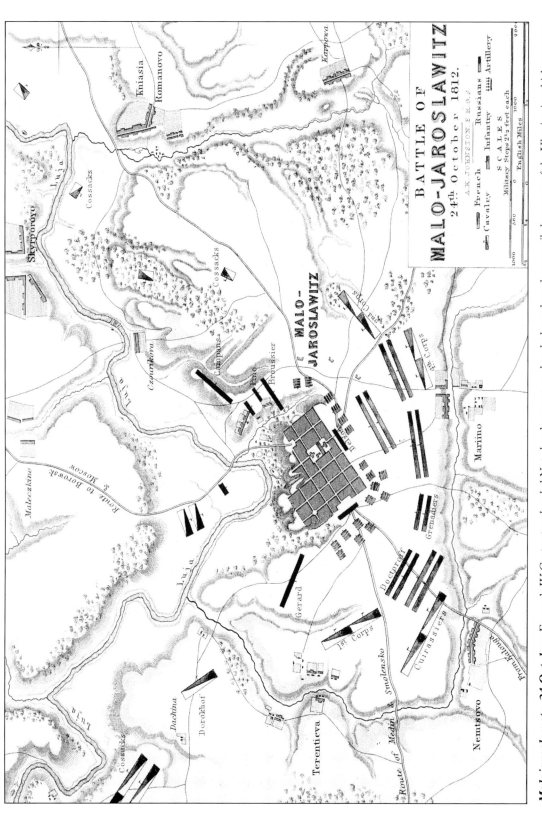

Malojaroslawetz, 24 October: *Eugene's IV Corps spearheaded Napoleon's attempt to break through to the unspoiled country of the Ukraine in which to retreat to the west. His opponent was Dochtorov's VI Corps. French losses were 6,000; the Russians lost 8,000, but Napoleon gave up his thrust to the south and turned*

Chapter 17

The central sector
in October and November

'I've had my fill of heroics! We've done far too much already for glory. The time has now come for us to turn our thoughts to saving the remains of the army.'

'Come on then, come on dandies of Paris!'

This was to be the scene of the notorious 'Retreat from Moscow' in all its misery and pathos.

This regiment, the 3rd Lithuanian Lancers of the Imperial Guard, was only formed on 5 July 1812, but it was not until early October that two squadrons were complete. Count Konopka was leading his regiment to join the *Grande Armée*, but decided to stop off in Slonim, his family home. He put out no sentries, a most lax attitude to the business of war.

> **The Ambush at Slonim, 20 October.** A small town in the southern-central sector, 190 km north east of Brest-Litowsk. A victory for the Russians (General Tchaplitz and the Pavlograd Hussars) over the 3rd Lithuanian Lancers of the Imperial Guard under Major-Colonel Count Jean Konopka.

General Tschaplitz's 18th Division, of A.P. Tormassow's 3rd Army of the West, discovered them and attacked. Konopka, 13 officers and 235 NCOs and men were captured. The rump of the regiment, some 500 men, formed in Grodno under command of Colonel Tanski. On 12 March 1813 they were incorporated into the 1st Light Horse Lancers of the Guard.

Meanwhile, out to the west of Moscow, Denis Davidov's partisans were operating north of the old Smolensk road between Wiasma and Gzhatz; on 11 October they came up with a convoy of seventy enemy wagons and its escort. They attacked it and took all the vehicles and 225 men as well as sixty-eight Russian prisoners.

Seslawin was another daring Russian partisan leader of 1812. After Napoleon had left Moscow, his army approached the crossing of the River Lusha at Malojaroslawetz. Seslawin crept through the woods at the roadside and managed to kidnap a second lieutenant of the Imperial Guard. He rode with him to General Alexei Petrovich Yermelov at Aristow, not far away. General Dorokhow's division was also here. Seslawin's prisoner corroborated his evidence of the position of the *Grande Armée* and this vital information was sent on to Kutuzov, precipitating the famous battle at that river crossing. The locals in Malojaroslawetz had demolished the bridge before

Eugene's IV Corps arrived and this delay made the clash even more certain.

> **The battle of Malojaroslawetz, 24 October.** A town in the central sector, on the River Luscha, 103 km south west of Moscow. Although Russian losses exceeded those of the French, the latter's attempt to return to the west by a more southerly route was stopped here. Prince Eugene commanded the I and IV Corps; Dokturov commanded the VI Russian Corps.

General Delzon's 13th Division, IV Corps arrived at Malojaroslawetz at six o'clock on the evening of 23 October and began to repair the bridge. The town was unoccupied at this point, so Delzons put two battalions into it, but kept the rest of his division north of the Lusha River.

When the news reached him that the French were falling back, Kutuzov guessed that they were making for Kaluga, about 150 km south west of Moscow, and at once set his forces in motion to catch them.

Dokturov's VI Corps arrived at Malojaroslawetz from Cziurikowa at five o'clock on the morning of 24 October and at once attacked the town. Soon all of Delzons's 13th Division was in the place, as Kutuzov deployed his army in a crescent south of the town. Delzons's men were forced to abandon the town, but then the rest of the IV Corps came up and retook it. Malojaroslawetz changed hands several times; Delzons was killed and replaced by General Guilleminot; at the height of the combat all of Eugene's infantry was in the town.

The day was drawing to a close when Davout came up with his I Corps, crossed the river and deployed to the right of the town. The firing went on until nine o'clock that night. Kutuzov pulled his army back south along the Kaluga road. The allies had won a tactical victory, but it was clear to Napoleon that he would not be allowed to advance further south. Thus ended Napoleon's hopes of pushing down south into the fruitful, unspoiled Ukraine; he turned back to the north west. Losses this day were about 6,000 allies to 8,000 Russians.

According to Segur, the Emperor now burst out with: 'I've had my fill of heroics! We've done far too much already for glory. The time has now come for us to turn our thoughts to saving the remains of the army.' Well, better late than never – or was it?

Early on the morning of 25 October, crowds of Cossacks appeared in the woods along the sides of the road along which the *Grande Armée* was retreating. One of their officers rode up close enough to the lancers of the guard to shout, in fluent French: 'Come on then, come on dandies of Paris!' The immediate response was that he was driven off by fifty Polish Lancers of the Guard. Later, at the hamlet of Uverofskoie, General Colbert sent Captain Schneither of the Dutch Lancers of the Guard, with forty-eight men, out ahead of the column as advanced guard. Some hours later, about 450 Cossacks charged and surrounded the squadron. General Colbert at once sent the 2nd Squadron of the Dutch Lancers, under Colonel-Major Dubois, to save them. They managed to reach their comrades, but were then themselves surrounded. Colbert had to lead the other two squadrons of the regiment to drive the Cossacks off. But the four-hour action had cost them dear; twenty-eight men killed and wounded and thirty horses.

According to Segur, Mortier returned to Napoleon one afternoon and brought the

The Russians reoccupy the Kremlin on 19 October. An engraving by I. Ivanov. Author's collection.

General Baron Ferdinand von Wintzingerode, who was the subject of Napoleon's wrath in the Kremlin. He survived that interview and was defeated at St Dizier by the Emperor on 26 March 1814. Author's collection.

captured General Baron Ferdinand Wintzingerode, ADC to the Czar, with him. At the sight of this German officer, Napoleon's hidden suffering came alive. His dejection turned to anger, and he vented on his enemy all the grief that had been oppressing him:

> Who are you? A man without a country! You have always been my personal enemy. When I was waging war against the Austrians, I found you in their ranks. Austria became my ally and you offered your services to Russia. You have become one of the most ardent abettors of the present war; yet you were born in one of the states of the Confederation of the Rhine, which makes you my subject. You are not an ordinary enemy – you are a rebel! As such, I have the right to have you tried! Guards, lay hold of this man!

The guards did not move, behaving like men accustomed to seeing such violent scenes come to nothing, and sure that they were obeying better by disobeying. Napoleon went on:

> Do you see the devastated countryside, sir? The villages in flames? Whom are we to blame for these disasters? Why, fifty adventurers like yourself, in the pay of England and turned loose on the continent by her. But the burden of this war will fall on those who instigated it. In six months I shall be in St Petersburg, and I shall get satisfaction for all this strutting and boasting!

Strutting and boasting? Napoleon could have taken out patents on both concepts. Segur now tells us that:

> At Borodino, on 30th October 1812, a few miles beyond Mozhaisk, we had to cross the Kolotcha, which at this point was little more than a broad stream… the rough bridge broke. The Emperor, stopped by so insignificant an obstacle as a broken bridge, did no more than make a gesture of discontent and scorn, to which Berthier replied by an air of resignation. As the details of this particular movement had not been dictated by the Emperor, he did not believe himself guilty; for Berthier was a faithful echo, a mirror, and nothing more. Always standing by, day or night, he reflected the Emperor's image, and repeating clearly and precisely exactly what he ordered, but added nothing, so that what Napoleon forgot was for ever hopelessly forgotten.
>
> In the evening of that long day, as the imperial column was approaching Gzhatsk, we were surprised to find a number of dead Russians, still warm, on the road in front of us. We noticed that their heads had all been shattered in the same manner and that their brains were scattered about. We knew that 2,000 Russian prisoners had gone before us, under the escort of Spanish, Portuguese and Polish troops. Some of our generals greeted this with indifference, others with indignation, others with approval.

In the Emperor's presence no one expressed an opinion. Caulaincourt could no longer contain himself and burst out:

> It's an atrocity! This then, is the civilisation we are bringing to Russia! What effect will such inhumanity have on our enemies? Aren't we leaving our wounded in their care, as well as thousands of prisoners? Will they lack provocation for horrible reprisals?

Napoleon maintained a gloomy silence.

There are several eye-witness accounts of this or similar incidents; in each case, the reporter attributes the murders to some nationality other than his own.

So, the dwindling force, which Napoleon led, joined up with their original entry route at the battlefield of Borodino on 30 October. Captain Morgenstern, with the 2nd Westfalian Infantry Regiment of the VIII Corps, has left us a vivid picture of the nature of the retreat even in these early stages. We will follow him along parts of his desperate trek westwards; his account may be taken as being typical for thousands who were now fighting for their survival.

> We bivouaced near the monastry of Kolotskoi. Despite the fact that the evacuation of the hospital here had been ordered well in advance, little had actually happened due to the lack of transport. We saw the pitiful fear of those helpless sick and wounded as they watched the convoy passing them by, to leave them to the mercies of the vengeful Russians. We felt the bitterness of those seriously ill who now gave up all hope of being moved from their pestilential cells. The possibility that poor Maibom [a companion of Morgenstern's wounded at Borodino – DGS] might still be alive, drove me to enter the place. Chaotic disorder met me at every turn; there were no staff left to answer my questions! I had exposed myself to all those horrors for nothing.
>
> The Emperor ordered that every vehicle in the endless convoy that streamed past the place should take as many sick and wounded with them as they could. The order extended to the sutlers' carts, to all the vehicles laden with the spoils of the city and even to the coaches of the generals themselves. Any contravention was to be reported to the Provost Marshal who was authorised to confiscate all vehicles of the offending persons. In spite of this, the order had but little effect. The unwelcome guests were grudgingly taken on board but within a few days many such wagons vanished from the convoy; despite the perils from the ever-present Cossacks, the owners took the risk of slipping off for a day to dump their helpless loads in the forest at the first opportunity.

General Wittgenstein's two corps from the northern flank, having broken through Saint-Cyr's blocking force at Polotzk, now fell into the main scene of the retreat.

The clash at Tschaschniki, 31 October. A village in the central (but Polotzk) sector, 70 km south west of Witebsk, on the River Ula. A Russian victory for General Prince Jaschwil's advanced guard of Wittgenstein's I Corps over Marshal Victor's IX Corps, hurrying eastwards to support Napoleon.

Victor had 18,000 men, the Russians only some 11,000. The combat was limited to an artillery duel; the IX Corps withdrew at nightfall. General Wittgenstein's I Corps had now advanced some 60 km south from Polotzk on the northern flank and was aiming to cooperate with Kutuzov in crushing the remnants of the *Grande Armée* as they hurried westwards. Victor's IX Corps lost over 1,200 men, the Russians lost 400. Victor now assumed command of Legrand's II Corps.

On 21 October, at midnight, Denis Davidov's partisans were north of the old Smolensk road; as they neared the village of Rybkov at dawn, they discovered the *Grande Armée*:

> ...total chaos! Carriages, carts, coaches, guns, horsemen and foot soldiers, officers, support personnel and all kinds of riff-raff – they were streaming through in droves. If we had been ten times stronger, we wouldn't have been able to capture even one tenth of what choked the road.

As there was no point in a direct attack on this huge mass, Davidov ordered his men to charge alongside the fugitives, yelling, screaming and hacking at whatever they could. They set to work with a will, spreading terror in the fugitives. This mayhem went on until the Imperial Guard appeared on the scene, with Napoleon in its midst, and serious resistance forced the Cossacks to pull back. They kept carrying out hit and run raids on the column all day and took two officers and 180 men.

The clash at Wiasma, 3 November. A town in the central sector, on the River Dniepr, 150 km north east of Smolensk. A victory for the Russian General Miloradovich (II and IV Corps and II and IV Cavalry Corps) over Prince Eugene (I, II, III, IV, V and IX Corps, I and III Cavalry Corps).

Even at this point, many regiments of the *Grande Armée* (now down to 25,000 armed men) had ceased to exist as tactical units. This was particularly true of the cavalry. Napoleon lost 4,000 killed and wounded and 3,000 captured as well as three guns and two standards of the Italian Guard Dragoons. The Russians had 24,500 men; their losses were 1,800.

Morgenstern, of the Westphalian infantry, continues with his telling account:

> The bonds of discipline fell apart within the first few days of the retreat; a dreadful omen of what was to come. We marched through Gschatsk, where we picked up our 3rd Battalion and on to Wiasma. In Griednowo our 8th Infantry Regiment met us and on 3rd November we reached Dorogobusch, where we were granted a rest day.

On 23 October, Davidov's partisans crossed the Osma stream and probed towards Slavko, where they ran into the Old Guard again. It was a repeat of the previous day and yielded three officers, 146 men and seven wagonloads of assorted loot.

Captain Morgenstern's account of the drastic effects of the first snowfall are of interest.

> On the 5th of November we left Dorogobusch. That same evening, we had a heavy snowfall; the snow fell in such large and dense flakes that even the nearest objects were unrecognizable. The wind raged and whipped the snow into deep drifts, covering ditches and streams into which the exhausted, heavily-laden soldiers collapsed. Anyone who managed to climb out of one of these deathtraps could count himself lucky. The icy blizzard whipped into our

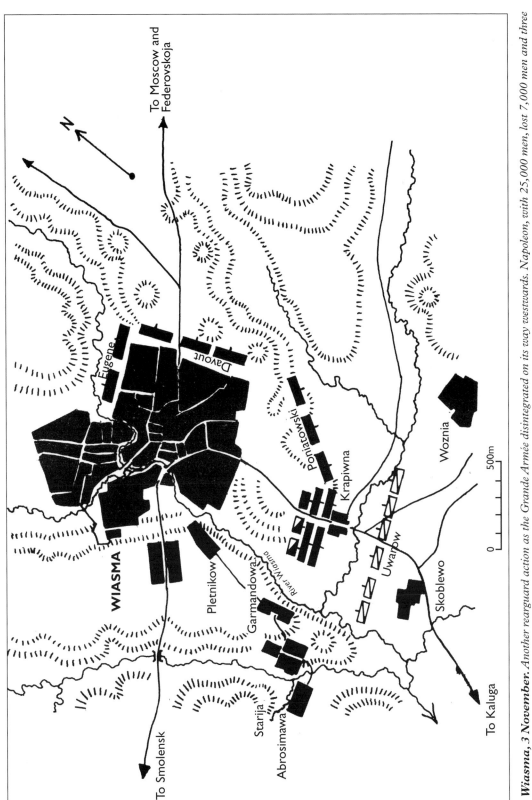

Wiasma, 3 November. *Another rearguard action as the Grande Armée disintegrated on its way westwards. Napoleon, with 25,000 men, lost 7,000 men and three guns. The Russians lost 1,800 casualties. This map is after Bogdanovich.*

faces, blinding us. The snow balled up under our feet and found its way through every layer of clothing to melt on the skin so that we were soaked through and frozen. The muskets slipped from our frozen hands; winter was disarming and destroying us much more effectively and quickly than the enemy ever could!

On 5 and 6 November, Napoleon's headquarters was in Dorogobusch. The Cossack partisan groups of Davidov, Platov, Seslawin, Orlov-Denisov, Figner and the militia forces of Prince Jaschwil Shepelev and Count Ozharovsky hovered around them. Figner was a sadistic fellow and had a habit of 'blooding' new recruits by letting them shoot unarmed prisoners. The total of his kill lay somewhere between 300 and 400 men. According to Segur, the first snow fell on 6 November. Segur relates how the effects of dwindling transport capacity were biting into the remnants of the once-great army:

> From Gzhatsk to Mikalewska, a village between Dorogobusch and Smolensk, nothing worthy of note happened... except that we were forced to throw all our spoils from Moscow into Lake Semlevo. The cannon, Gothic armour, works of art from the Kremlin and the cross of Ivan the Great were sunk beneath the waters of the lake. Trophies, glory, all those things for which we had sacrificed so much, had become a burden. There was no longer any question of adorning or embellishing our lives, but merely of saving them.

Segur also tells us of the day on which they reached Smolensk:

> At length the army came within sight of Smolensk again... Here was the end of their suffering, here was the land of promise, where famine would be changed to abundance, and weariness would find rest. In well-heated houses they would forget the bivouacs in sub-zero cold. Here they would enjoy refreshing sleep, and mend their clothes, here shoes and uniforms, adapted to the Russian climate, would be distributed among them.

According to Segur, the rate of attrition between Moscow and Smolensk had been dramatic:

> The army left Moscow 100,000 strong; in twenty-five days it had been reduced to 36,000 men. At the sight of the city [Smolensk] only the corps d'élite, reduced to a few soldiers and the required officers, kept their ranks. All the others dashed madly ahead. Thousands of men, mostly unarmed, covered the steep banks of the Dniepr, crowding together in a black mass against the high walls and gates of the city. But the unruly mob, their haggard faces blackened with dirt and smoke, their tattered uniforms or the grotesque costumes that were doing the duty of uniforms – in short, their frenzied impatience and hideous appearance frightened those inside. They believed that if they did not check this multitude of hunger-maddened men, the entire city would be given over to lawless plunder. Therefore, the gates were closed against them. It was also hoped that by such rigorous treatment these men would be forced to rally. Then, in this poor remnant of our unfortunate army, a horrible conflict between order and disorder took place. In vain did the men pray, weep, implore, threaten, try to batter down the gates, or drop dying at the feet of their comrades

who had been ordered to drive them back; they found them inexorable. They were forced to await the arrival of the first troops still officered and in order. These were the Young and the Old Guard; the disbanded men were allowed to follow them in. They believed that their entrance had been delayed in order to provide better quarters and more provisions for these picked troops. Their suffering made them unfair, and they cursed the Guard, asking themselves, 'Are we to be forever sacrificed for this privileged class, for this useless ornament never seen in the front rank except at reviews and festivities, or at the distribution of awards? Is the army never to get anything but their leavings? Must we wait for ever to be fed until these favourites are satiated?... Finally, all the unfortunate creatures were in Smolensk – Smolensk, city of their dreams! They left the river banks strewn with the half-dead bodies of the weak, who had succumbed to impatience and the long hours of waiting. They left still others on the icy slope they had to climb to reach the upper part of the town. The survivors rushed to the regimental storehouses, where many more died outside the doors, for they were repulsed again. 'Who were they? To what corps did they belong? How could they prove it?' The quartermasters were responsible for the rations. They were not to deliver supplies except to authorised officers bringing receipts for which they exchanged a stipulated number of rations. But these disbanded men around the doors had no officers, nor could they tell where their regiments were. Fully two-thirds of the army were in this predicament... No winter quarters had been prepared, no wood provided. The sick and wounded were left out in the streets in the carts that had brought them in. Once again the deadly high road was passing through an empty name! Here was one more bivouac among deceptive ruins, colder even than the forests the men had just left.

For some regiments there were bright spots in the gloom. The 2nd Dutch Lancers of the Guard numbered 330 men with only 130 horses when they entered the city; there they were joined by the 130 men of the 5th Squadron, coming forward from the depot.

Having been on outpost duty outside Smolensk for two days prior to the arrival of the fugitives from Moscow, Westphalian Captain Morgenstern, his sergeant and three men tried to go back into the city to draw more rations from the magazines there. By now, the survivors were beginning to reach the town; at the prospect of food, the starving hordes lost all control and discipline and stormed the place. Morgenstern described the scene as follows.

> The only thing to do in this chaos was to help ourselves. The conditions were far worse than any of the rumours that we had heard. We five, still fairly strong men, clung together in the maelstrom of men, horses and vehicles which was trying to squeeze through the narrow gateway into the city. We let ourselves be carried forward in the crush over the remains of wrecked vehicles, harness, discarded equipment, dead horses and even human corpses. At the gate itself however, any further progress was impossible. Formed bodies of armed troops cut their way into or out of the city with bayonet and butt; mounted men spurred their horses directly into the throng, regardless of whom or how many they trampled underfoot. By use of all our strength, we managed to extricate ourselves from this dangerous press to one side at the

cost of some bruising and ripped clothing. Bitterly disappointed, we scanned the high city wall which separated us from the mountains of supplies inside. We then saw a spot where the walls had been badly damaged. With great exertion, we scaled the minor breach with the help of the ropes that we had brought with us to tie up the bundles of supplies that we hoped to get. Once inside, we managed to locate a minor food store where the crush was not so great. Here we managed to bully one of the commissaries into issuing us with a sack of flour, a bag of much longed-for salt and some large pieces of salted meat. In another store, which seemed already to have been looted, we fought our way into possession of several pairs of shoes. We left Smolensk over the damaged wall again and made our way back to camp where we all enjoyed the spoils of our perilous exploit.

Major von Lossberg was also in the city; he recorded a brighter side to the grim events that were played there:

> I cannot leave Smolensk without mentioning the 'annual market', which was set up in the great square in front of the magazine from which I drew rations. Hundreds of soldiers (mostly of the Imperial Guard) traded here in the booty, which they had gathered, mostly in Moscow.
>
> This consisted mainly of articles of clothing, women's dresses and shawls of all types, but there were also many items of church jewellery. An NCO in green uniform, from his appearance and French accent an Italian, offered me such a piece of church treasure for two thousand francs and assured me that it was worth ten times that. He went into great detail on each of the precious stones it had and seemed to be an expert in this field.

The clash at Witebsk, 7 November. A town on the River Dwina, in the northern central sector, about 130 km north west of Smolensk. The Russians under General Harpe (part of Wittgenstein's I Corps) captured the French garrison. Exact details of the garrison are unknown; some 2,000 were captured for a Russian loss of forty killed and wounded. It was here that General Harpe heard the news of the abandonment of Moscow and passed it on the Wittgenstein. On 8 November Prince Eugene wrote of his IV Corps:

> Three days of suffering have so dispirited the men that at this moment I believe them incapable of any serious effort. Numbers have died of hunger or cold, and many more in their despair have permitted themselves to be taken by the enemy.

The clash at Liakhovo, 9 November. A village in the central sector, 40 km south east of Smolensk. A Russian victory over General Augereau's brigade. The Russian partisan leader, Denis Davidov, had learned that General Jean-Pierre Augereau[1] and some 2,000 men of the 1st Division, I Corps were in Liakhovo; he informed Orlov-Denisov and suggested a combined raid. During the fight, news came that another French force of about 2,000 men was coming from the east behind them. There was a brief skirmish and the French force of one general, sixty officers and 2,000 men surrendered. From 2 September to 23 October Davidov's partisans had captured forty-three officers and over 3,500 of the enemy.

> **The clash at Axensi, 13 November.** A village in the central sector, 40 km east of Tschaschniki and 60 km south west of Witebsk, in Belarus. A Franco-German victory over the Russians. This was General Partouneaux's 6,000 strong 12th Division of Victor's fast-vanishing IX Corps, advancing eastwards to aid Napoleon and the survivors to escape. They were opposed by Wittgenstein's advanced guard of 10,500 under General Alexejev. Losses were about even at 500 on each side.
>
> **The clash at Mir, 13 November.** In the central sector. A town between Brest and Minsk. A successful Russian raid (General Orurk's advanced guard of 1,300 men the Army of the Danube) which captured the French garrison. The entire French garrison of 500 men was captured by General Count Lambert's force, which lost forty-three men.
>
> **The clash at Smoljaentzi, 14 November.** A village in the central sector, 70 km south west of Witebsk. A victory of Wittgenstein's I Corps over Marshal Victor's IX Corps. Victor, with some 5,000 men, was badly beaten and lost 3,000 men. The Russians, with 30,500 men, lost about the same, but they could afford it. Victor withdrew south to Tschereja and stayed there until 22 November. Wittgenstein did not follow.

Westphalian Captain von Morgenstern gives us a picture of his division in Smolensk at this point:

> Next day, our pitifully weak division led the army's retreat. Our halt in Smolensk meant that the pursuing Russians were now very close behind us. Junot and von Ochs decided to regroup the [24th] division into three weak battalions and a 'squadron' of about 40 horses to which many mounted officers of all ranks attached themselves. This reorganization took place at the village of Korytina. General von Ochs commanded the troops; Junot was not to be seen outside his coach.

The scales had fallen from Phillipe de Segur's eyes:

> So great expeditions are crushed by their own weight. Human limits had been exceeded. Napoleon's genius, seeking to transcend time, climate, and distance, had, as it were, got lost in space. Great as his capacities were, he had gone beyond them. He had no illusions concerning this destitution. Alexander alone had deceived him. Accustomed to overcoming everything by the terror of his name, and the admiration inspired by his daring, his army, himself, and his fortune, he had staked everything on Alexander's first move. He was still the same man as in Egypt, at Marengo, Ulm or Esslingen. He was Hernando Cortez; he was the Macedonian burning his ships and in spite of his soldiers striking out into an unknown Asia; he was Caesar entrusting his whole fortune to a fragile bark.

It was on 14 November, according to Segur:

> ...that the *Grande Armée* began to leave Smolensk. Many disheartened men, some women, and several thousand of our sick and wounded were left behind. The Old Guard and the Young Guard together could muster no more than nine or ten thousand infantrymen and two thousand troopers. Davout

and the I Corps had five or six thousand; Prince Eugene and the army of Italy, five thousand; Poniatowski, 800; Junot and his Westphalians 700, and Latour-Maubourg with the remains of the cavalry 1,500. There might also be added to these about one thousand light-horse and 500 dismounted cavalry that we had succeeded in getting together. This army had numbered 100,000 combatants on leaving Moscow. In twenty-five days it had been reduced to 36,000!

The *Division Princière* was composed of the regiments of Frankfurt, Würzburg, the Ducal Saxons, and the Thuringian states of the Confederation of the Rhine. They were in Marshal Augereau's XI Corps, which only entered Lithuania in mid-November. On the 14th of that month, they numbered 14,000 men; by 10 December they had dwindled away to just 1,500 men with the colours. This climbed back to 2,000 by the 25th.

The accounts of conditions even in Lithuania, in mid-November, are related by Bernays, who covered the progress of the Frankfurt Regiment:

> The cold, made much worse by a strong north east wind, was almost unbearable. In addition, in the absence of any snow cover, it whipped up great clouds of dust, as high as church towers, which threatened to choke the marchers.

Captain von Soden of the regiment wrote:

> Past Tilsit the quarters got progressively worse. We kept meeting isolated French officers who told us that they were going to Spain, like the others (we had met in the previous days).
>
> In Kowno there were thousands of wounded in terrible conditions. The hospitals in which these unfortunates lay were just there to hasten their passing. Long lines of carts, filled with frozen corpses, took the road to the nearby River Niemen. Holes were hacked in the ice and the bodies thrown in to find cold, watery graves.
>
> At this time several troops of lightly wounded French soldiers arrived in Kowno; many of them seemed to have inflicted their wounds themselves, as they were wounded in the left hand. They were commanded by an officer of the 92e[2] who told us of the evacuation of Moscow, but not much else.
>
> A far worse sight were the 'Isolierte', as they termed the men who had left their units, who appeared staggering towards us in the snowstorm. Silently, with staring eyes, they stumbled past us, looking like ghosts. Some of them were amputees, who had fashioned themselves crutches and false legs so that they could escape from this chamber of horrors. Along the road lay masses of dead horses, half buried in snow and little mounds covered by shrouds of snow.

But what a wonderful thing 'timing' is. Having read the countless harrowing stories of the unfortunates who trudged back from Moscow when that city was evacuated on 19 October, let us look briefly at the almost incredibly different story that is to be found in Albrecht Adam's autobiography. Adam was one of the two famous artists that survived the Russian campaign. He left Moscow about four weeks before the *Grande Armée*, but it may as well have been four months or four years judging from the very different journey that he had. On 25 September he revisited the battlefield of Borodino:

> Despite this, I stopped my wagon for a time and took a walk over what seemed to me to be an interesting part of the battlefield, but I saw so much that was hideous and shocking, and found the air so polluted, that I soon turned round.
>
> Most of the corpses of men and horses had been left unburied and it was a horrific picture, if I am to give you a true account of the field 18 days after the battle. The most touching scene was that of seven men, who had crawled together next to a dead horse. Five of them were out of their misery; death had ended their martyrdom; but two were still alive and could speak and move a little. I couldn't take them with me, nor could I get them help. I confess, that for a moment, I had the idea that I should put them out of their misery. Horror-struck, I ran from this scene of hell. Breathing heavily, I said to myself: 'Yes, war is the most terrible thing!' Those unfortunates were Russians, who had lain helplessly on the ground for 18 days in such a state.
>
> Whenever I told this tale, I was asked what had kept those men alive for so long. I cannot answer this question, as I did not speak their language and they were not in any condition to talk much, but I think that they must have been eating the horse by which they lay.
>
> The battlefield of Borodino is of very gloomy formation, but now it appeared to be a hideous desert. I met no one for hours; it seemed that no one wanted to be here; they all passed by as quickly as possible. This impression that everything made on us was heightened by the melancholy weather. My vet was pleased when I returned; he had no wish to walk around the battlefield and was sitting impatiently in the wagon.
>
> I was deeply depressed and we went silently on our way along the devastated road, which everywhere showed the traces of the fighting. Later we came upon an abbey, which gave us hope that we might find quarters there, but we found it was a field hospital, which gave us another horror show and urged us on our way.
>
> Towards evening a large barn offered passable quarters for us and the horses for the night. We made tea, without sugar or milk, as we had neither, and we ate the rest of the mutton. But the terrible things that I had seen that day kept filling my dreams with awful fantasies.
>
> Next day brought us a terrible storm; we trudged on amid wind, rain and snow showers through the 29th on the muddy road. It was the sixth day of our continuous journey. Due to the poor diet and the bad road, our horses began to show fatigue. The prevailing westerly wind caused us great discomfort. Strange to say, the days were very stormy, but the nights were mostly calm and fine.
>
> That afternoon we met some travelling companions; Jewish salesmen from Glogau. Business-like as they were, they had followed the army to Moscow to find trade and seemed to be returning in a quite happy state. They looked well and in good spirits, three fairly young men-of-the-world who knew how to conduct themselves; from their dress and appearance, they were not – at first sight – members of the Jewish class. They had studied

and – although not perfect – were well on the way to becoming part of the intelligentsia.

Their transport consisted of a canvas covered wagon pulled by four good horses. They seemed very keen to attach themselves to me; I was not overjoyed at this, for I like to travel alone on principle; but I could not stop them.

The hope that we might find reasonable quarters in the town of Wiasma was soon dashed; it was so bad that we could scarcely wait until morning to have this place behind us; a spot, in which we had been a month before, in fine autumnal weather, full of high hopes of success.

We moved off in better weather and got to know our new travelling companions better. They seemed to appreciate travelling with an officer from the retinue of the Viceroy and paid me a certain respect.

I also wanted to convince myself – in the modesty with which I undertook everything – that they would help bring some more courage and hope into our journey. They had some coffee and sugar and offered to sell some to us quite cheaply.

At midday we made a lucky find of forage in a village; that was a great gift; we fed the poor horses, which ate with gusto, and took a goodly supply with us. Towards evening we spotted a small village on a hill and made for it. At least the horses were out of the wind and rain and had a good supper.

Here we found several poor French soldiers, sick and helpless, who had sought shelter in the huts. Two of these sidled up to our fire like ghosts and asked to be allowed to warm themselves a little. They looked awful and I felt very sorry for them; I gave them some hot soup, which they took with shaking hands and gulped down greedily. Then they curled up under my wagon and seemed to go to sleep; I didn't want to disturb them and let them lie. Next morning one of them was dead and the other dying.

On the next day, 1 October, Adam learned of rumours that Cossacks were raiding the road. His Israelite travelling companions took fright at this news, and began to drive faster, which Adam was unwilling to do because of his horses and his much heavier wagon. However, good fortune smiled on Adam when he met a group of French soldiers with three horses on their wagon: he haggled for some time before managing to secure a fine horse that was immediately harnessed up. His account continues:

Now we had four horses and made better speed; towards evening we reached the town of Semlewo. Here things looked really bad. The entrances were blocked with palisades and all sorts of obstructions and we had difficulty getting them to let us in. The small garrison were scared of being raided and were surprised to hear that we had come from Moscow. We found some miserable lodgings; we were almost always in such a state in the towns. At least, in the country we had fresh air; in the towns the atmosphere was poisonous.

As we reached Semlewo early, I went to garrison headquarters and found some good types there. They were most interested to hear from me all about the conditions in Moscow and of our experiences on the way back. 'I am really very surprised,' said the commandant, 'that you got here so easily, but I have to tell you, that you won't get to Smolensk; we hear that the Cossacks are stopping everything from twelve hours out from the city, and they're frequently on our backs here. We have to send out large military parties to find food and forage, for we have nothing here and our situation is miserable.'

'That's bad news,' I answered, 'but what do you want with me here? You say yourself, that you are short of everything, why do you want to add two more guests to your problems? I do not doubt the truth of that which you have been kind enough to tell me, but since I left Moscow I have heard the same story, and you have to admit, that the same dangers which lie before me, are behind me as well. No-one knows what Napoleon will decide to do and I cannot convince myself that I should stay here in indecision. I am determined to continue my journey to Smolensk.'

There were three French officers here, who had been lightly wounded at Borodino. They were now well enough to travel. They had been hanging around in Semlewo for days already. They listened to our conversation keenly; agreed with me and decided to join me on the journey.

We left Semlewo early in a cold mist and soon met a Chasseur à cheval, who was a sentry on the road. He looked gloomy and frozen and shouted to us in a deep bass voice: 'You'll meet Cossacks within a quarter of an hour!' But he made no effort to stop us. My new companions were visibly shaken. They said that to continue in such mist was dangerous; we should at least wait until it had cleared, as we might bump into the Cossacks before we were aware of them.

I answered that we should not let ourselves be so easily scared. The mist also hid us from the Cossacks; they wouldn't be directly on the road; that was how I interpreted their operational tactics. Anyway, I had not the slightest intention of talking them into coming along with me; I was not responsible for them and was acting in my own interests; they might do as they pleased, I was going on. That was what I did, and the officers trailed along, someway behind us, as slowly as snails.

We had not gone far, when our situation seemed really to be getting serious. An officer on foot hurried out of a side road to meet us; I slowed up a little. He caught up with us and asked us in French to stop. He was a tall, well-built man, of commanding speech and appearance. After the usual questions; 'Where have you come from? Where are you bound?' he began to tell us that he was: 'the colonel of a Polish infantry regiment, that is on the march here. Yesterday evening, I left the main road to spend the night in a chateau that I know. I found lodgings there and had no suspicions of staying there, as I had a strong military escort with me. But during the night I was woken by gunshots; the Cossacks had attacked in force; my men were captured after a brave fight, and I lost my horse and all my belongings. I escaped in the dark and, as you see, I have nothing else apart from my sword. You will meet my regiment; the Cossacks will let it pass – they always avoid combat with large bodies of infantry. It is a fine regiment and would fight to the last. Tell the officers what has happened to me and tell them to speed up their march; I will await them in Semlewo. If you have the courage to continue on your way, I wish you better luck than I had!'

So they parted company with the officer. His story caused Adam and his fellows to reconsider their plan. About an hour later they met the regiment, which was surprisingly still in good order and well-manned. The officers were disturbed to hear Adam's tale, and told him that the Cossacks had not dared to attack them, but all trains and wagons that they met were lost and fell into their hands. The escorts had defended themselves; some had been killed and the rest wounded or captured. All the horses following the regiment had also been taken. The Cossacks had taken post in a wood so that it was not possible for infantry to get near them. Adam goes on:

> So we parted. This tale certainly caused us to reconsider our plan; we could expect nothing good today. After about an hour, we met the regiment, which to our surprise, was still in good order and very numerous. They took up the whole road, and there were strong patrols to each side. The officers were very disturbed to hear my story, and told me that the Cossacks had not dared to attack them, but all train and wagons that they met were lost and fell into their hands. The escorts had defended themselves, some were killed, the rest wounded or captured. All the horses that had been following their regiment had also been taken. The Cossacks had then taken post in a wood so that it was not possible for infantry to get near them.
>
> This was now too much for the three officers from Semlewo who had dared to come this far. One of them turned to me and said: 'Now, young man, what do you say to that?'
>
> 'It looks very dangerous, but I am not turning back.' I replied.
>
> 'Allez,' he said scornfully, 'You are an idiot!'
>
> They had a small Russian wagon with three horses with them. As they were now in the middle of the regiment, they could not turn around. They unhitched the horses, swung themselves up on them and rode for Semlewo for all they were worth.
>
> Afterwards, I often thought about these three gentlemen, and whether that were as lucky as I was, to see their homeland again. I doubt it; they were not over-endowed with courage and resolution.
>
> After the regiment had passed, we went slowly and carefully on our way, and in half an hour we came to the site of the Cossack attack. Two dead lay in their blood, and the smoking wreckage of ammunition wagons and other vehicles showed where the fighting had been shortly before. I cannot deny that this scene affected our courage, neither can I conceal our relief that the Cossacks had vanished; we didn't see them all day long.
>
> Happy that my guardian angel was watching over me, I set my journey forth. I always seemed to come upon these battlegrounds after the crisis had passed. A couple of hours earlier or later and the situation might have been very different.
>
> Without further trouble, we moved on and towards evening we came upon a sizeable inn, off to the side of the road. I would have passed on, but the noise of a mighty row took my ear. I halted, listened, and established that a serious argument was taking place. Soon a well-known voice was heard. It was so loud, that you could have heard it from a quarter of an hour away. I clearly recognized that Swabian accent; I dismounted and went inside. Here I found the baggage of the Crown Prince of Württemberg. Some of the light cavalry

troopers of the escort had fallen out and were fighting among themselves. At my appearance, the noise gradually abated.

My Jews were there and added their voices to the row. They had been scared by the rumours yesterday and had hurried on and met the Württembergers. In the inn I made good friends with a royal horse-breaker, who was with the escort. He was an educated man, with whom I later spent many hours. I travelled on with this escort, which included the servants, some fine riding horses, vehicles and some mounted Jaegers.

However pleasant I found the company – for the Jews had also joined in – I could not help thinking, that it was always the larger convoys that were attacked by the Cossacks, and I was safer if I went on alone and less likely to be noticed.

On the tenth day of our journey the sky lightened up, the air turned mild and we enjoyed one of the best autumn days in the whole of October. There followed days on which one could discard one's overcoat and not even think of one's fur. Unhindered, we went on and reached a small village at evening, where we found good lodgings. The next day was the same; we wandered along in a large group without any alarms. With such good weather, we didn't even try to find a village. We set up camp at the most appropriate spot and sat around the fire, in the best of spirits, eating, drinking and talking until midnight.

On the twelfth day of the journey I hit a big snag; the horses' strength suddenly dropped off and my driver was difficult. We had great difficulty to get on and lost our company, as we could not keep up. We spent the night in a wood. Next day we met the Württembergers again and spent a pleasant evening in a chateau in a pleasant setting, that regaled us with a splendid sight as the sun set. At moments like this, one forgets one's past troubles and draws new strength.

On the 14th day we had to combat many problems. Our horses were so weak that they could scarcely walk. The harness kept breaking apart and to crown it all, we lost our way, lost our company and reached Smolensk with difficulty only at the evening. Here, we had put the greatest dangers and the worst problems behind us, but great difficulties still lay ahead.

What efforts it had taken us to travel 130 hours distance in 14 days! What distances still lay between us and our beloved fatherland!

In Smolensk Adam found himself in good health despite his arduous journey. He stayed there two days, having his harness repaired as well as possible, and laying in some supplies, although there was not much food to be had. Both men and horses benefited from the rest. Adam noted that Smolensk was pretty full of French soldiers, mostly stragglers and convalescents from the hospitals, and that there was no large garrison. He was not tempted to stay there long, and soon continued his journey:

On 10 October, with well-fed and rested horses, we set off again in beautiful weather and made good progress. I had taken the road to Minsk and aimed to go on via Grodno and Warsaw. That would have been the most direct route, but in Minsk I met new difficulties.

The first two days march from Smolensk to Minsk went very well. On the first night I found good lodgings in a pretty village, but on the second it was very bad. But you don't really bother about this sort of thing as long as you find some sort of shelter from wind and rain.

On 13 October we came upon two abbeys fairly close together. The first was for monks and looked very inviting from the outside, so we tried to find accommodation there. But right at the gate, a priest appeared and forbade us entry. His whole being radiated holiness, so we moved on. Shortly afterwards we came to a convent; here, no one barred our entry into the walled courtyard; the gate was missing. The main building was shut, so we didn't bother to disturb the nuns, but took up quarters in one of the outbuildings in the yard. We could at once tell, that we were not the first guests that had been here. It was wrecked and dirty and had neither doors nor windows. Here we had a peculiar, almost comical adventure, but it did not seem so funny at first.

As there were no stables, I had the horses let into one of the rooms in which there was not much to damage. Leading off this was a small cubby-hole with place for a bed – but no bed; the vet and the driver settled in here, using our small remaining supply of hay as pillows. I settled down in the wagon, as the room was too dirty and the night was mild.

Suddenly I was woken by a great scream of fear and the stamping of the horses. I felt sure that my men were being beaten or killed. With my sabre in my hand I jumped down from the wagon. By the pale glow of a light in one of the convent windows, I saw my horse dragging my driver around the floor by his hair. He had smelled the hay under the driver's head and tried to get it. Now the hair was snagged in his teeth and he could not let go. This is due to the fact that the driver had long, curly hair, that was in a bit of a mess due to our style of life. My vet tried to help, but as the horse kept walking backwards, pulling and pulling, and as the other horses were stamping around, he could not do the job alone. Even the two of us had great difficulties to free the driver. Thus our night's sleep, in the solitude of the convent, which we had looked forward to so much, was rudely disturbed. The driver got off with a few kicks and a shock. A Polack like that can put up with a lot!

The 14 October was an ominous day; we lost our way early on, went far astray and upset the vehicle, but did no real damage, and at midday we reached a small village, where we found food and forage in abundance. We thought that we could help ourselves, and the horses obviously enjoyed the hay. But we were soon taught otherwise.

A group of peasants appeared with the landowner at their head. They seemed very aggressive and wanted nothing better than to beat us up. The landlord came forward and asked me why we had left the main road? There were magazines there. This was not a military road and so on.

There was nothing for it but to outwit him. I acted more aggressively than the peasants. I shouted at them that I had left the road because there were insufficient supplies in the magazine there, as I had a train of 60 horses that were coming up behind. I had come on ahead to scout out the way and to find

French dragoons guarding Russian prisoners. Albrecht Adam. Author's collection.

quarters for the night. This story, and my confident manner, worked the trick.

They decided to negotiate. The landlord assured me that we could reach a large chateau easily before nightfall, where the lodgings would be much better than here. He painted a really rosy picture of it.

Initially I played the sceptic and took out a four-page map of Russia from the wagon and spread it out on the ground. I poked about on it and played the situation out as long as possible, so that the horses could eat their fill.

This ploy worked so well, that in the end they offered me money to go away. I rejected this indignantly; then wrote some lines of Italian on a piece of paper and gave it to him, saying that he could give this to a sergeant when my men arrived; they were Italians, who had great difficulty making themselves understood, but this would tell them to keep moving.

Thus we were out of a fix and went off with our well-satisfied horses as fast as possible. A good hour before darkness we reached the chateau that we had been promised. The lord and his wife were of the educated class. I entered politely; explained that we were lost and requested to be able to enjoy their hospitality until next morning. They welcomed me in and treated me as a not unwelcome guest. The food was very good.

We set off again next morning and that evening we found a very pretty little village off to the side of the road. My driver told me that everything was not quite what it seemed here. All sorts of men were creeping around the wagon, and he had overheard some remarks, which made him prick up his ears. I ought to be watchful and have someone else sleep in the wagon as well.

I told him that it was not so dangerous; they would scarcely murder me, and I could guard against robbery. As a precaution, I laid two loaded pistols on the seat beside me. My driver was right; during the night I felt someone fiddling with the box and heard murmured voices.

I did not move, but grasped my pistols and cocked them both, which they outside could hear clearly. At that, all fell silent; then someone tried to enter the wagon, putting his hand through the leather curtain. I gave it a heavy blow with the barrel of the pistol, whereupon he fell back; I then heard many footsteps running away. I was not disturbed again.

Next morning we met a poor Jew, who acted as our guide for some hours for a little money and led us back to the military road, that I had to follow according to my marching orders.

Since he had left Moscow, Adam had learned that leaving the military road was dangerous. In the two days he had been off the road, he had not met a single French soldier, and could thus have been murdered without anyone suspecting. Now back on the road, he found that what the landlord had told him was true: magazines had been set up on the military road. He continues:

We drew forage and fed the poor horses; it was just such a shame that they had almost died on the journey here. We went on wearily, but without event, for the next six days, until the 22 October, when we were three hours from Minsk.

It had taken us four weeks of countless difficulties and dangers to cover a journey of 200 hours. You can easily imagine what damage such a trip does to one's clothing and equipment. The condition of the horses was really pitiful; it broke my heart just to look at them. They were in such poor state, that they could scarcely walk. On that last day, it took them a whole day to cover the distance that a pedestrian could cover in three hours.

When we left Moscow, a beautiful moonlit night had followed a stormy day. Having escaped the perils of that day, we had sought out a quiet, secret camping spot, to hide from the eyes of men like thieves, not even daring to light a fire. Now, four weeks later, we were again camping, for the last time, under a starlit sky, also at the full moon. But how the conditions had changed.

After sunset we reached a small copse by the side of the road, in a pretty little spot where a fire burned brightly, and where I could see various cooking vessels. A lot of people seemed to be in a good mood there, and I said: 'I must see who those people are, they seem to be having a good time.' I got down from the wagon and walked over to them. I was astonished to find my previous Israelite travelling companions. They were also surprised and greeted me with joy when they saw who I was. 'Well, this is going to be a fine evening and we can all swap our memories!'

One of them drew a fine coffee set from his wagon and coffee was prepared, as they knew that I liked it. We added to the meal from our supplies and later we made grog. We were all very relaxed and the evening turned into a party, which went on until late in the night.

It is always a pleasant experience, in such a hazardous situation, to meet people who exhibit such loyalty. That is what these merchants did whenever I met them, and it was never with any selfish motivation.

It may have pleased them that I had showed none of the prejudice, that is generally shown in society to the Jews. This was not hard for me; I have always seen only the human being in a man, without regard for religion, nationality or class, and have always found it easy to make friends as soon as I recognised a good heart and fine feelings in anyone. This policy has never let me down.

The day after this meeting with the Jews (who begged me to stay with them if I should ever get to Glogau) I finally reached the sizeable town of Minsk. It was the evening of 23 October.

I stayed here for some days, to put some matters in order; to sell my horses (for a real song), because there was no way that I would be able to get on with those poor animals.

I could not expect to get new horses, so there was nothing for it but to go on to Wilna by post-horse.

The day after my arrival I called on the governor, who received me in friendly fashion and talked with me for a long time. He gave my papers to an officer of his staff, in order to have them signed and to make out the necessary passes so that I could get post-horses. When I had returned to my lodgings, I noticed that he had given me a route card, which took me via Wilna and Koenigsberg, and listed every post station through which I had to pass. The marching order was the same.

I went straight back to the governor and pointed out this error; I had asked to be allowed to return through Grodno and Warsaw. He looked at me seriously and said, very clearly: 'There is no mistake; this is what I intended. You cannot take that route! Go the way that I have given you. I wish you a pleasant journey!' I could see from his manner, that there was nothing to be done.

'Odd behaviour by this man. Why on earth does he want me to make such a diversion?' I said to myself. Then I bowed to the inevitable and set off. It soon became clear why I had been given this route in Minsk. Some days after I left the place, the advanced guard of the Russian army under Tschitschagoff's command out of Turkey, appeared close to the town. And in the second night of my journey to Wilna, the post commander was unwilling to give me any horses, as there were rumours that there were Cossacks in the area. If I had taken the road to Grodno, I would have run straight into their arms.

That second night, before he reached Wilna, Adam had what he would later call 'the most wonderful and joyful adventure of my entire journey'. He explains:

We were still two stations from Wilna, when I came to the post-house to change horses. In front of me was a loaded stage-coach, which attracted my attention, as the silhouette seemed familiar to me. But I thought no more of it and went into the post-house to register my name in the Post Book, as was required, until my horses had been changed. On the long benches, which ran round the walls, lay two officers covered in blue greatcoats. I thought no more of them and didn't want to disturb them, but I asked who they were. I was told that they were a French general and an officer of cuirassiers, who had arrived an hour beforehand. I climbed into my wagon and soon fell asleep, dreaming of my dear de Saive, when I was woken by a shout from outside my vehicle.

I couldn't believe my ears and thought that I was still dreaming, but again and again I heard: 'Mr Adam! Mr Adam!' I threw back the leather curtain of the wagon and saw the valet of my friend de Saive. He told me that his master had woken up just after I left and had signed his name under mine in the Post Book. He had ordered him to saddle up a courier horse at once and to ride after me until he caught me up. He added that de Saive was beside himself with joy at this wonderful coincidence. He would follow and hoped to catch me at the next post-house.

Anyone who understands the deep feelings that existed between me and this nobleman, who understood the emotions that attached me to him, the significant moments of my life that he had shared with me, always there at my side as partner and protector, will have some faint idea of the joy which I felt when I heard this in the middle of the night in a foreign land.

Was it the familiar shape of the coach, in which I had so often travelled, was it the two sleeping figures, which attracted my attention, or was it the mental image of de Saive of whom I was just dreaming? I don't know myself, but it was a wonderful meeting, with all the surrounding circumstances.

From then on I travelled at a walk, but it was not until we reached the next post-house that we met. The joy of our unexpected meeting was indescribable. From there we travelled together on to Wilna. Here, I spent the three happiest days of my journey; they went all too quickly. We had such a lot to tell each other! How many memories of happier days were awakened in these rest days. But dark thoughts for the future and for the fate of the army cast a dark shadow over our meeting.

De Saive had been sent by Prince Eugene to Wilna on business and was to stay there when I left after those three days.[3]

Wilna is a very fine town, and the lifestyle which existed there was of the liveliest; a great confluence of all sorts of troops. You could get anything here if you had the money. I improved parts of my costume and bought a new hat; I could not be seen anywhere in my old one.

To continue the journey with post-horses seemed to me to be too expensive. I feared that my supply of cash would run out. I thus made a contract with a Jew, to drive us to Koenigsberg for 40 Thalers. These people do all sorts of business, especially transportation. He had five horses, harnessed abreast, and we really moved along.

This Jew, I should say, was gifted with endless plots and stories, as are most people of his sort. You could well have believed that he had taken lessons from an Italian Vetturino. Luckily, I had learned how to handle such fellows; on one or two occasions it came to blows, as there was no other way to solve the impasse. Then we made it up again. It was always about money and swindling.

I had left my Polish servant in Wilna; he soon found a new master, with whom he went to Paris. Three years later, he visited me in Munich.

We left Wilna on 28 October, reached the Niemen at Kowno, and carried on up the right bank of the river to Tilsit. Here we left Russia. I shall never

Denis Davidov, Russian cavalry officer and extremely successful partisan commander. Author's collection.

forget that wonderful feeling that I had, when I bade farewell to the Russian border post.

There is little to tell of our journey from Wilna to Tilsit, even though it took us eight days. We usually had bad lodgings and bad roads, but the weather was still very fine. To my great joy, we met up with the baggage of the Crown Prince of Württemberg on the road again.

On 5 November we arrived in Tilsit. With the first step on the left bank of the Niemen, we were back on the soil of our German homeland, which we greeted with a joy and happiness that can only be understood by those who have lived among foreigners for a long time.

As luck would have it, the contrast between this first German town and the far bank of the Niemen hit me in the eye. I was quartered on a family of the educated class; a widow with three daughters, who competed in beauty, the freshness of youth and the grace of their manners. Their mother was still fairly young and her speech and manner was gentle and attractive. This was all in incredible contrast to the life, the houses, and family conditions that I had seen on the Russian bank of the Memel.

I was received politely, and invited to enter the family parlour, sit down and warm myself, until my room would have been warmed up. I was offered coffee. Initially, the atmosphere was a little frosty, as the French eagles on my uniform buttons and cuffs were repugnant to these ladies. Despite this, they were friendly, and became more so when they realised that under this French uniform there beat a German heart.

They were very attentive, looked after me very well and regretted that I would be with them only for a day. They would have liked me to stay longer, so that I could recover from the privations. That meant me going to the town commandant to obtain special permission; which he gladly gave me. I thus spent three pleasant days there, which did me the world of good, psychologically.

On the other hand, I had to wean myself gradually off the long, wild nomadic lifestyle, learn to sleep in a proper bed and to clean myself up. I was so hardened to the open air and rough weather, that after I returned to Munich, I worked for most of that hard winter of 1812–1813 in an unheated room.

Notes

1 This was the brother of the marshal.
2 13th Division, IV Corps.
3 The two friends never met again, but exchanged many lively letters. De Saive settled in Belgium, his homeland, as a farmer, and lived to a ripe and happy old age with his wife and many children. Finally, the strains of his earlier life caught up with him; he became lame and almost blind. He retained his love of art and of the church to his dying day.

Chapter 18

Winter in Latvia – the last phase

Hartwich, now established as Prussian ADC to Marshal Macdonald in Eckau castle, takes up the story of the Latvian front again, on 14 November.

I returned to HQ [in Stalgen] just as lunch was about to be served. The Duke of Tarento stood there in undress uniform, with a powdered toupé, and welcomed me to the gathering. He asked after my comfort, took my despatches, read them and discussed them with Colonel Terrier, his chief of staff, who then withdrew in order to answer them. We then went in to dine, and I was placed opposite the marshal. He conversed with me frequently in a most friendly manner and I had to give him a run-down on my family background.[1] Colonel Terrier came in with some prepared papers, which the Duke read attentively, making the occasional note on them in pencil, before handing them to Major Segnier(of the 4e Hussars) for delivery. I returned to Eckau at about 8 o'clock.

Next day, the Prussians attacked the Russians at Dahlenkirchen, Gallenkrug and Tomoschna; Macdonald advanced with seven battalions to Eckau; the Bavarians[2] were in Friedrichstadt. We took three battalions of Russian infantry and about 70 cavalry prisoner.

It was bitterly cold. The men were accommodated in Dahlenkirchen church and the surrounding buildings… the ice on the Duena could already support cannon… The fighting continued on 16 November, but was indecisive. We were now aware that the Russian forces opposed to us were much stronger than we were.

On 18 October we withdrew to Tomoschna. My general[3] sent me across to the Russian outpost at the Neue Mühle, as he had lost a valued keepsake of the Princess Pauline Borghese, a valuable box. The enemy were in position with four battalions and ten guns; I was received in most friendly fashion and almost drowned in brandy. Lieutenant von Goerbel, a Russian artillery officer, a Courlander who spoke German very well, promised to search for the item. Lieutenant General von Massenbach raided Friedrichstadt this day and had captured 300 men of Schmidt's Freikorps cavalry.

On 19 October Oberst von Hühnerbein succeeded in driving a Russian force into some woods at Wallhof, where they were forced to surrender to the Poles and Westphalians. Their artillery escaped over the frozen River Duena. On 23 November, a groom appeared at Corps HQ with an English thoroughbred, chestnut with white markings, as a present for Colonel von Horn from Marshal Macdonald, as thanks for his efforts at Dahlenkirchen.[4]

Hartwich left us with some observations as to Marshal Macdonald's staff methods: 'When any of us were sent off on a mission, we first had to repeat exactly what we had to do to the marshal. He listened intently and, if satisfied, dismissed us with a friendly: *"Partez, mon cher!"'* [Go, dear fellow!]

The 2nd Clash at Dahlenkirchen, 15 November. A village in Latvia, on the River Duena, 14 km south east of Riga. A Prussian victory for Colonel von Horn's 2nd Brigade group over part of General Steinheil's Army of Finland. The Russians employed ten battalions, five squadrons and many guns in this engagement; according to the bulletin, they lost 1,200–1,300 prisoners, including twenty-five officers, 1,500 muskets and fourteen drums. Apart from the Prussians, the 7th Division was engaged here this day. The Russians lost over 1,000 men; allied losses were 'light'.

The blockade of Riga, Latvia, 24 July–18 December. The Russians successfully resisted all efforts of Macdonald's X Corps.

As this desperate drama was being played out in the central sector, up in Latvian dreamworld, the young Prussian officer, Julius Hartwich recorded what was happening there:

> On 27 November I was again sent over to the Russian lines, to deliver some letters to the new Governor of Riga, Marquis Paulucci. Baron Essen had been removed and hauled before a court-martial for burning down a suburb of the city for no good reason.
>
> We stayed in Eckau, in comfort, until 19 December. Each morning I would drink my cup of coffee, which my servant brought to me in bed, then go to Colonel von Horn. Today, he was reading the daily papers and Russian bulletins, which he received from the outposts, who had found them scattered on the road by the Russians.
>
> Officially we knew that the Emperor had withdrawn to Smolensk; we regarded Russian reports of their victories as being just fabrications for our consumption and laughed at them. I usually had to translate them for the general[5], who sent them on to the Duke. Gradually, however, even the French began to lend credence to these reports. The general would stand by his map, tracing out the places mentioned and comparing the names of the generals reported captured with his table of army establishment.
>
> At this time, the differences between General von Yorck and the duke became more noticeable, as the failures of the French commissariat caused more frequent shortages among the troops, particularly of forage [for the cavalry]. In revenge, the French Intendant of X Corps, M. Chambaudoin, accused the Prussians of indulging in large scale smuggling [of forbidden English colonial goods].
>
> There was an open breach between the men; it was suspected that the duke wanted to remove von Yorck from command so as to have tighter control of the Prussians.

Looters attacked by a swarm of bees. Albrecht Adam. Author's collection.

One night…Colonel Terrier[6] arrived at von Yorck's HQ with despatches. The duty ADC woke the general, who came out to read them. One letter was full of personal accusations and insinuations against von Yorck. Von Yorck read it through, twice, carefully, then folded it up and laid it down behind him on the table on which he was sitting.

Terrier was apparently expecting some outburst of rage from the general, that he could use as an excuse to have him removed from command. But Yorck was cunning, and said that he would only reply next day. Terrier was nonplussed and just stood there. The general gave him a sardonic smile. Terrier tried again and asked what answer he should give the marshal? What had the general decided to do? The general just said *'De me coucher sitôt que vous serez parti'* [To go to bed as soon as you leave]. The baffled colonel then left.

One evening, after dinner with Colonel von Horn there was the habitual merry round of the officers of X Corps staff at Eckau, fuelled with the usual glasses of grog. On this occasion, a [French] Captain Salentin came up to von Horn and said that he wished to show him something. Expecting a joke, von Horn followed him over to a fine copper engaving on the wall. It showed a rampant lion standing atop a defeated hyena. Salentin pointed to the lion: 'That is the Duke of Tarento; that,' pointing at the hyena, 'is the General Yorck.'

The colonel's expression flashed from humourous to enraged. He stabbed his finger first at the lion and then at the hyena. 'That's me and that's you!' he spat out. He then grasped Salentin by the chest, opened the door of the room, threw him out and slammed the door shut behind him.

General von Yorck became more concerned about the strategic situation. The news came of Wittgenstein's advance, the losses of Oudinot, St-Cyr and Wrede; but of the *Grande Armée* we heard nothing. Lieutenants Behm and Menzisepki were sent off to Wilna to get news. Both came back within a few days; they had been unable to get through and had only just managed to avoid the numerous Cossack patrols by means of good luck.

On 18 December the Schmidt Freikorps attacked our outposts at the Wehrschen Krug...We began to make preparations for our withdrawal. On this day, Major von Schenck... returned from Wilna, to deliver to Marshal Macdonald the order from the Viceroy of Italy, to fall back slowly on Tilsit; the army would stand in Kowno.

Two hours later, another courier arrived from Kowno, with another order, telling us to withdraw as quickly as possible on Koenigsberg. It was dated the 9th of December, 12 o'clock midday, and stated that Kowno could no longer be held and was being abandoned. Next day I left Bausk with a frost-bitten fusilier in a sledge that I had 'commandeered', together with five horses and my servant, Lobes and plenty of supplies. In Bausk was Grandjean's division, including the Polish and Westphalian troops, who had come in from Eckau.'

Hartwich describes General Grandjean thus:

General de Division Grandjean was a small, unpleasant man. His chief of staff, Colonel Nowitzky, was a real joke; in his personality and mentality he was a gossip-loving washerwoman. Like all of Grandjean's ADCs he was closely related to him and they shared an intimate relationship. They called one another by the familiar '*tu*'; a rarity among the French. Here it was that I came to know a Prince Radziwill, who commanded a brigade of the 10th and 11th [Polish Infantry] Regiments.[7]

It was also here that I came to read the infamous 29th Bulletin, which Major von Schenk had brought from the Viceroy and which admitted monstrous losses.

We moved off on 20 December at 4 o'clock in the morning... it was unbearably cold. Marshal Macdonald had traded his plumed bicorn for a bearskin Colpack, as had many other staff officers. Many even wore bearskin coats and trousers, with the fur on the outside.

On 21 December we rested in Schawli... next day we reached Kielmy, where we bumped into two squadrons of the Isum hussars (grey uniforms) and the Isum hussars (blue and red)[8] in the town square. We threw ourselves at them and they fled; we chased them and took some 80 horses from them.

On 23 December we reached Niemokszty... wherever we arrived, the Cossacks had been there before us; and all of them had asked the way to 'Parischi'. To us it was clear that they wanted to get to Paris, but the French officers just could not believe that these sons of the Black Sea coast had even heard of their capital city. The poor inhabitants were closely interrogated as to where this mysterious 'Parischi' lay, some of them were beaten to extract the information. The [French] staff in every hut were studying their local maps furiously to find the place.

On 24 December I celebrated Christmas Eve with a bottle of wine in

Skaudwile. On 25 December we captured two Isum hussars in a sledge near Tauroggen. We found very comfortable quarters with a Polish depot commissar, who was well supplied with everything. The hussars that we had captured were carrying letters from corps HQ to General von Diebitsch in Memel. These gave us a clear insight into the strategic situation around us. General von Yorck was most pleased.

On 26 December we left Tauroggen and crossed the Prussian frontier at Meldiglauken, to the loud cheers of the troops. Tears came to my eyes when I thought of all that I had survived.

We marched on Piktupoenen.

The skirmish at Piktupoenen, 26 December. A small village in Latvia between Tilsit on the River Memel and Tauroggen. A skirmish between Prussian cavalry and a small force of Cossacks. This was the last action of any note, a pathetic whimper, of the Russian campaign, which had begun with such a dramatic show of overweening power, on the River Niemen, just six months before.

We bumped into a Russian picket and rushed them, capturing two battalions, a gun, an ammunition wagon and 60 cavalry. We learned that Tilsit was occupied by the enemy.

On 27 December Grandjean's division arrived in Piktupoenen. We entered Tilsit at 10 o'clock at night; the Russians had left. The astounded inhabitants told us that the Russians had been there for eight days and had conducted themselves perfectly.

Marshal Macdonald came in on 28 December... The Leib-Husaren had a clash with about 2,000 Kalmucks and a regiment of dragoons and lost quite a few men. We then entered Ragnit, where we stayed until 31 December. All hospitals in the place were full of unfortunates who had managed to drag themselves back out of Russia; most of them died.

I was sent off to the Russian lines to try to bring about an exchange of prisoners; it was here, from Colonel von Benckendorf, that I learned of the pact agreed between Generals von Yorck and von Diebitsch.[9]

At first, the Russians would not let me leave, as they feared that I would tell the French of this event and this might have negative consequences for the remaining Prussians, still with the X Corps. Eventually, they agreed to let me go, as I had promised to say nothing.

Back at X Corps HQ, I told General Bachelu the story agreed with the Russians, that the prisoners had already been sent back to St Petersburg and that nothing more could be done. I then met Marshal Macdonald walking down the street; he asked me where I was going. I replied that I wished to return to my battalion. '*Retournez! Je vous souhaite tout le bonheur possible pour votre personne, remerciez à tous les braves Prussiens pour la bravoure qu'ils ont montré dans les temps que je les ai commandé. Adieu.*' [Return! I wish you all the best, please convey my thanks to all those fine Prussians for the bravery which they showed while under my command. Adieu.] He then embraced me and kissed me.

From this it is clear that the marshal already knew of the Convention.

Napoleon had left orders for the remnants of the army to be rallied on the line of fortresses along the River Vistula: Danzig, Thorn, Graudenz, Plock, Modlin; to protect most of the Grand Duchy of Warsaw. This was just not credible, given the massive losses and the pitiful condition of the few survivors. To quote Segur:

> The rallying of the army on the Vistula had been illusory. The Old Guard numbered 500 combatants at most; the Young Guard was practically non-existent; of the I Corps there remained 1,800 men; of the II, 1,000; of the III, 1,600; and of the IV, 1,700. Moreover, the majority of these soldiers – all that was left of an army of 600,000 – were just about able to use their weapons. While we were in this powerless state the right and left wings of the army broke away at the same time, Austria and Prussia having deserted us; and Poland became a trap which could be easily sprung on us. On the other hand, Napoleon, who had never willingly surrendered anything, expected us to defend Danzig; and we were obliged to rush all the forces that could still keep the field to that city.

On 16 January 1813 Murat abandoned the wreck of the *Grande Armée* in Marienwerder to return to Naples; Prince Eugene took over command.

Notes

1 The marshal referred to Hartwich as 'Artwick'.
2 13th Infantry Regiment.
3 Von Yorck.
4 Von Horn's horse had been cut in two by a cannonball during the action.
5 General von Yorck.
6 Macdonald's Chief of Staff.
7 In the 28th Polish Division.
8 II and III Russian Cavalry Corps.
9 The Convention of Tauroggen.

Chapter 19

The central sector – build-up to the Beresina crossing

'In that case, there is no choice left to us but to cut our way through with our bayonets!'

In Dombrowna, in mid-November 1812, Segur tells us:

> The Emperor knew that his army was destroyed... That night we heard groaning and muttering, 'The misery of my poor soldiers breaks my heart! Yet I cannot help them, unless I establish a permanent base... But where can we rest without ammunition, food or artillery? I am not strong enough to stay here; we must reach Minsk as soon as possible.'

While he was speaking a Polish officer rushed in with the news that Minsk – Minsk, his storehouse, his retreat, his only hope – had just fallen into the hands of the Russians! Napoleon said coolly: 'In that case, there is no choice left to us but to cut our way through with our bayonets!'. Minsk fell on 17 November.

Napoleon stayed four days in Smolensk, mainly to allow the wreck of his army to close up. But in doing this, he allowed Kutuzov to gain much ground; in fact, the Russians overtook the allies in that city, passing to the south to take up position at Krasnoi ahead of them.

Up to Smolensk, Davout had formed the rearguard; now Ney's much-reduced III Corps took over this thankless task and the stage was set for one of the most famous acts of the entire tragic farce of 1812. Ney left Smolensk only on the morning of 17 November, although it is thought that he might have left the day before. This delay proved fatal for his unfortunate corps, as we shall see.

The raid on Minsk, 17 November. Capital city of Bielo Russia, in the central sector. A victory for Count Lambert's advance guard of the Army of the Danube, 3,600 men, which captured most of the 2,000 strong Polish garrison under General Bronikowski, 2,000 sick and wounded and a huge magazine of two million rations. Lambert's losses were light. This was a major blow to Napoleon's hopes.

The 2nd clash at Krasnoi, 14–18 November. A village in the central sector, 40 km south west of Smolensk. A victory for the Russians under General Miloradovitch (III, V, VI, VII and VIII Corps of Kutuzov's army), over the remnants of the *Grande*

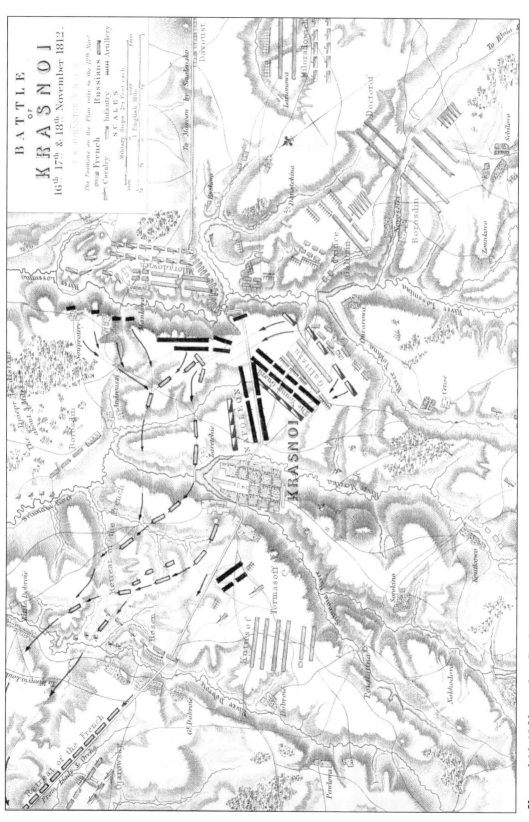

Krasnoi 14–18 November. By this point, most regiments were reduced to handfuls of men. The well-fed Imperial Guard were the exception. Over these four days, Napoleon's fugitive army ran the gauntlet of the Russians who adopted a flanking position and bombarded the enemy as they staggered past. Napoleon lost 39,000 men, 123 guns and fifteen eagles and colours. Marshal Davout's baton was also taken. The Russian losses are not clear. This is a Blackwood map.

continued...

Armée under Napoleon. This four-day action saw the remnants of the *Grande Armée*, some 50,000 men in all, strung out over a column four days long, hurry their way past the 90,000 Russians. The Russians claimed 13,000 killed, 26,500 captured, 133 guns and fifteen colours, standards and eagles taken, as well as Marshal Davout's baton. Kutuzov reported his losses as 700 killed and wounded. No serious effort was made to try to stop the fugitives; Kutuzov could have annihilated Napoleon here. For some reason he let most of them go.

The Russians recorded the losses of their enemy day by day as they hurried past through the artillery fire:

14 November. Advanced guard of the Imperial Guard and the 3e Leger – 400 killed, 3 generals, 24 officers and 1,220 soldiers captured.

15 November. Imperial Guard – 800 killed, 1 general, 20 officers and 1,100 soldiers captured.

16 November. The Viceroy of Italy – 1,800 killed, 1 general, 53 officers, 2,700 soldiers, 5 eagles, 24 cannon and 30 caissons captured.

17 November. The Prince of Eckmühl – 4,000 killed, 2 generals, 58 officers, 9,160 men, 6 eagles, 60 cannon and 30 caissons and one marshal's baton (M. Davout) captured.

18 November. The Duke of Elchingen – 6,000 killed, 100 officers, 12,000 soldiers, 4 eagles, 27 cannon and 18 caissons captured.

Totals – 30,000 killed, 7 generals, 2,052 officers, 26,180 men, 15 eagles, 133 cannon and 98 caissons.

Russian losses at Krasnoi were given as 2,000, which may be an understatement.

The entry for 18 November marked the effective end of Ney's III Corps. He assaulted the Russian army, but failed to make any impression on it and lost most of his corps for his troubles. Fate saved him by allowing him to slip off with his survivors into the dusk, back to the east. Setting up camp that night, he then abandoned his fires and marched north, seeking a way to cross the frozen River Dnieper, 16 km away. The ice on the river was too thin to bear horses or artillery, so all were abandoned. Next morning Ney's group of survivors were attacked by some of Platov's Cossacks, but beat them off.

A Polish officer had managed to slip through the Russian lines and brought the news of Ney's desperate plight to Prince Eugene and his IV Corps. Eugene turned back and miraculously met up with Ney, armed with a musket, and the 900 men that now represented the III Corps. The legend of the 'bravest of the brave' had been born.

Napoleon meanwhile, had decided to abandon his rearguard to save what was left of the main body of his army; a hard but correct decision. The Emperor's joy at the reappearance of Marshal Ney at Orscha on the evening of 21 November was great and genuine.

On 3 November, Davidov's group raided the main road between Anosov and Merlin and took Generals Almeras[1] and Burthe[2], 200 men, four guns and a number of supply wagons. That same day, they saw Napoleon in the midst of the Old Guard and skirmished, unsuccessfully, with them.

Three days later (18 November according to Six), Davidov's men captured General

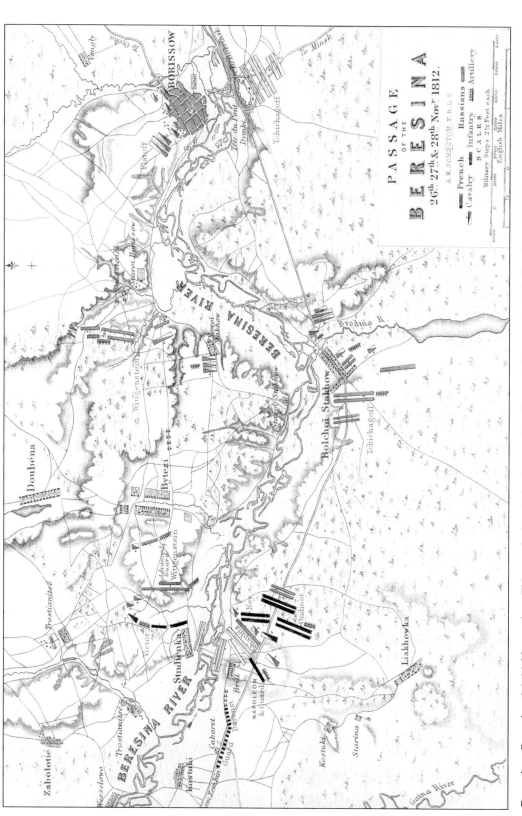

Beresina Crossing 26–28 November. *This was the last clash of any serious degree of the campaign. The four days of fighting have been compressed onto one sheet. Kutuzov had a chance to crush Napoleon here, but failed to risk it. Victor's IX Corps bore the brunt of the fighting and was largely destroyed. Blame for this failure to catch Napoleon was placed on Admiral Tschitschagoff, but there was plenty to go around all the senior Russian commanders. This is a Blackwood map.*

Martushewich[3] at Krasnoi, together with 700 prisoners and countless vehicles. Having only Cossacks with him, Davidov was unable to offer serious resistance to the Imperial Guard, who, with the Emperor in their midst, 'ploughed through [them] like a 100-gun ship [of the line] through fishing skiffs.'

Acording to Segur, Napoleon entered Orscha on 18 November with 6,000 Guards – all that were left of the original 35,000. By now Eugene's 42,000 had been reduced to 1,800; Davout's 70,000 to 4,000... As Davout said: 'Only men of iron could bear such hardships! It is physically impossible to hold out any longer! Human strength has its limits, and we have gone beyond them!'

But worse was to come. The Beresina had yet to be crossed.

And now the weather turned against Napoleon. The bitter cold, which had convinced him to order his bridging train to be abandoned and burned, now gave way to a relatively warm spell. The Beresina, a lazy river, meandering through swampy banks, thawed; the ice would no longer support even a man. It became a serious obstacle again.

Luckily for Napoleon, the true state of his army was not known to Kutuzov, who was following slowly, some distance behind him. Even more luckily for the Emperor, his Commander of Pontonniers, General Count Jean-Baptiste Eble, had disobeyed his orders to destroy all the bridging equipment. He had kept two field forges, two wagons of coal and six wagons loaded with beams, nails, clamps and tools. Also, each pontonnier still carried his tools and a quantity of nails. In the coming days, these, and the dedication of the French pontonniers, would provide the golden escape route for Napoleon and his men.

General Count Poitr Pavlovich Pahlen, of the Army of the Moldau, had learned from French prisoners on 22 November that Napoleon was close by and would try to cross the Beresina at Borisov very soon. He sent news of this to Tchitschagoff and to Kutuzov. Neither believed him. Neither moved in for the inevitable kill with any semblance of urgency.

Bavarian General von Preysing-Moos' cavalry brigade had vanished by now. The surviving officers received permission to march with the Imperial Guard. His account continues:

> On 18 and 19 November we went on to Orscha and crossed the Dniepr there; as there was no room in the town, I went on for half-an-hour on the road to Minsk, where I found a barn to sleep in. From all those officers who still had horses, the Emperor formed a single squadron – 'The Sacred Squadron' – under his personal command and headed by the King of Naples.
>
> From 21st to 26th, the march (or more correctly the headlong flight) went on under constant enemy attack and pursuit. Colonel von Rassler and Major Gaddum, who were sick, were stabbed by Cossacks.

The first clash at Borisov, 21 November. A town in the central sector, on the left bank of the Beresina River, 58 km north east of Minsk. A Russian victory for Count Lambert's advanced guard of the Army of the Danube over General Dombrowski's 17th (Polish) Infantry Division. Most of Dobrowski's 5,000-strong division was captured. The Russians had now seized the vital bridge over the river at the cost of 2,000 killed and wounded. Next day, Tschitschagoff's Army of the Moldau closed up to the town.

On 9 November Denis Davidov's partisans raided Kopys on the River Dniepr, east of Orscha, taking some 600 prisoners. They now moved on towards the Beresina crossing points – the crisis of the entire 1812 fiasco was about to be played out. On 14 November, they raided an enemy outpost in the village of Belynichi, together with Lieutenant-Colonels Khrapovitsky and Chechensky. There was a sharp fight, but eventually the enemy decided to evacuate the place and set off in column towards the bridge over the River Oslik to Esmony. Once they were in the open, one determined Cossack charge, supported by several discharges of canister, broke them up; the rearguard was cut off, yielding three officers and 96 men captured.

The bridge over the Oslik had by now been demolished and the relatively warm weather had melted the ice covering. A party of Cossacks lay in ambush; the rest of the column was killed or taken. The day also yielded a field hospital with 290 sick and fifteen medical orderlies, a supply depot with considerable grain stocks and a collection of wagons.

> **The second clash at Borisov, 23 November.** A victory for the French General Castex's 5th Light Cavalry Brigade of Oudinot's II Corps, which retook Borisov from General Count Pahlen's brigade of the Army of the Danube.

Castex's determined raid scattered the Russian garrison, inflicting 2,000 casualties on the 3,000-strong garrison for the loss of 1,000. The Russians still held the bridgehead on the western bank of the river, so Napoleon was forced to find a new site.

On 23 November, Napoleon sent for General Colbert and asked him to show him the ford across the Beresina, which he had discovered on 13 July[4]. The *Grande Armée* recrossed the Beresina at the same spot at which the Red Lancers had crossed in their advance. The general was certainly possessed of an incredibly retentive memory.

> **The clash at Cholopenitsche, 23 November.** A village in the central sector, near Borisov. A victory for the Russians of Colonel Gerngross's brigade of Wittgenstein's I Corps, which overran Partouneaux's 12th Division, IX Corps four days later. The Russians claimed to have broken the square of the 126e Ligne here and destroyed the regiment.
>
> **The clash at Baturi, 24 November.** A village in the central sector, near Borisov. A victory for the Russian General Harpe's division of Wittgenstein's I Corps over General Daendel's 26th Division. Exact losses are not known.

Three Russian armies were now closing in on the *Grande Armée* as it stumbled towards the fateful Beresina River. They included Kutuzov's main army, Wittgenstein's I Corps, Steinheil's Finland Corps and Admiral Tschitschagoff's Army of the Moldau, coming up from Minsk to the south west. But this last army had detached 27,000 men to observe the Austrian corps under Schwarzenberg and brought only 31,000 to the Beresina. Bavarian General von Preysing-Moos recalled the events:

> On 26th we crossed the Disna and passed through the little town of Beresino in order to leave the Minsk road. The whole day we could hear heavy artillery and musket fire to all sides. It was clear to us all that we were approaching another catastrophe.

On 27th November we passed through Borisow and reached the site where they had just thrown two bridges over the Beresina, at exactly the spot used by Charles XII [of Sweden].

The scene was dominated by the pathetic hordes of stragglers, huddling in the snow and ice, waiting for a miracle to save them. For Preysing-Moos and a couple of other Bavarian officers, that miracle arrived and they crossed the river that afternoon, even though they lost most of their remaining possessions.

> **The battle of the Beresina crossing, 26–28 November.** Including the following clashes: **first Brili** (26 November), **Staroi-Borisov** (27 November), **Studianka** (28 November), **second Brili** (28 November). The dramatic escape of the remnants of the *Grande Armée* from the clutches of the three converging Russian forces.

General Claude-Juste-Alexandre Legrand, commanding the 6th Division in Oudinot's II Corps, was to be instrumental in enabling Napoleon to slip out of the trap. Wittgenstein led the chase from the east with his I Corps; he clashed with Legrand's division and the stiff resistance that he encountered caused him to stagger back a little, as he overestimated the strength and determination of the force opposing him. Kutuzov was some way behind Wittgenstein, off to the east, and Tschitschagoff was on the west bank of the river, around Borisov, south of the vital bridging site.

Meanwhile, the desperation of the situation had galvanised Napoleon's great mind into action. Learning that certain bridging tools and materials still existed, he planned to build two bridges over the river between the villages of Studianka on the east side and Brilowa on the west. The houses in the former village would provide the materials needed. As Napoleon now said: 'I have been emperor long enough; it is time now to be a general.'

Michel Ney, Duc d'Elchingen, Prince de la Moskwa

Born on 10 January 1769 in Saarlouis as the son of a cooper, Ney entered the 4e Hussars 'Colonel General' (later the 5e, then the 4e) in February 1787 as a trooper and worked his way up to captain by the time he left in December 1794.

He was involved in many military campaigns and actions and in March 1799 he was promoted *General de Division* after having distinguished himself at the capture of Mannheim by the *Armée du Bas-Rhin* under Bernadotte. Ney then served as a cavalry commander in the army *d'Helvetie-et-du Danube* in Switzerland under Oudinot. He was wounded at Winterthur and had to quit his field command. In October 1802 he was appointed minister plenipotentiary to Switzerland, where he occupied Zurich and signed the Act of Mediation with the Swiss government on 19 February 1803.

Michel Ney, Marshal of France, 'bravest of the brave'. Author's collection.

Despite having associations with Moreau, Kleber and Hoche – all Napoleon's rivals – he was well trusted by Napoleon. Ney had been a committed republican but was an ardent supporter of the emperor. In 1803 he commanded the VI Corps in the camp at Boulogne and he was created Marshal of the Empire in 1804. In 1805 he was created *Grande Aigle* of the *Legion d'Honneur* and fought at Austerlitz.

In the 1806 campaign he received several annuities paid from the governments of various conquered states for his deeds, although he was defeated at Guttstadt and Deppen by Bennigsen and was lucky to escape complete destruction. In June 1808 he was ennobled as the Duc d'Elchingen.

After extensive action in Spain, including an episode in which Ney burned and destroyed 27 towns as he withdrew from La Romana thinking he had been betrayed by Soult, a fellow commander, and a dispute with Massena that led to Ney being relieved of his command for insubordination, he took command of the III Corps for the 1812 campaign in Russia.

He fought at Krasnoi in August, where Neverovski's 27th Division escaped destruction due to Murat's stupidity, and at Smolensk, Valutina Gora, Borodino and Wiasma on the retreat. From Smolensk Ney formed the rearguard and was cut off at Krasnoi on 18 November. Then began his epic trek to escape and rejoin the rest of the army. When he at last cut his way through to Napoleon's side, the Emperor said: 'I would have given anything rather than lose you.' For this campaign he was dubbed 'the bravest of the brave'.

He again commanded the III Corps in 1813 and after the retreat he returned to France to recover from his wounds, but he served throughout the 1814 campaign. By now his loyalty to Napoleon had largely evaporated and he was in the forefront of these advocating his abdication. He accepted service under the Bourbons and was created Peer of France and appointed to command the 3rd Military Division. He was sent by them to stop Napoleon's return to Paris in 1815. Ney promised to bring Napoleon 'back in an iron cage', but at their first meeting the old magic worked once more and Ney changed sides again.

He was rewarded with a vital command, but failed badly at Quatre-Bras on 16 June. His poorly coordinated assaults at Waterloo contributed to the French defeat there two days later. Ney was arrested by the enraged Bourbons, court-martialled, tried by a jury of his peers, convicted of treason and shot on 7 December 1815 in the Luxembourg Gardens in Paris.

The *Grande Armée* owed its salvation to the foresight of General Eble, and to the dedication of his 150 pontonniers, many of whom died in the icy waters of the Beresina as they built these two bridges across it. To mask his plans from the immediate enemy, on both sides of the river to the south, Napoleon staged a diversion. On 26 November he sent General Junot, with the remnants of his VIII (Westfalian) Corps, to the area of Borisov to make loud and obvious bridging attempts. Local Russian peasants were leaked the information that this was the Emperor's chosen bridging point. This information was passed quickly on to Wittgenstein and was regarded as credible. The main Russian forces thus remained in this area and only light Cossack patrols were left to observe the Studianka site.

It was at Staroi-Borisov, on 27 November, that General Count Louis Partouneaux's 12th Division of Victor's IX Corps was surrounded by the Russians of Wittgenstein's corps and surrendered. He was personally blamed for this by Napoleon and not re-employed by him. His career flourished under the Bourbons and he died in 1835.

Some idea of the state of this once-great army may be gleaned from the fact that the entire VIII Westfalian Corps spent the night in one house in Borisov during this operation. That same day, Napoleon had some rafts built; he also sent a detachment of cavalry wading through a shallow spot in the Beresina, each with a Voltigeur behind his saddle. Some 300 infantry ferried themselves over the river on the rafts and together, these men drove off the Cossack patrols. The construction of the two bridges began with feverish haste at eight o'clock in the morning; the river was about 100 metres wide at this point.

Victor Perrin, Marshal of France, Commander, IX Corps. Author's collection.

The bridges were sited about 200 metres apart. The northern one was to be for artillery and cavalry, the other for infantry. The infantry bridge was finished at one o'clock in the afternoon; that for the artillery was ready by four o'clock. The two structures were fragile; their surfaces often dipped under the level of the water under their loads and each had to be repaired on several occasions.

Oudinot's II Corps (5,600 infantry, 1,400 cavalry and two guns) was rushed across and took post on the west bank, facing south. Their aim: to fend off any Russian attack and to keep the vital withdrawal route to Sembin open. Soon, Tschaplitz's 5,000-strong advanced guard of Tchitschagoff's army came up from Borisov; but Oudinot's men held firm, supported by the fire of a fifty-gun battery that Napoleon had set up on some high ground east of Studianka. As fast as possible, Ney's III Corps and the Imperial Guard doubled over the river to join Oudinot. The Russian assault was beaten back; the way to the west was now open.

By midnight on 27–28 November, all formed units of the *Grande Armée* had crossed the Beresina using these two flimsy bridges. Only then was the great mass of stragglers and fugitives allowed to cross. The regimental history of the Baden Hussars recounts events on 28 November as follows:

> Colonel von Laroche charged the Russian infantry, which had formed square and had their artillery with them. He also commanded the Hessian Chevau-legers and these followed his regiment at a trot. The battalion of the 34th Russian Inf.-Rgt [sic][5] fired a volley only when the hussars were very close. Despite this, the square was broken, the infantry either cut down or captured. After the hussars had handed over 500 prisoners to the Chevau-legers, they went after a string of enemy infantry in extended skirmishing order. They then fell on the Nizhoff and Voronesch Infantry Regiments and the Depot Battalion of the Pavlov Grenadier Regiment. Soon after this, two squadrons of enemy Kuerassiers [a provisional regiment made up of depot troops] appeared; Laroche gathered in his hussars and charged them.
>
> In the wild mêlée, Sergeant-Major Martin Springer[6] of the hussars, although wounded already by sabre cuts and bullets, went to the aid of Colonel von Laroche[7] and cut down his opponents, thus freeing the colonel.

As the Germans were fighting the Kuerassiers, they were taken in flank by a Russian hussar regiment,[8] which sealed their fate.' The official report by General Wilhelm Graf Hochberg[9] recorded the events as follows:

> The Hussar Regiment was almost destroyed in this honourable combat. Only 50 horses out of 350 returned over the Beresina. The brave Chevau-legers shared the same fate. It was a stroke of destiny that these two fine regiments were able to close their battlefield careers with such a fine action which saved the lives of so many of their comrades by their sacrifice, in this campaign, where the deprived cavalry, in the bitter climate, were facing their end.

The fight went on for five hours until darkness fell, after which the Russians ceased their assaults. The cost had been heavy. The Baden Hussars and the Hessians had effectively been destroyed. Only fifty hussars were still present. The Baden infantry brigade now consisted of twenty-eight officers and 900 men. The Berg infantry brigade had only Colonel Genty and sixty men. The 28th Polish Division counted just 300 men. But they had bought the time required of them. Of the two Saxon regiments, 109 men remained.

Marshal Victor, and Generals Damas, Gauthier, Girard and Fournier were wounded. In the dreadful scramble to get back over the bridges to safety, Colonel von Dalwigk, commander of the Hessian Garde-Chevau-legers, became separated from his men and was pushed into the icy river by the crush. A Hessian driver recognized the colonel by his white greatcoat and pulled him out. Lieutenant Lippert, of the same regiment, was unable to reach the bridge, so he and one of his troopers swam their horses across.

At midnight, the IX Corps began to withdraw over the river. General Wilhelm Graf Hochberg of Baden was one of the last to cross on the morning of 29 November; the bridges were then fired. About 10,000 unarmed refugees on the eastern bank, men, women and children, fell into Russian hands, to say nothing of the vast collection of booty, including the imperial treasure chests. The surviving German cavalry of IX Corps was detailed for orderly duties in Victor's headquarters because, as of this day, they were too weak to be of further tactical use.

The infamous 29th Bulletin contained not one word of praise for the efforts of the Poles and Germans of IX Corps. In mid-December 1812, the IX Corps returned through Kowno 3,500 strong; in four months they had lost almost ninety percent of their strength.

The good General Daendels survived to become governor of the fortress of Modlin, where he capitulated on 25 December 1812. In the Waterloo campaign he served in the Anglo-Dutch army.

Russian losses on 27 and 28 November here are estimated at 4,000. French losses are generally put at 13,000 men, four guns and two colours. On 29 November the Russians took a further 5,000 prisoners, twelve guns and hundreds of vehicles.

Thus ended one of the most tragic and dramatic rearguard actions in military history. The survivors of the *Grande Armée* were now allowed to drag themselves out of Russia with little further interference. On the Russian side, once full realisation dawned of the chance that had been missed, recriminations began to fly. The upshot was that Admiral Tschitschagoff was blamed for the fiasco. It should be remembered, however, that Tschitschagoff was not the only Russian commander to ignore Count Pahlen's information.

On 16 November, Denis Davidov received the following note from Colonel von

Toll, an officer on Kutuzov's staff, in the village of Somry:

> The whole French army is on the march towards Borisov. You will do well to occupy Ozyatichi quickly and open the road leading to Borisov through the woods. It is desirable that this point be occupied completely and that patrols be sent out along the Borisov highway. Orlov has been dispatched with 150 Cossacks towards Tchitchagov; try to open communications with him. You will thereby earn the favour of the field marshal. All your brave men will be rewarded.

Having made his own tactical assessment of the situation, Davidov decided to ignore von Toll's advice and to march to occupy Smolevich, between Igumen and Minsk, to try to block any attempt by Napoleon to march north west to retake that depot city. In the event, Napoleon passed north of Minsk and made for Wilna.

Having arrived in Borisov, Wittgenstein was overcautious in tackling the remains of Victor's IX Corps on 28 November, as they defended the two vital bridges over which the viable wreckage of the *Grande Armée* escaped. For his own part, Kutuzov, not believing the real degree of destruction of Napoleon's army and having a healthy respect for his opponent, hung back at Kopys, some distance upstream from Borisov and on the eastern bank, and let events take their course. Tschitschagoff, isolated from the other Russian formations on the western bank of the Beresina, was blamed for allowing Napoleon to escape, but it seems that there was enough guilt to allow everyone to have a share. Kutuzov's tardy pursuit of Napoleon in 1812 has been a perennial subject for discussion ever since.

Davidov's partisan group were now (1 December) redirected to pursue the enemy army through Borisov, Logoisk, Ilya and Molodechno. These Russians were now in Poland and the natives were very hostile to them. Our Bavarian commentator, General Preysing-Moos, continued his adventure:

> At 7 o'clock in the morning of 2 December, accompanied by just a few officers, I reached a bridge near the village of Ilija. By the bridge was a mill, burning fiercely. I had to make a detour and – without knowing it – walked across a pond, hidden under the snow. My companions, and a large number of soldiers with small Russian ponies, were all safely across, when the ice broke under me and the horse I was leading.
>
> Up to my waist in water, frozen to the marrow and weighed down by my wet fur coat, I could not help myself. This went on for about half an hour; I saw my horse and my companions dead in the water. Then a shout went up that a general was in the water and my ADC, von Flotow, and my servant rode back and dragged me out. They took me to a nearby hut and were busy exchanging my wet things for other rags, when the cry: 'Cossacks!' went up.
>
> My companions hoisted me onto a horse, but then I found myself surrounded by about 20 Cossacks who shouted 'Pardon' to me. A few paces away was a whole regiment of Cossacks. An officer who spoke some German came up and asked me, very politely, to accompany him to General Martinow, Platow's son-in-law and commander of the advanced guard of the Cossack corps. Martinow had a fire lit for me and gave me some brandy, which revived me.
>
> Meanwhile, several regiments of Ulans and Cossacks, with infantry and artillery, passed by. The general gave me a demonstration of their discipline, in that he had several miscreants beaten with small rods. Many officers from

the passing column came up to see a Bavarian general; all were polite and sympathetic to my plight, especially a Lieutenant-Colonel Baron Igelstrom, commander of a regiment of Ulans[10] and a Courlander, who gave me a piece of bread, some meat and his only pair of gloves. He also insisted on giving me – despite my protests – eight ducats.

After two hours an order came that I should be taken to General Platow; I met him at the edge of the village. Due to sickness, he was in a troika; after talking with me for some minutes, he ordered one up for me.

We passed by some 300 of our prisoners and a lot of wounded who had been stripped and were dying. After midnight we reached a village, where I was shown into a hut with two Cossacks and some straw.

As soon as day dawned, on 3 December, my two Cossacks beckoned me to follow them into the garden; here I found my whole escort, eating soup, of which they offered me a bowl in friendly fashion. It was a 'Cossack soup' with various types of meat; I found it very tasty. They gave me sun-dried Tuna fish, but I couldn't eat it. Soon I was called to Platow, where they gave me tea and some bread and butter; it was the only food that they had.

We then marched to the village of Latiga; on the way, we passed a very fine horse artillery battery commanded by Captain Bracke, a Courlander, who gave us some saugages and a package of biscuits. He also wanted to give me money, as we wouldn't get any for eight days.

On 4 December we again met a large convoy of prisoners; despite their obvious poverty, the infantry escorts searched them roughly and took what little they had left. I noticed that the infantry were much more brutal to the prisoners than the Cossacks.

At midday an order arrived that I was to be taken to General Kutuzov. Platow gave me as escort a Cossack officer, Strabusch, who had studied in Leipzig and spoke German and seemed to be a fine fellow. Seven or eight Cossacks came along as well. I mounted Flotow's horse and he and Auditor Ries were given small Cossack ponies.

We rode back to Latiga and met Admiral Tschitschagow's army corps; he and General Langeron each spoke with me for some time. The troops were very well dressed and held themselves well. The horse batteries were astoundingly well equipped; their teams were superb.

On 7 December, in bitter cold, we came to the headquarters in Radomirskowitschi at three o'clock in the afternoon. I was taken to the General of the Day, Kanawitzow, who took me to the commander, who was dining with all his staff. Many generals and ADCs were there; all were very kind, especially Prince Dolgoruki. At 7 o'clock I was taken to Kutuzov, who spoke with me for an hour. I found an oldish man, full of spirit and benevolence, to whom I owe thanks for my good treatment during my captivity. He had us paid 500 rubels. He allowed me to write not only to General Graf Wrede and my family, but sent these letters off by a special messenger.

As a special concession he designated Jaroslawl[11] as my place of captivity and gave me a letter of introduction to the governor there. The town was so full of troops, that it was impossible to find quarters, so General Oppermann gave us his own room...

On 9 December the temperature dropped to 26 degrees and the wind was fierce. We would have frozen to death in our rags, had we not come upon a castle at Nowidwor, where Count Udoladkowitz received us very kindly. Here were Kutuzov's cabinet, including Chief Secretary Fuchs, who had been in Bavaria with Suworow and wore the Order of Saint Hubertus[12]...

On 10 December we reached Minsk, where I was quartered on the Catholic Bishop, Dredenkow.

So much for the adventures of this Bavarian general and the condition of the Russian troops. Preysing-Moos returned to Bavaria in February 1814, commanded the 2nd Light Cavalry Division in 1815 and died in Moos on 25 November 1834.

On 3 December, at Molodeczno, Napoleon – according to Segur – said:

I no longer feel strong enough to leave all Prussia between myself and France. And why should I remain at the head of a retreat? Murat and Eugene are well able to lead it and Ney to protect it. It is absolutely necessary that I return to France, to reassure and arm the people and to ensure the alliegance of all the Germans.

He actually left two days later at Smorgoni. Berthier was also to stay with the army; this shocked him. Segur attributes this to it being the first time in sixteen years that he would be separated from Napoleon. Napoleon informed France of the success of his 1812 adventure with the notorious '29th Bulletin':

29th Bulletin, 3rd December, at our Headquarters at Molodetchna.

Until the 6th of November the weather was perfect and the movement of the army was carried out with complete success. On the 7th the cold set in; from that moment we lost several hundred horses at each night's bivouac. On reaching Smolensk we had already lost an immense quantity of cavalry and artillery horses. The cold became more intense, and between the 14th and the 16th the thermometer fell to zero. The roads were covered with ice, the horses were dying every night, not in hundreds but in thousands. More than 30,000 horses died in a few days; our cavalry was dismounted, our artillery and transport had no teams. Without cavalry we could not risk a battle; we were compelled to march so as not to be forced into a battle, which we wished to avoid because of our shortness of ammunition.

The enemy, marching in our footsteps of the frightful calamity that had overtaken the French army, tried to profit by it. All our columns were surrounded by Cossacks who, like the Arabs in the desert, picked up every cart or wagon that lagged behind. This contemptible cavalry, which only knows how to shout and couldn't ride down so much as a company of light infantry, became formidable from the force of circumstances!

But the enemy held the passage of the Beresina, a river 80 yards wide; the water was full of floating ice, and the banks are marshy for a distance of 600 yards, which made it a difficult obstacle to overcome. The enemy had placed four divisions at four points where they supposed the French army would attempt to pass. After having deceived the enemy by various manoeuvres on the 25th, the Emperor marched on the village of Studienka at break of day on the 26th, and, in the face of a division of the enemy, had two bridges thrown across the river. The army was crossing all through the 26th and the 27th.

It may be concluded from what has been said that the army needs to re-establish its discipline, to be re-equipped, to remount its cavalry, its artillery, and its transport. During all these events the Emperor constantly marched in the midst of the Guard, the cavalry commanded by the Duke of Istria, the infantry by the Duke of Danzig. Our cavalry was so reduced that it became necessary to form all the officers who were still mounted into dour companies of 150 men each. Generals acted as captains, and colonels as corporals. This Sacred Squadron, commanded by General Grouchy, and under the orders of the King of Naples, kept the closest watch over the Emperor.

His majesty's health has never been better.

NAPOLEON.

That put matters into the correct perspective.

Notes

1 Commander 14th Division (vice Broussière), IV Corps.
2 7th Light Cavalry Brigade, II Cavalry Corps.
3 Chief of Artillery of Ney's III Corps.
4 Pawly, p48.
5 This should be 'Jaeger Regiment'; Russian infantry regiments bore titles, not numbers. The 34th Jaegers were originally in the 4th Infantry Division, II Corps, of the 1st Army of the West.
6 The brave Sergeant-Major Springer was rewarded with a commission and retired as a lieutenant of artillery in 1829.
7 Colonel von Laroche, badly wounded, was saved by some men of his regiment and returned safely to Baden.
8 The only Russian hussar regiment to be recorded as being in action at the Beresina this day is the Alexandria Regiment. This regiment was in General Tormassoff's 3rd Army of the West, attached to the 15th Division.
9 General Wilhem Graf Hochberg of Baden, as the only general officer left fit for duty, took command of the 'IX Corps'.
10 The Wolhynian Ulans.
11 Jaroslawl lies 248 km east of Moscow; many unfortunate prisoners ended up deep in Siberia.
12 The Order of Saint Hubertus was a Bavarian order.

Chapter 20

Wilna – Tinseltown revisited

'If I had been born on a throne, if I were a Bourbon, it would have been easy for me not to make any mistakes!' [1]

Captain von Soden of the Frankfurt Regiment[2] tells us of one of the oddest aspects of this island of apparent normality in the floods of the dissolution of the army:

On 22 November, the regiment climbed down the hollow way of the Ponary hill and onto the plain of Wilna. At this point, Wilna presented a peculiar scene. Seldom can splendour and need, pomp and misery, pride and despair have cohabited as at this point in this crowded town. With few exceptions, the entire diplomatic corps accredited to Napoleon's court was present. Hugues-Bernard Maret, the Duke of Bassano, presided over it all.

As nothing was yet known (or supposed to be known) of Napoleon's defeat, the glittering diplomats carried a carefree air and expressed the usual wonder at his deeds. Dazzling balls and receptions followed one another in rapid succession. The starving, freezing troops stared in amazement at the expensive coaches that trotted past, their richly dressed occupants wearing that air of pampered boredom, so peculiar to the diplomatic corps.

The governor of the city, General Thierry van Hogendorp, also kept an open house. The German officers were invited to balls and dinners, at which the luxury reminded them of Paris.

On 2 December Napoleon's birthday was celebrated with a parade, gun salute, the ringing of church bells and an illumination. A great, crowned 'N' in hundreds of lanterns, had been set up over the city gate; suddenly, it fell and smashed to pieces. We regarded this as an omen. In fact there were immense magazines accumulated in Wilna. But even now, the slovenliness of the French officials was showing through. The German troops were refused the rations to which they were entitled, so that their commanders saw themselves forced to storm the bread and brandy storehouses with armed parties. There were then bloody clashes with French troops, which the officials called up to their aid.

Time passed, and Captain von Soden's journal assumed a grimmer tone.

On the morning of 5 December, we found some frozen bodies, almost in a state of mummification. If one lifted a limb of one of these unfortunates and then let it fall back, it splintered apart, like glass.

On the afternoon of that same day, the division reached Ozmiana, a town

A grenadier of the Portuguese Legion. The infantry served in the 6th, 10th and 11th Divisions.
A plate by Martinien. Author's collection.

of several hundred wooden houses. Most of the inhabitants – mainly Jews – had fled; the houses looked awful, but at least they offered some protection from the cold, even more so as the village lay in a shallow valley, under the biting east wind. During the march General Gratien formed us into column and had us fix bayonets. This precaution amazed us, for where should any enemy come from? For as far as we knew, the *Grande Armée* was holding them off at least twenty German miles away.

The atmosphere relaxed when we got into Ozmiana and no sentries were posted; everyone was sent off to find there own quarters, wherever they could. There was going to be an issue of rations – amazingly enough there was still food here – and even the pigsties were full; there were even some cattle. We were all busy lighting fires, when there were shots, the general alarm was beaten and, for the first time, we heard the dreaded shout of: 'Cossacks, Cossacks!'

A band of about eighty of these riders of the steppes, with two small cannon, mounted on sledges and commanded by the tireless Hetman Seslawin, had entered the town through an unguarded side street. As chance would have it, the farmhouse that they first entered was that in which General Gratien had set up his headquarters. He only just managed to rush out of the door and take refuge in the square of the Ducal Saxon regiment, which was on duty there. This unit now opened up a rapid, if ragged, fire on the Cossacks. These calmly replied by firing their pistols back at a range of only a few paces, then rode off. Once out of the village, they fired two or three rounds of canister and killed or wounded some 60 men who had run after them.

The Cossacks left behind a few dead, but no wounded, that we might have been able to interrogate. The immediate result was that General Gratien got all the men out of the houses – totally needlessly – and had them bivouac in the gardens of the town.

There now came a rumour that Marshal Lefebvre, commander of the Old Guard, had arrived in Ozmiana. Then it was said the Emperor himself was following him on foot. This amazing news proved to be true.

Colonel von Egloffstein, commander of the 4th Regiment, Confederation of the Rhine (the Ducal Saxon contingent) led his men into Kowno on 18 November after a strenuous march through a blizzard. They spent the night in a deserted monastery, with no doors or windows, but at least were issued with bread and brandy. It was here that stragglers brought the first news of the evacuation of Moscow. The regimental band was sent back to Koenigsberg.

On 20 November, the 4th Regiment set off for Wilna in blustery snowstorms; they reached the town six days later, and were overjoyed to hear that they would be given billets. However, the billets were not issued until ten o'clock that night and they were found to be written in French or Polish, which most of the men could not read. Some unfortunates did not find their accommodation until the next morning.

The regiment had already lost 120 men through exhaustion and 640 of those in Wilna were sick with dysentery, scurvy, lung infections and bilious fever. The twenty hospitals in the town were full, so the sick of the regiment were looked after in the billets. In a letter of 27 November, von Egloffstein wrote: 'I fear that we shall suffer the same fate here as was our lot in Spain[3]... Our young soldiers are very downhearted.... we can expect to perform no heroic deeds here.'

There was still no reliable news of the *Grande Armée*, but the Duke of Bassano issued a proclamation:

> The Emperor left a strong garrison in Smolensk and, having set himself at the head of his army at the Beresina, and having beaten the Russians at all points and destroyed Tschitschagov's army, will enter Wilna and take up winter quarters in Lithuania.

The 34th Division was now sent to Miedniky. Two ration wagons accompanied the 4th Regiment and the Light Battalion left three officers and sixty men sick in Wilna. The 4th Regiment now numbered 2,000 men. General Loison was now sick, so General Baron Pierre-Guillaume Gratien took command of the 34th Division. By 8 December the 4th Regiment's strength had dropped to forty officers and 998 men, but of these, only twenty-six officers and 213 men were fit for duty.

Two days later, Captain von Grayen and one hundred men of the regiment were wounded or captured by Cossacks, and later the entire 2nd Battalion were cut off and captured. A further twenty-nine officers and 800 men were lost at the hill of Ponari on 10 December, and next day Colonel von Egloffstein could muster less than fifty men under arms. By 21 December, von Egloffstein had gathered some 163 men of his regiment in Koenigsberg; a week later this had risen to 550, half of them without weapons.

Napoleon had left the army at Smorgoni on the evening of 4 December, and handed over command to Murat. At 10 in the evening he arrived in Ozmiana, escorted by the very weak remnants of a squadron of Polish lancers. He was travelling in a coach lined with fur and drawn by six Lithuanian stallions. Caulaincourt was at his side; the Mameluke Rustan and the interpreter, Captain Vukasovitsch of the Guard, were on the driving seat. Duroc and Mouton were in a second sledge. Doctor Geissler recalled the moment:

> Napoleon wore a green fur coat trimmed with golden tassels and a matching cap. He looked serious but healthy. We watched this mighty mortal from a few paces distance, while Generals Gratien and Vivier [sic], and the colonels of the regiments stood in a half circle around him. The talk was of the deep cold and the recent attack. This upset the Emperor, who thought it meant that the Russians already knew of his departure...
>
> The Emperor was travelling under the unlikely name of 'Monsieur de Rayneval'. The Cossack raid had alarmed the Emperor, and he took some squadrons of Neapolitan cavalry with him from Wilna to Kowno; the vast majority of these men died on the way.

The 6th Regiment of the Confederation of the Rhine was made up of the contingents of the mini-states of Schwarzburg (1st Battalion), Waldeck and Reuss (2nd). Colonel von Heringen, of Waldeck, commanded the regiment, which was part of the Princes' (34th) Division, XI Corps and entered Russia in late November, as escort to a military treasury chest. On 2 December they staggered into Kowno in a snowstorm. Despite being relatively well-fed, they lost several men from exhaustion on the march.

Their accommodation was a deserted monastery outside the town; it had no doors, no windows, no ovens and even the floorboards had been torn out. To their general relief, they were ordered on 5 December to march on to Wilna. This was an eight-hour march, during which more men were lost; some just falling out of the ranks to slump down and sit in the snow until they froze to death. Those who could still march just stumbled on by. They ran into more and more isolated stragglers, heading back to the west. Then the entire diplomatic corps, the Duke of Bassano in the lead, swept past them. The unfortunate men staggered into the village of Riconti, two hours from Wilna, that evening. All they found was empty houses. Colonel von Heringen addressed his men:

> Comrades. I have led you so far and looked after your needs as well as I could. But now my powers have ended. Find a place to sleep where you can. Try to find food where you can. Your commander is helpless himself and does not know where to lay his weary head.

Later that night, another contemporary account confirms this:

> On 5 December, in the village of Riconti, just west of Wilna, on the road to Kowno, Napoleon met the 6th Regiment of the Confederation of the Rhine, in the Princes' Division. The officers of the regiment were gathered together in a barn; a small man in a green fur coat came in, stepped up to the fire and asked, in authoritative manner: *'Quelles sont ces troupes?'* Captain Wiedburg, who noted that this must be a senior officer, answered this and several other questions, and then suggested that he should waken Colonel von Heringen. The small man forbade this with the words: *'Non, camerade, ne le derangez pas.'*

The 6th Regiment of the Rhine re-entered Kowno on 8 December; since leaving it three days before, it had lost half its strength. By 6 December, the entire Princely Division, gathered in the town of Ozmiana, was 10,000 men strong; at the end of October it had been 14,000. That same day, at Miedniki, Napoleon burst out to Maret, the Duke of Bassano:

> I have no army any more! For many days I have been marching in the midst of a mob of disbanded, disorganized men, who wander all over the countryside in search of food. We could still rally them by giving them bread, shoes, uniforms and arms; but my administrative personnel has not provided against anything of the sort, and my own orders have never been executed.[4]

More self-pity. Why had he not ensured that his orders had been properly carried out? This is, surely, the most basic principle of good management.

On the night of 6 December, the survivors of the *Grande Armée* began to shuffle through Ozmiana. Up to the crossing of the Beresina, there had been some semblance of order in many regiments; now this had all been swept away. The sight made the senses reel. There was now nothing more than a herd of half-crazed refugees, motivated only by the barest urge of self-preservation. As they flooded past the survivors of the Princely Division, the Germans gave them their own bread; without a word of thanks, it was snatched by filthy, skeletal hands and devoured at once.

As the corps of Oudinot and Victor had also been destroyed at the Beresina, the 600 men of the Princely Division, still under arms, were the last disciplined, armed formation between the Russians and Europe. At midnight that night, the order arrived for the 'division' to march back to Wilna. Ozmiana was set on fire and they trudged off in the bitter darkness. The Ducal Saxon Regiment and a battery of artillery formed the rearguard. The starving horses could no longer pull the guns; they collapsed on the icy road and the battery was left for the Russians. Long fuses were left smouldering into the ammunition wagons in the hope that they would take plenty of Russians with them when they went up.

The men of this vanishing division had been healthy and well fed up to now; but the shattering events of the last day seemed to have crushed their spirits. Silently, one man after another dropped out of the ranks and sat down in the snow; in a few minutes they had frozen to death. When the dwindling column reached a bivouac fire at Miednicki, scores of men fell out of the ranks and ran to it, and nothing could induce them to move on.

The terrible shock of being confronted with the truth about the state of the once-mighty *Grande Armée* had the same effects on the Bavarian VI Corps, when it rejoined them after coming down from Polotzk. General von Wrede recorded that after marching only three or four hours in the presence of the wretched survivors of the main body, and despite all his efforts and those of the senior officers, he had lost half his strength and six guns.

By the evening of 7 December, the remnants of the Princely Division (now down to 500 men) reached Wilna; there had been 10,000 of them in Ozmiana two days earlier. But the city had changed since they were last there. The expensive restaurants, where famous Parisian chefs had plied their trade for high prices were empty, the diplomatic corps gone. The streets were full, it was true, but there was a palpable air of fear, despair and confusion.

Murat, King of Naples and now commander of the shambling mobs flowing thought the city, was in Wilna, as were marshals Berthier, Bessières, Davout, Gouvion-Saint-Cyr, Mortier, Ney and Victor. Ney was the only one of them to make any attempt whatsoever to bring some order to the chaos that they witnessed.

In Wilna the magazines still included bread, biscuit and flour for 100,000 men for forty days; as well as meat for thirty-six days, much of it in the form of live animals. There were also large stocks of brandy, beer, vegetables, grain and forage, 42,000 pairs of shoes, large stocks of uniforms, greatcoats, saddlery and harness, 34,000 muskets, great stocks of ammunition and even a large herd of remounts under General Boercier. The vast majority of these supplies were abandoned without the surviving soldiers even knowing that they were there. But in some cases, the news got about and vast mobs of freezing, starving men besieged the stores.

At one, a French general appeared at an upper window and said: '*Entendez-moi, je suis general!*' [Listen to me, I'm a general!] Back shot the answer: '*Il n'y a plus des generaux, il n'y a que des malheureux!*' [There are no more generals, there are only unfortunates!] The general quickly saw that there was nothing for it but to push out sacks of bread and flour through the hatches into the frenzied mob, which at once dissolved into a heaving sea of fighting, scrambling men as each sought his own share.

But this was not enough. The desperate mobs stormed the storehouses and sacked them, in which process, three-quarters of the stocks were destroyed or spoiled, and the storehouses themselves went up in flames. The worst scenes took place in the brandy stores. Many men knocked back as much spirit as they could, as fast as they could, then fell senseless to the floor, or in the street, and died.

For two days, the Princely Division rested in Wilna; at the end of that time, there

A drum major of French line infantry; his uniform and shako well adorned with gold lace. He wears red plume, epaulettes and sabre fist strap. A plate by Weiland. Author's collection.

were some 1,000 men back in the ranks of the Ducal Saxon Regiment and about 800 in the Frankfurt battalion. Only about a third of these were capable of performing duty; the rest were suffering from wounds or frostbite. The state of the other regiments was even worse. It was here that General Lioson joined his 34th Division from Koenigsberg, as replacement for General Joseph Morand, who had been retained as governor of Pomerania. His command now consisted of some 3,000 armed men. There was no cavalry, except some sixty Bavarian Chevau-legers with the Bavarian General von Wrede, the last remnants of the 40,000 horsemen with which Napoleon had started this disastrous adventure.

When the news of Napoleon's departure spread among them, even those veteran warriors were unsettled, and soon fell into disorder. 'Accustomed to being directly commanded by the conqueror of Europe, they scorned to serve another', wrote Segur.

On 8 December Seslavin's partisans mounted an assault on Wilna, which was beaten off and Seslavin was wounded.

On the evening of 9 December the rest of the Bavarian VI Corps, the rearguard of the army, which had been holding back Wittgenstein's corps, stumbled into Wilna. They were closely followed by the Cossacks. Wilna was to be evacuated without a fight. The troops were ordered to draw bread for four days from the surviving storehouses. Again, the French storekeepers tried to deny all non-French units access to their stocks. Again there were violent scenes. In one instance, there was a gunfight between some of the Old Guard and some Germans, in which several were killed. The temperature was minus 27 degrees. Lieutenant Jacobs of the Frankfurt Regiment left this record:

> Bread was distributed in the marketplace, but it was frozen solid and inedible. Some soldiers attempted to thaw the loaves out in the bivouac fires. This experiment usually went badly wrong and the loaves were burned. All around us lay dead and dying; many with gangrenous, frost-bitten limbs. From all sides we could hear the groans and curses of the unfortunates. It was a night of pure horror, but we were all so numbed by our circumstances, that we scarcely noticed the drama that was played out before our eyes. All feelings of sympathy and mercy had been driven out of us. If, as often happened, one dropped dead around the fires, the only reaction was that there would be a scramble among those still living to grab a seat on the corpse, which was warmer than sitting on the snow.

By the next morning, the strength of the men in the ranks of the Ducal Saxon Regiment had fallen to 700 men; that of the Frankfurters was down to 600. The 5th Regiment of the Rhine[5] had been escorting a convoy of treasure wagons back to Koenigsberg; two of them lost their teams in Kowno and it was decided to let the men take what they wanted, rather than leave it to the Russians. There were scenes of wild conflict as hundreds fought for the coin. Some members of the Imperial Guard tramped past the scene and were invited to join in. 'The Guard does not rob their Emperor!' came the retort.

They were joined by the remnants of many regiments, which by now consisted only of a handful clustered around their eagles. The troops paraded at dawn, but only moved off an hour later. Behind them, in Wilna, they could hear shots and the sounds of sporadic combat as the Cossacks gradually spread into the city. For some inexplicable reason, Ney felt that he had to hang on to Wilna until 10 o'clock!

As the west gate of the place was blocked by a mass of abandoned vehicles of all sorts, the column had to defile through side streets and alleys to reach the road to Kowno. Some 15,000 prisoners were taken in the city.

But the refugees from Wilna then found this road blocked by crowds of refugees. The cause was the Cossack Pulks of Lanskoi, Seslawin, Tettenborn and others, some thousands, drawn up on a small hill to one side of the road, with four cannon mounted on sledges.

Fearing a cavalry assault, Loison ordered his division to march in a thick column. The Cossack gunners rubbed their hands with glee. This was a target that they just could not miss! Rapid salvoes of canister ripped through the column; one of the guns was driven off to the rear of the mass of fugitives and fired down the axis of the road into them. The Frankfurt Regiment was the rearguard and suffered very heavy casualties this day.

One hour's march west from Wilna lay the village of Ponary – and a steep hill. This obstacle – minor in any other weather – was a major challenge at this point. The road surface was frozen solid and polished to a glass-like state. None of the divisional vehicles (which included a number of wagons loaded with gold and coin) could be brought up the slope.

General Loison now thought to have the division form into battalion squares and to retire in chequerboard formation, alternately firing and moving. Under better conditions, with troops with firmer spirit, this might have had a chance. On 10 December 1812, with the Cossacks in thousands swarming left and right, it didn't. The 34th Division broke apart and dissolved; many of the squares were broken and cut down.

When Marshal Ney saw the chaotic mess on the hill, he gave orders for the cash wagons to be broken open and the money to be given to the troops. Even in this desperate predicament, greed caused many of the soldiers to stuff their pockets with gold coins and five franc pieces, so that they soon were so weighed down, that they could not run away from the ubiquitous Cossacks. Indeed, the extraordinary spectacle was seen of friend and foe, peacefully plundering the same wagons beside one another. Let us see how Segur reported this same incident.

> On the most exposed spot of the hill a colonel of the Emperor's staff, Count de Turenne, held the Cossacks at bay, disregarding their wild shouts and their shots, while he distributed Napoleon's personal treasury among the guards who stood within sight and hearing. These brave men, fighting with one hand and holding the riches of their leader in the other, succeeded in saving all of it. Long afterwards, when we were out of danger, each one returned the amount that had been entrusted to him: not a single gold coin was lost.[6]

Pure fantasy. Who would have possibly accounted for the money issued under such circumstances? Did all the grateful recipients survive the trials of war to repay the coins? Did not one of them spend even one coin to buy himself food? Shelter? Clothing? Transport? 'Fighting with one hand and holding the riches of their leader in the other.' Stirring stuff! Penny dreadfuls would pay handsomely for such copy.

The only way for the men of Loison's division to climb this notorious hill was to wade through the snow to the south of the road, where many of the vehicles were now ablaze. Once on the plateau, the survivors of the division were attacked by Cossacks and kuerassiers, but were able to beat them off. By evening they reached the village of

Mikiti, next day Zizmory. Denis Davidov, the intrepid Russian partisan commander, was also at this dramatic scene; he left this account:

> From Novi Troki to the village of Ponari the road was clear and smooth, but from Ponari, where the road branches off to Kowno, mountains of dead men and horses, a host of carts, gun carriages and caissons left barely enough room to get through. Piles of enemy soldiers, barely alive, lay in the snow or sought shelter in the carts, awaiting a cold and hungry end. My path was lit up by blazing wooden huts and hovels whose wretched occupants were being burned alive. My sledge kept bumping against heads, legs and arms of men who had frozen to death, or were close to dying. My journey from Ponari to Wilna was accompanied by a strange chorus of moans and cries of human suffering, which at times dissolved into something more akin to a joyous hymn of liberation.

In Zizmory on 11 December, the remnants of Loison's division bumped into Berthier's column. The 'Major General of the Army' accused Ney of losing his grip and retreating too quickly. Ney retorted that he would not withdraw again unless forced to do so by a superior force. Herewith the fate of the remaining Bavarians was sealed. They were to form the rearguard. They fought until their ammunition ran out. Only twenty men of the original 12,000 of the once-proud VI Corps lived to see Germany again, but they had secured the title 'bravest of the brave' for Marshal Ney.

On the evening of that same day, the remnants of the 34th Division reached the village of Rumszisky, near Kowno. There they were taken up by the Anhalt battalion of the 5th Regiment of the Rhine, which had been retained in Kowno as garrison. Next day they marched into the city. All the scenes of dissolution and chaos, which they had witnessed in Wilna, were played out before their eyes again.

Marshal Ney, with his uncrushable spirit, organised a new rearguard from the Princely Division, based on the Lippe Battalion, and occupied a weak, pallisaded redoubt just outside the Wilna gate. In it was a single gun, which did good service until it was dismounted by the Cossacks' sledge-borne battery.

Now the redoubt was subjected to a veritable hail of shot, which killed and wounded dozens at a time. The German officers wanted to fall back, but Ney shouted: '*Un bon grenadier doit se faire tuer sur son poste!*' (A good grenadier should be killed at his post!'); shortly after this, a cannon ball took off both the legs of Captain Barkhausen of the 5th Regiment. He pulled his pistol and shouted to Ney in a firm voice: '*Marechal, voyez comme un grenadier allemande meurt à son poste!*' (Marshal, see how a German grenadier dies at his post!) and blew out his brains.

This event caused Ney to order a withdrawal. As they fell back, he shouted to another German officer (Captain Wiedburg): '*Viens camarade – vous êtes tous brave garçons!*' (Let's go comrade – you're all brave boys!). Segur recounts a slightly different version:

> Ney called upon his infantry: but only one of its weak battalions, the garrison of three hundred Germans, was armed. These he disposed, shouting words of encouragement, and was about to give the order to fire when a Russian cannon ball came crashing over the stockade and shattered the thigh of their commanding officer. This brave soldier fell to the ground and, knowing that he was lost, coolly seized his pistol and blew his brains out, in

full sight of his troops. At this stroke of misfortune the soldiers lost their heads, and threw down their arms and fled in terror.

Still Ney, deserted by everyone, surrendered neither his person nor his post. After a vain attempt to check the flight of the Germans, he gathered up their muskets and faced the horde of Russians alone. His boldness halted them and shamed some of his own artillerymen who followed the example of their marshal.'[7]

As they fell back into the town, a fire broke out and spread rapidly. There was one incredible incident, in which a church, converted to a small arsenal to store 40,000 muskets, was set on fire by the Lippe Battalion on orders from General Antoine-Joseph Bertrand. Four hundred freezing soldiers stormed into the burning building to warm themselves and could not be moved to leave it. They died when the blazing roof fell in.

The 6th Regiment of the Rhine left the burning town of Kowno late on the night of 12 December; a member described the scene:

The road, lit by the flames, was covered all along by the dead and dying. Every step went over dead men and horses and everywhere lay those who had frozen to death in their sleep. The march was slow, but then we came to a hill upon which carts, wagons, guns and refugees had become so entwined, that no progress was possible. The chaos was indescribable. We had to spend the rest of the night here.

At last dawn came. The sky flashed with electricity and became a sea of blood-red flames, heaving and roiling back and forth. Great columns of fire rose, like funeral pyres out of Kowno, scattering clouds of sparks around.

Again and again ammunition wagons exploded, throwing shells in all directions, like a living volcano. Great balls of fire rose through the black smoke into the sky. A horrible, infernal light illuminated the scene, turning the snow pale pink.

The entire town was burning. It was a fascinating, terrible sight, which shattered the onlookers.

Kowno – or what was left of it – fell to the Russians on 13 December. They captured thousands of prisoners and a mass of vehicles. The retreat from Wilna to Kowno effectively destroyed the last, formed vestiges of the *Grande Armée*.

Three men of the 6th Regiment of the Confederation of the Rhine, who had fallen out of the march in these last days, were captured by the Cossacks. They entered the newly-formed Russo-German Legion under General von Tettenborn, fought in Saxony, the Netherlands and France and returned home in 1814.

Notes

1 Napoleon, in Smorgoni on 5 December 1812, according to Segur; was this imperial self-pity?
2 Loison's 34th Division, XI Corps.
3 The 4th Regiment served in Catalonia from 1809 to 1811; of the 2,292 men who marched off to Spain, only 292 survived.
4 Segur, page 267.
5 The Lippe contingent was the 2nd Battalion, 5th Regiment of the Confederation of the Rhine.
6 Segur page 271. Dramatic fiction at its best.
7. Segur page 271.

A gunner of Polish foot artillery by C. Weiland. Dark green uniform, black facings piped red, yellow buttons and cap plate, red pompon, cords and epaulettes. The Poles served mainly in Poniatowski's V Corps. Author's collection.

Chapter 21

Back to the beginning

The Red Lancers of the Guard had started the campaign with 1,090 NCOs and lancers; they received 401 reinforcements during the fighting and on 13 December their strength was sixty men. They had lost 1,341 horses. Of the fifty-six officers, only thirty-two were still fit for duty.

Denis Davidov was called to Kutuzov in Wilna on 13 December; he recalled the sudden change from visions of hell to near normality:

> What changes in headquarters! Whereas previously a ruined village and a smoky hut surrounded by sentries, or a log cabin with folding stools, served as a setting, I now saw a courtyard filled with fancy carriages and a crowd of Polish grandees in dress uniforms, captured generals, and our own generals and staff officers roaming all over the place!

It seems that Kutuzov's field headquarters bore no comparison at all with the pomp and circumstances of that of Napoleon.

Kutuzov gave Davidov the task of marching south west from Wilna to Grodno on the River Niemen to urge the Austrians to evacuate Russian territory. On 20 December, his men bumped into an Austrian patrol and took two prisoners. According to instructions, he returned them to Austrian General Frelich, who was holding Grodno with his cavalry brigade. After some negotiations, Frelich agreed to hand over the town, intact, with its considerable depots, and withdrew into Austrian territory. For his daring exploits during this campaign, Denis Davidov was awarded the Order of St George, 4th Class and the Order of St Vladimir, 3rd Class.

The road to the west forked after Kowno; one road led to Koenigsberg, the other down the Niemen to Tilsit. Marshal Ney had signposts erected showing the survivors of the various corps to which towns they should go. Many of the isolated refugees preferred, however, to strike off on their own to try to get home. The Russians did not press their pursuit.

The 6th Regiment of the Rhine, under Colonel Heringen, escorting a treasure wagon back to Koenigsberg, was attacked by a group of French lancers, on the pretext that they had not received any pay for months and felt entitled to help themselves. Heringen had his men drive them off with musketry. Just then, Murat arrived and managed to bring the lancers back to their senses. On another occasion, Marshal Berthier and his ADC came upon a broken down wagon with a German detachment guarding it. '*Allons en prison avec ce Jean f… d'Allemande, avec ce traitre!*' growled

Berthier. (Throw those f...ing Germans into prison, the traitors!).

The Austrians in the southern sector also fell back westwards, as Ulan Captain von Boehm's account relates:

> In early December – after the crossing of the Beresina – we reached the area of Slonim, but there we began to receive madly fictional despatches from the Duke of Bassano's rumour factory (*'l'Empereur avait complètement battu l'ennemi sur la Beresina'*) [the Emperor has completely defeated the enemy at the Beresina] and the Prince began to smell a rat. At this time the thermometer fell to minus 27 degrees on the Reaumur scale[1] and we were losing a lot of men on the outposts.
>
> Lieutenant-Colonel Graf Latour, two other officers and I were sent out in different directions to establish what the real situation was. My task was to go back as far as Warsaw if necessary, to talk to the French ambassador to the Grand Duchy, Baron Dominique Dufour de Pradt, Napoleon's Aumonier, and to find out what was really going on. After delivering this vital information to Vienna, I returned to the army.
>
> The Austrian and Saxon corps had by then withdrawn to the area of Bialystock; this movement was continued and we soon crossed the River Bug at Brest Litowsk. By this time, we had formally been authorised by Marshal Berthier to begin negotiations with the Russians on an armistice, in order to save the Saxons and Durutte's[2] division from total destruction. We then took up winter quarters in the Duchy of Warsaw; headquarters was at Pultusk.

In Gumbinnen Murat assembled the general staff and addressed them.

> It is no longer possible to serve a madman! There is no hope of success in his cause. In all Europe there is not one prince who still has faith in his treaties. I am sorry that I rejected the proposals of the English. If I had not done that, I should still be a great monarch, like the Emperor of Austria or the King of Prussia!

He was interrupted by Davout.

> The King of Prussia and the Emperor of Austria, are princes by the grace of God, the age, and the acceptance of their people. But you – you are only a king by the grace of Napoleon and your French blood! The only way you can keep your title is through Napoleon and by remaining faithful to France. Black ingratitude has made you blind. I swear I will denounce you to the Emperor!

The survivors continued to trickle off westwards, to the grudging safety of East Prussia, and soon the once high-and-mighty of Imperial headquarters limped gratefully into Koenigsberg. To quote Segur:

> We were soon forced to drag our abasement through Koenigsberg. The *Grande Armée* that for twenty years had been marching triumphantly through the capitals of Europe was reappearing for the first time in full flight, mutilated, disarmed, in one of the cities it had most humiliated by its glory. The inhabitants ran out as we went by to count our wounds, to evaluate their hopes of liberation by the extent of our misfortune; and we had to satiate their

A Polish general in the traditional uniform of that country; slate blue jacket, crimson piping, silver buttons, red breeches. The band around the square-topped Czapka and the waist sash are crimson and silver. A plate by C. Weiland. Author's collection.

greedy eyes with the sight of our misery, bear the insults of their hopes, parading our failure before their odious merrymaking and marching under the crushing weight of disaster... But the poor vestige of the *Grande Armée* did not sink beneath the burden. This mere shadow managed somehow to make an imposing show, to preserve its air of sovereignty. Though defeated by the elements, we paraded before man our victorous dominating formation. The Germans, inspired either by fear or sluggishness, received us submissively. Their hatred was confined to a show of cold indifference, and as they rarely act of themselves, they were obliged to minister to our distress while awaiting some signal.

The 6th Regiment of the Rhine, which had not even seen a Russian soldier, arrived back in Koenigsberg only 300 men strong. But even now the survivors were not safe; typhus and other ills raged among them.

Loison's 34th Division, which had left Koenigsberg with 14,000 men on 1 November, re-entered the city on 28 December with scarcely 2,000. The Frankfurters had suffered most casualties, but despite this, they managed a '*Vive l'Empereur!*' as they filed past Murat. The 5th and 6th Regiments of the Rhine tramped past in silence.

Notes

1 Rene-Antoine-Ferchault de Reamur (1683–1757) invented a temperature scale in 1730, in which water froze at 0 degrees and boiled at 80 degrees.
2 32nd Infantry Division.

Epilogue

So the great adventure was over. Napoleon's refusal to admit that he had committed an error had not made it all come right. On the contrary, he had caused a military disaster to accompany his economic shambles. And the cost was catastrophic. Some ninety percent of the men who marched into Russia in June 1812 died. Of course, one's chances of survival increased the more senior a rank one held; his marshals and most of his staff managed to escape. He also lost all his horses and almost all his guns. Only the contingents of Hessen-Darmstadt and Warsaw brought their cannon out.

Murat and several others began to realise that Napoleon was a megalomaniac, who would stop at nothing to achieve his own aims; to him, they were all as expendable as the half a million whose bones were now whitening in Russia.

By this great poker game, he caused all of Europe to realise that he was vulnerable after all. They would bring him low in 1813 and force his first abdication in 1814. 1815 was but a last, dramatic, twitch of the corpse. He had had his day – but he would not admit it, even on St Helena. It was there that he wrote the following passage, which allows us to judge just how far removed from reality the man was:

> The Russian war should have been the most popular war of modern times. It was a war on the side of good sense and sound interests, to bring peace and security to all. It was purely pacific and conservative. It was a war for a great cause, the end of uncertainties and the beginning of security. A new horizon, and new labours would have opened up, full of well-being and prosperity for all. The European system was established; all that remained was to organize it... In this way Europe would have become in reality but a single people and every man travelling anywhere would have found himself in a common fatherland... Paris would have become the capital of the world and the French the envy of the nations.

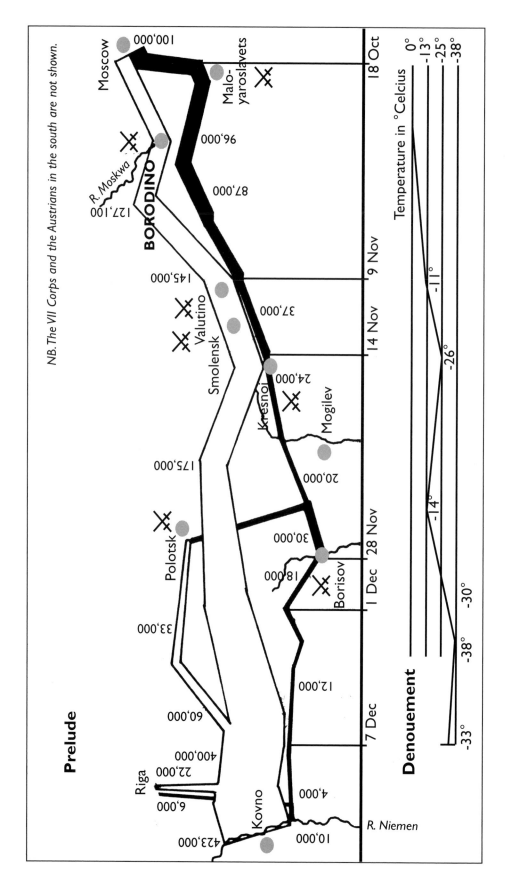

Appendix

The diminishing strength of the *Grande Armée* in 1812

The main body (Imperial Guard, I, III, IV, V, VIII, IX, XI Corps and I – IV Cavalry Corps)

24 Jun	4 Jul	3 Aug	19 Aug	9 Sep	12 Nov	25 Dec
298,000	244,600	183,300*	142,500	137,000	70,500	19,800

The northern flank guard (II and VI Corps)

24 Jun	4 Jul	3 Aug	19 Aug	9 Sep	12 Nov	25 Dec
70,000	65,000	49,500	22,000	16,000	11,000	3,800

The southern flank guard (VII Corps and the Austrians)

24 Jun	4 Jul	3 Aug	19 Aug	9 Sep	12 Nov	25 Dec
19,300*	16,300	14,000	11,400	11,000	12,500	13,200
34,248**	?	30,000	?	26,000	?	20,937
		Kosinski's Polish div.		5,500	4,000	2,000

* VII (Saxon) Corps.
** Austrians.

The Riga front (X Corps)

24 Jun	4 Jul	3 Aug	19 Aug	9 Sep	12 Nov	25 Dec
32,497	27,253	?	?	24,000	23,000	23,00

Bibliography

Adam, Albrecht *Croquis Pittoresques Dessinés d'après Nature dans la Russie en 1812*, Munich.

Baden-Hochberg, Wilhelm Markgraf von *Denkwürdigkeiten*, Bearbeitet von Karl Obeser, Heidelberg, 1906.

Baumgarten-Crusius, Oberst z. D. *Die Sachsen 1812 in Russland*, Georg Wigand, Leipzig, no date.

Bernays, Guillaume *Schicksale des Grossherzogtums Frankfurt und seiner Truppen*, E.S Mittler & Sohn, Berlin, 1882.

Barschewisch, Hauptmann von *Geschichte des Grossherzoglich Badischen Leib-Grenadier-Regiments 1803–1871*, Karlsruhe, 1893.

Bogdanowitsch, M. Generalmajor *Geschichte des Feldzuges von 1812*, Leipzig, 1863.

Borodino 1812, Izdatelsvo Misl, Moscow, 1987.

Chandler, D.G. *The Campaigns of Napoleon*, London, 1967.

Chlapowski, Dezydery *Memoirs of a Polish Lancer*, Emperor's Press, Chicago, 1992.

Clausewitz, General Carl von *The Campaign of 1812 in Russia*, John Murray, London, 1843; Greenhill, London 1992.

Clausewitz, Carl von *Hinterlassene Werke Vol. VII, Der Feldzug 1812 in Russland*, 1843.

Davidov, Denis *In the Service of the Tsar Against Napoleon*, Greenhill Books, London, 1999.

Ditfurth, Maximilian Freiherr von *Die Schlacht bei Borodino am 7. September 1812*, Marburg, 1887.

Duffy, Christopher *Borodino, Napoleon Against Russia, 1812*, Sphere Books, London, 1972.

Duncker, Oberstleutnant Karl von. *Oesterreichische Militaerische Zeitschrift, Vol I*, 1894, Vienna.

Fezensac, General de *A Journal of the Russian Campaign of 1812*, London, Parker, Furnival and Parker, 1852. Reprinted by Ken Trotman, Cambridge, 1988.

du Four, Faber *Blaetter aus Meinem Portefeul 1812*, Leipzig, 1897.

Gabler, K.K. Feldmarschal Wilhelm Edler von *Das K.K. Oesterreichisches Auxiliarcorps im Russland-Feldzug 1812*, Vienna, 1863.

George, Hereford, B. MA *The Moscow Expedition*, Oxford, 1904.

Gerdes, A. *Die Geschichte der Truppen Bergs und Westfalen 1812 in Russland*, Langendreer, 1914.

Gerhardt, O. *Die Württemberger in Russland 1812*, Stuttgart, 1937.

Hartwich, Julius von *1812 Der Feldzug in Kurland*, R. Eisenschmidt, Berlin, 1910.

Heilmann *Die Bayerische Division Preysing im Feldzuge von 1812* in the *Jahrbuch für die Deutsche Armée und Marine*, Vol 17.

Hellmueller, C. Theodor, Oberst. *Die Roten Schweizer 1812*, Verlag A. Francke, Bern, 1912.

Hohenhausen, Leopold von *Biographie des Generals von Ochs*, Kassel, 1827.

Holzhausen, P. *Die Deutschen in Russland*, Berlin, 1912.

K.B. Kriegsarchiv. *Darstellungen aus der Bayerischen Kriegs-und Heeresgeschichte*, Heft 21, Munich, 1912.

Kausler, Franz von and Professor J.E. Woerl *Die Kriege von 1792–1815 in Europa und Aegypten mit Besondere Rücksicht auf die Schlachten Napoleons und seiner Zeit*, Karlsruhe and Freiburg, 1842.

Kraft, Heinz *Die Württemberger in den Napoleonischen Kriegen*, Stuttgart, 1865.

Leyh, Dr Max *Die Feldzüge des Koeniglich Bayerischen Heeres unter Max I Joseph von 1805 bis 1815.*

Lossberg, Friedrich, W. von *Briefe in die Heimat Geschrieben Waehrend des Feldzugs 1812 in Russland*, Berlin, 1912.

Lünsmann, Fritz *Die Armée des Koenigsreichs Westfalen*, Berlin, 1935.

Maag, Dr A. *Die Schicksale der Schweizer-Regimenter in Napoleons I. Feldzug nach Russland, 1812*, Verlag Ernst Kuhn, Biel, 1890.

Malibran, A. and J. Chelminski *L'Armée du Duche de Varsovie de 1807 à 1815*, Paris, 1913.

Morgenstern, Franz, Oberst *Kriegserinnerungen aus Westfaelischer Zeit*, Wolfenbüttel, 1912.

Pawley, Ronald *The Red Lancers*, Crowood Press, Ramsbury, 1998.

Pivka, Otto von *Armies of 1812*, PSL, Cambridge, 1977.

Preysing-Moos, Generalmajor Graf von Maximilian, *Tagebuch 1812*, Munich, 1912.

Roeder, Franz *Der Kriegszug Napoleons Gegen Russland im Jahre 1812*, Leipzig, 1848.

Roos, Heinrich von *Mit Napoleon in Russland*, Stuttgart, 1912.

Roth von Schreckenstein, Generallieutenant Freiherr *Die Kavallerie in der Schlacht an der Moskwa am 7. September 1812*, Münster, 1855.

Schubert, F. von *Unter dem Doppeladler : Erinnerungen eines Deutschen im Russischen Offiziersdienst 1789–1814*, Stuttgart, 1962.

Schuler *Geschichte des schwarzburg-rudolstaedtischen Contingents in den Kriegsjahren von 1807 bis 1815*, Verlag Hermann Stroh, Rudolstadt, 1874.

Segur, Count Philippe-Paul de *Napoleon's Russian Campaign*, Michael Joseph, London, 1959.

Smith, Digby *The Greenhill Napoleonic Wars Data Book*, Greenhill Books, London, 1998.

Stein, F. von *Geschichte des Russischen Heeres vom Ursprunge desselben bis zur Thronbesteigung des Kaisers Nikolai I . Pawlowitsch*, Liepzig, 1895.

Thiers, Louis A. *The Moscow Expedition*, Oxford, 1904.

Tolstoy, L.N. *War and Peace*, Jena, 1907.

Vossler, Lieutenant H.A. *With Napoleon in Russia 1812*, The Folio Society, London, 1969 and 1998.

Walter, Jakob *Denkwürdige Geschichtsschreibung über die Erlebte Militaerdienstzeit des Verfassers dieses Schreibens (The Diary of a Napoleonic Footsoldier)*, Windrush Press, 1991.

Württemberg, Herzog Eugen von *Erinnerungen aus dem Feldzuge des Jahres 1812 in Russland*, Breslau, 1846.

Württemberger im Russischen Feldzug 1812 in *Wuerttembergische Volksbuecher*, Stuttgart, 1911.

Index